MANY
PATHS:
ONE
GOAL

OTHER BOOKS AND BOOKLETS BY J.P. VASWANI

In English

10 Commandments of A Successful Marriage
101 Stories For You And Me
108 Pearls of Practical Wisdom
108 Simple Prayers of A Simple Man
108 Thoughts on Success
114 Thoughts on Love
25 Stories For Children and also for Teens
A Little Book of Life
A Treasure of Quotes
Around The Camp Fire
Begin The Day With God
Break The Habit
Burn Anger Before Anger Burns You
Dada Answers
Daily Appointment With God
Daily Inspiration
Daily Inspiration (Booklet)
Destination Happiness
Dewdrops of Love
Does God Have Favourites?
Formula For Prosperity
Gateways to Heaven
God In Quest of Man
Good Parenting
Hinduism
How To Embrace Pain
I am a Sindhi
I Luv U, God!
It's All A Matter of Attitude
Joy Peace Pills
Kill Fear Before Fear Kills You
Ladder of Abhyasa
Life After Death
Living Legend
More Snacks For The Soul
Nearer, My God, To Thee!
Peace or Perish
Positive Power of Thanksgiving
Sadhu Vaswani : His Life And Teachings
Saints For You and Me
Saints With A Difference
Secrets of Health And Happiness
Short Sketches of Saints Known & Unknown
Sketches of Saints Known & Unknown
Snacks For The Soul

Swallow Irritation Before Irritation Swallows You
Teachers are Sculptors
The Heart of a Mother
The King of Kings
The Little Book of Freedom From Stress
The Little Book of Prayer
The Little Book of Service
The Little Book of Success
The Little Book of Wisdom
The Little Book of Yoga
The Lord Provides
The Magic of Forgiveness
The One Thing Needful
The Patience of Purna
The Perfect Relationship: Guru and Disciple
The Power of Good Deeds
The Power of Thought
The Seven Commandments of the Bhagavad Gita
The Terror Within
The Way of Abhyasa (How To Meditate)
Thus Have I Been Taught
Thus Spake Sadhu Vaswani
Tips For Teenagers
Trust Me All in All or Not at All
What You Would Like To know About Karma
Whom Do You Love the Most
Why Do Good People Suffer?
You Are Not Alone God Is With You!
You Can Make A Difference

In Hindi

Dainik Prerna
Dar Se Mukti Paayen
Mrutyu Hai Dwar… Phir Kya?
Santon Ki Leela
Sadhu Vaswani: Unkaa Jeevan Aur Shikshaayen
Safal Vivah Ke Dus Rahasya
Prarthna ki Shakti
Laghu Kathayein
Bhakton Ki Uljhanon Kaa Saral Upaai
Bhale Logon Ke Saath Bura Kyon?
Aalwar Santon Ki Mahan Gaathaayen
Atmik Jalpaan
Atmik Poshan

Ishwar Tujhe Pranam
Krodh Ko Jalayen Swayam Ko Nahin
Chahat Hai Mujhe Ik Teri Teri! (Booklet)

In Marathi:

Krodhala Shaanth Kara, Krodhane Ghala Ghalnya Purvee (Burn Anger Before Anger Burns You)
Jyanchya Jholit Aahe Prem (Jiski Jholi Mein Hai Pyaar)
Yashasvi Vaivahik Jiwanaachi Sutre (10 Commandments of Successful Marriage)
Karma Mhanje Kay? Samjun Ghyaychey (What Would You Like to Know About Karma)
Mrityu Nantarche Jeevan (Life After Death)

In Kannada:

Burn Anger Before Anger Burns You
Life After Death
Why do Good People Suffer
101 Stories For You And Me

In Telugu:

Life after Death
Burn Anger Before Anger Burns You

In Spanish:

Bocaditos Para el Alma (Snacks for the Soul)
Mas Bocaditos Para el Alma (More Snacks for the Soul)
Queme La Ira Antes Que La Ira Lo Queme A Usted (Burn Anger Before Anger Burns You)
Inicia Tu Dia Con Dios (Begin The Day With God)
Sita Diario ku Dios (I Luv U, God!)

In Arabic:

Daily Appointment With God

In Chinese:

Daily Appointment With God

In Dutch:

Begin The Day With God

MANY PATHS: ONE GOAL

J. P. VASWANI

GITA PUBLISHING HOUSE
Sadhu Vaswani Mission,
10, Sadhu Vaswani Path, Pune – 411 001, (India).
gph@sadhuvaswani.org

Published by:
Gita Publishing House
C/o. Sadhu Vaswani Mission,
10, Sadhu Vaswani Path,
Pune – 411 001, (India).
gph@sadhuvaswani.org

Second Edition
ISBN : 978-93-80743-11-0

Printed at:
Mehta Offset Pvt. Ltd.
Mehta House,
A-16, Naraina Industrial Area II,
New Delhi – 110 028, (India).
info@mehtaoffset.com

Dedication

To

Gurudev Sadhu Vaswani

The Teacher (Guru) who urged:
Religion? Let us *talk* of it less, *practise* more!

– J. P. Vaswani

There are so many who can believe only one thing at a time. I am so made as to rejoice in the many and behold the beauty of the One in the many. Hence my natural affinity to many religions; in them all I see revelations of the One Spirit. And deep in my heart is the conviction that I am a servant of all prophets.

– Sadhu Vaswani

INVOCATION

In all Religions, the Light is Thine!
In all the Scriptures, the Inspiration is Thine!
In all the Saints, the Picture is Thine!
In all the Races, the Song-flute is Thine!
In all the Countries, the Rose-dust is Thine!
Master! Sing the Song of Union anew
And re-kindle the Light of love!

– Sadhu Vaswani

CONTENTS

FOREWORD

In the fourth chapter of the Bhagavad Gita, we find a beautiful *sloka*:

> *However men approach Me, even so do I greet them as Mine own;*
>
> *For all the paths men take from any side are Mine, verily Mine!*
>
> *(IV – 11)*

Speaking to his dear, devoted disciple Arjuna, the Lord says: "At the end of each path do I stand. All ways are My ways. All men everywhere walk to Me!"

Gurudev Sadhu Vaswani's comments on this *sloka* are truly memorable:

His Path, indeed, is the One Path: there is no other. He is the One Bridge that spans the sea of sorrow, the Bridge of Light. The Bridge has diverse colours, and each is called by a different name. The Bridge has different sections or stages. Gnana, bhakti, karma are some of the names used by men to indicate what helps them to cross: but the path for all is still His path.

All paths lead us to God. Therefore, fights, feuds, arguments, discussions, debates and differences in the name of the religion are futile. You can follow the path that draws you; let another follow the path that draws him; yet another can take the path that he chooses – ultimately, all of you will arrive at the same destination.

In a world torn by strife and violence, religion is exploited by unscrupulous elements that fan the flames of hatred in the name of their faith and belief. At the same time, it has become habitual for vested interests to blame religion for all the evils of society. Thus, religion today has been made a convenient scapegoat for all the atrocities perpetrated by man. Fundamentalism, intolerance, bigotry and fanaticism have crept into religious faith. Terrorism, bloodshed and killing of innocent men and women are all labelled as "religious" strife.

A man came to Sadhu Vaswani and said to him, "You say: God is Love; God is Mercy. Why is it that your God stands by and watches while there is so much violence and suffering in the world?"

Sadhu Vaswani pointed to a tablecloth. At the back of the cloth was a mishmash of crisscrossed stitches, with knots and ties and tangles. It all looked so untidy. But when the cloth was turned right side up, the man saw on it beautifully embroidered, the words, *God is Love.* "It is we who turn religion inside out," the Master explained. "In truth, God is Love; God is Mercy."

Today, in the name of religion, we have fights and feuds, sectarian strife, hatred and violence. But let us not forget that religion came to unite, to reconcile, to create harmony among men. It is not religion which has failed us, it is *we* who have failed religion!

Sadhu Vaswani, constantly urged us, "Let us *talk* of religion less, *practise* more!" We need to follow his wise counsel now, more than ever before. We need to put into practice the great truths and ideals of religion in our daily life. And if we really take the trouble to study the great religions of the world, we will come to know that they emphasise the ideals of Love, Peace, Service, Piety, Prayer and Brotherhood.

I humbly submit to you, that rivalry in religion is meaningless. There can be no rivalry among true religions. If such rivalry has become rampant today, it is due to want of knowledge and lack of reverence.

There are some who believe that they have the one full and final revelation of the truth; so that those who stand outside the circle of their own faith must necessarily be in error. Again, there are others who approach religious issues without the spirit of sympathy; they fix their attention on what they regard

as aberrations and extravagancies of a particular religion and say, "This religion is a monstrosity!" Saddest of all, we have people who hurt and kill in the name of religion. They are ignorant of the fact that they are killing their own brothers and sisters!

This is why discord and hatred have entered the sphere of religion; and religion, which was meant to be a bond of union, has become a source of sectarian strife. Little wonder then, that young men and women today, are turning away from true religion.

India is the land of many religions and has always respected every religion. For India has profoundly believed, through the centuries, that God is One, though the ways to reach Him are many. The Hindus do not merely tolerate, but accept every religion, knowing that so many religions are but so many ways of the human soul to grasp and realise the Infinite!

We can indeed be proud of India's inspiring history in this regard. India has always stood for religious harmony and understanding. Today, India is passing through a difficult period. But this is only a temporary, transitional phase. The history of India bears ample testimony to the fact that through the centuries, the truth and message of religious harmony has influenced the Hindu people, Hindu society, Hindu political thought and Hindu state policy – both of large empires and small kingdoms – all over India. Not only is India home to the world's oldest extant religion, Hinduism; she has also been the cradle of other great faiths of the world like Jainism, Buddhism and Sikhism. Unroll the pages of the past, and you will find that among all the nations of the earth, India alone has greeted and welcomed with love and respect every foreign religion that entered the country. Judaism, Christianity, Islam, Zoroastrianism, Baha'ism, have all become naturalised in India, have become religions of India and have been influenced by the Indian environment. When they first entered India, they were all received with respect and love. This is an outstanding example of tolerance and liberalism in world history. And it is this spirit that this book is meant to reflect.

WHAT IS RELIGION?

Even as I attempt to answer that question, the unforgettable words of Gurudev Sadhu Vaswani echo in my heart:

Religion! Let us *talk* of it less, *practise* more!

Sadhu Vaswani was right! Religion is not merely a matter of words; it is practice of the art of living; it permeates every aspect of our lives.

When human beings first became capable of thought, surely they must have wondered about themselves, the natural environment that was their habitat and the vast sky above them, and then again, they perhaps asked themselves how such phenomena as day, night, lightning, thunder, rain and the various seasons occurred, and by what laws they operated; and who was in charge of it all . . .

When questions arise in the mind, answers follow after reflection and contemplation.

If we turn to etymology, we are in a way, taking refuge in sophisticated linguistic abstractions: for let us admit, faith and belief preceded speech and language. The words we are familiar with today arose much later than the ancient religions of this world.

To return then to the question: What is religion? The Latin word *religio* translates roughly as "careful" "scrupulous" or "things done with great attention to detail".

The Latin root *liga* means to bind; *religare* thus means to bind something to something else. Thus religion could mean binding man to God; binding people together in a common faith; binding us to a tradition of belief and worship.

Interestingly both *culture* and *cult* are derived from the Latin root *cultus,* which means worship of a Higher Power. Thus we may infer that belief in and worship of a Higher Power formed the very basis of culture; or, to put it differently, religious worship was the foundation of the great cultural systems of the world.

Consider for example, Stonehenge in Britain; the Acropolis in Rome; the Parthenon in Greece; the Pyramids of Egypt; the Archeological Excavations of the Indus valley; the Sun Temple at Konark; the Ka'bah in Mecca; and to move to modern examples, St. Peter's Basilica; Juma Masjid; the Pearl Mosque; the Pallava Cave Temples . . . the list is endless. All these architectural marvels are nothing but the expression of man's faith and belief in the Supreme Being whom, for want of a better word, we call God.

Religions also came to regulate man's lives through their moral and ethical laws – rules and prescriptions that were meant to be respected and observed scrupulously. Thus we find many of the world faiths telling their adherents what to eat and what not to eat; whom one can and cannot marry; what people could do and must not do. Not only did this regulate and govern human conduct, but also brought peace and harmony into human lives. It would be no exaggeration to say that religions came to protect, order and preserve the survival of humanity. They also contributed to tradition and continuity, for faith and belief were nurtured and carefully passed down from one generation to another. In this sense, we could also say that religions constituted the earliest information systems of the world.

Somewhere along the way, religions also acquired a specific organisational structure. Special people were chosen to lead worship and rituals, and perhaps, to intercede with the Gods on behalf of humans. Thus hierarchical systems gradually arose and religions became institutionalised.

One of the earliest definitions of religion in English, comes from Dr. Johnson's Dictionary, which simply calls it, "a system of faith and worship". The German philosopher Hegel defined religion with more feeling as, "the Divine Spirit becoming conscious of Himself through the finite spirit". The sociologist Lindbeck defines religion as, "a kind of cultural and/or linguistic framework or medium that shapes the entirety of life and thought… it is similar to an idiom that makes possible the description of realities, the formulation of beliefs, and the experiencing of inner attitudes, feelings and sentiments."

What all religious scholars agree on is that there can be no unitary definition of religion that is acceptable to all.

Thus we can see, from being "a strong belief in a supernatural power or powers that control human destiny", religion gradually evolved into "an institution to express belief in a Divine Power". Today, we even have a branch of metaphysics called the philosophy of religion which asks and tries to find answers to questions on the world of nature, the presence of God, the problem of evil, and the complex inter-relationship between religion and morality. The philosophy of religion must be distinguished from religious philosophy, which is specific to individual religions. Of all these issues we may say that God is primary and central to religious belief.

In what is regarded as the first and fundamental work on the subject, Aristotle's 'Metaphysics' refers to God as "the unmoved mover", "the most divine of things observed by us", as "the thinking of thinking". Today God is variously referred to as Brahman, Ishwar, Allah, YHWH, and so on. God is sometimes given a personal name, a proper noun to emphasise His personal nature, as in Krishna-Vasudeva in *Bhagavad* or later *Vishnu* and *Hari*. While the Abrahamaic religions are monotheistc, Hinduism is polytheistic within the framework of belief in a Supreme Being; religions like Buddhism and Jainism are virtually non-theistic.

Once again, I must recall Sadhu Vaswani's words: *God defined is God denied!*

The word "pantheism" derives from the Greek words *pan* meaning *all* and *theos* meaning *God*; *pantheism* literally means "all is God". Essentially, pantheists believe that the Universe as a whole is divine, and that there is no divinity other than the Universe and Nature.

Closely allied to pantheism is animism, the belief that every object in the universe is, in a sense, alive, and that every object has a spirit or a soul, and that every object is divine in its own right.

There are many people too, who view religion primarily as a collection of myths, stories and legends. Myth is a much debased word today, but twentieth century developments in anthropology and psychology have brought out the centrality of myth in human culture and civilisation. Myths are, in fact, stories that embody profound truths that are too complex to grasp in abstract terms. Myths are deeply significant stories that are shared by the people of a particular culture. Myths hence form an integral aspect of their cultural identity. Thus every religion has its own 'myth of creation'. Let me caution you, I use myth, not in its debased sense as a false notion or a lie, but in the sense of a deeply held belief. The myth of creation is allied to the religion's world view as a whole. Other myths may include stories of critical stages, such as the story of Noah's Ark in the Bible or the churning of the ocean in the Vishnu Purana.

Closely allied to myth are rituals. Ritual is yet another word that is now used in a debased sense, to denote empty, meaningless religious practices. But in early religions, rituals were deeply symbolic actions, performed in compliance with sacred beliefs and ideals. When performed with such dedication and pure motives, they fulfilled the spiritual and emotional needs of the people, and brought them great satisfaction. Today, rituals of various kinds are a feature of almost all known religions, and in fact, have also been incorporated into secular activities: e.g. flag hoisting ceremonies, lighting of the Olympic torch, singing the national anthem, etc. They are certainly not empty actions, but have become very meaningful and valuable traditions and customs.

I have until now, given you some theoretical aspects of all world religions; but close to my heart is a view of religion which is derived from the *rishis* of ancient

India: *Ekam, Satyam, Shivam, Sundaram.*

Sarva-ruupa-dharam Shaantham
Sarva-naama-dharam Shivam
Sath-chith-aananda rupam Adhvaitham
Satyam Shivam Sundaram

(The One Absolute, who is Being, Awareness and Bliss, is the embodiment of peace in all His forms. All His Names are auspicious and He manifests the threefold attributes of Truth, Auspiciousness and Beauty).

Ekam – for there is but One Light pervading all. There is but One Light that thrills the universe from end to end – the One Eternal Light.

Satyam – for the central note of religion is Truth: not *your* version of truth or *my* version of truth, but the truth of the One, the truth of the soul and the Oversoul, the Supreme Being and the rest of creation, the *paramatma* and *jivatma*, as Hinduism puts it so beautifully.

Shivam – or goodness, unalloyed and pure goodness, for the third note of that beautiful melody of faith is purity of thought, word and deed.

Sundaram – or beauty. The realisation that God is One, that He is the Truth and the Only Goodness we all need, leads to the ultimate beauty of God-realisation, which is the goal of all religions.

In India, we use the word *dharma* to denote religion. *Dharma* is derived from the Sanskrit root *dhri*, meaning 'to hold'. *Dharma* is a power that holds – it upholds, it sustains, it maintains the universe from end to end. It does this by means of certain laws, the Laws of the Spirit, which are closer than you think, to the laws of science. Schilling, the well known physicist asserted that both science and religion have "a threefold structure of experience, theoretical interpretation and practical application." Therefore, our ancient rishis described religion as *atma vidya*, or the science of the Spirit.

Religion then is a study and application of the laws of life. These are laws to which we must conform, if we wish to be happy. Do you live according to the laws of the Kingdom of God? Do you bear witness to these laws in deeds of daily life?

"What is your religion?" This was a question that people repeatedly asked Gurudev Sadhu Vaswani. And he would answer, "I know of no religion higher than the religion of unity and love, of service and sacrifice."

On one occasion, he said, "Religions are worth no more than a straw if they do not teach man to love God and serve the God-in-man. For God dwelleth in every man."

The Kingdom of God is within you. Your religion, your faith must help you reach this world within!

WHY DO WE NEED RELIGION?

Do we really need God or indeed a religion in this day and age?

This is a question that has been repeatedly asked by people at various fora, at discourses by spiritual leaders and at gatherings of thinkers and scholars.

I am not going to take the standpoint of the atheists on this issue: they are people who are certain of their unfaith: they do not need religion or God, and do not need an answer to this question.

The distinguished humorist Mark Twain answered the question in his own way: "Man is a religious animal. He is the *only* religious animal. He is the only animal that has the True religion – several of them.

For the sake of those who are genuinely troubled and disturbed by what they see as the condition of the world today, for those who seek reassurance, this question must be tackled.

Here are a few answers that emerged when I invited some of my friends to answer the question:

1. We need religion for the sake of our own salvation. After all, death cannot be the end of the life of the soul.

2. We need religion because we all need to stay connected with a Higher Reality.

3. We need religion to live life in the right way.

4. We need religion because if there is one relationship we cannot do without, it is our relationship with God.

5. We need religion because it is only the sense of a Higher Authority, a Superior Power that can guide us through the vicissitudes of life.

6. We need religion because we need to have a sense of order, a sense of belonging, and also a sense of protection and security that a Higher Power affords us. Without this belief we would be lost in nihilism.

7. To quote St. Augustine, "We are restless until we find our rest in God."

8. God and Religion give meaning to our life. Why would anyone want to lead a life that is meaningless?

Religion is response to the God-within and the God-around you!

As we may see from the above, lots of people have very clear thoughts about why they need God and Religion in their lives. (You may have noticed too, it is impossible to speak of one without the other; so closely are God and Religion intertwined in our lives.)

And yet, when we see the decline of values and morals in society, when we see people ready to kill innocents in the name of faith, when we see the threat of a Third World War looming, we begin to wonder: how can such things happen in a world ordered by religion? What is the significance, the role of religion in such times? Is religion being hijacked by a few people to serve their vested interests in the name of God and faith?

Let us not stop with professing faith: let us *practise* the great ideals of religion in our daily life.

All that is best, all that is wise, all that is beautiful and worthwhile, all that is true and radiant, comes to us from God.

As I have studied the religions of the world at the feet of my beloved master – Sadhu Vaswani – a great seer, sage and prophet; of the New Age; as I have imbibed the teachings of the great founders of the different faiths under his benign wisdom, it seems to me that there is a beautiful similarity in their message. To study different religions in the light of sympathy

To abolish religion would be to tear the very heart of humanity.

and understanding is to know that they emphasise the same fundamental truth. This often makes me wonder why some people claim that their own religions are true and others are not!

As religions advance in time, they tend to become more and more rigid and create differences. What we really need today is that people belonging to different faiths should join together in the creative and constructive task of building a new world order, based on unity and love and universal brotherhood.

We live in an age of science and we are proud of our achievements and the 'progress' we have made; and indeed, science has given us many comforts, conveniences and gadgets. So many of us today are apt to take the sanctuary that science offers, almost as an article of faith! But the problem is that science has also inflated our ego and skewed our vision. We are beginning to think: "What is there that man cannot do on his own? We have no need of God or religion!"

True it is that man is exploring the moon for the purpose of a settlement; true it is that our rockets are trying to reach the distant planets; our satellites are stationed in space and bring us minute-to-minute details of what is happening in the firmament and in the nooks and corners of this vast world. But does this make us feel safe and secure? Are we truly happy? Are we at peace with ourselves? Are we at peace with our own neighbours and the rest of the world?

Let me remind you, that one of the greatest scientists of our time, Albert Einstein, observes: "True religion is real living, living with all one's soul, with all one's goodness and righteousness." Whoever the God we choose to believe in, whatever the faith we follow, there can be no compromise on this: we must *be* good; we must lead a good life and as far as possible; we must do good to others.

The eminent psychiatrist, Karl Jung observed that civilisation today has become sick because man has alienated himself from God. I believe that God is the source and the sustainer of all life and we cannot live a happy and healthy life – physically, spiritually, emotionally and morally – so long as this alienation persists.

The cure to the many maladies that affect us today, is certainly not to reject religion, but to practise religion in its truest sense, true to the spirit, rather than the letter. How is this to be done? Take a U-turn to God!

The eternal *Sanatana Dharma*, the way of life I practise, teaches me to believe not in the survival of the fittest, but in the glorious ideal: *Sarve bhavantu sukhinaha* – may all beings be happy!

If there is one thing I wish this book to convey to you, it is this. All religions are pathways to the One Eternal God. All we need to do is see to it that every Hindu is a true Hindu, every Christian is a true Christian, and every Muslim is a true Muslim. All religions are true, and everyone must be true to the religion they are born into.

Historians and scholars of religion agree that the Baha'i Faith is the world's youngest independent religion. Its Founder Baha'u'llah (1817-1892), lived and preached his faith in times that are still in people's living memory. Today over five hundred million people all over the world owe allegiance to this faith. The word Baha'i is both a noun and an adjective, used respectively to describe the faith, and also a follower of the faith. The term Baha'ism is not generally encouraged, and Baha'i Faith is the preferred choice.

Awe-inspiring Lotus Temple, Delhi

THE BAHA'I FAITH

Throughout history, God has revealed Himself to humanity through a series of divine messengers. Baha'u'llah, regarded as the latest of these messengers, brought new spiritual and social teachings for our time. His essential message is of unity. He taught the oneness of God, the oneness of the human family, and the oneness of religion. He said, "The earth is but one country and mankind its citizens," and that now is the time for humanity to live in unity. Baha'is believe that the crucial need facing humanity is to find a unifying vision of the nature and purpose of life and of the future of society. Such a vision unfolds in the writings of Baha'u'llah.

Never become angry with one another…Love the creatures for the sake of God and not for themselves. You will never become angry or impatient if you love them for the sake of God.

A new or independent religion does not arise in a vacuum. Thus Buddhism and Jainism grew out of Hinduism. They were in one sense, reactions to Hinduism in their own historical and social context. Similarly, Jesus Christ was born a Jew, and followed the Jewish faith, before his teachings evolved into the new religion of Christianity. We can also say that Buddhism and Christianity acquired their independence and distinct identity, only when they moved out of the land of their origin, into the wider world arena, and became the accepted faith of 'outsiders' other than Indians or Jews. This is true of the Baha'i Faith too. It may be said to have originated in the matrix of Islam, although it subsequently became quite independent of the originating religion.

The new Faith first began in Persia or Iran. From there it spread to many neighbouring countries like Turkey, Russia and Northern India. Some Jews, Christians and Zoroastrians embraced the new Faith, although its early followers were predominantly Muslim. Many of its ideas were drawn from the Holy Qur'an, although they differed in matters of interpretation.

The Baha'i Faith is unique in this respect – that it unreservedly accepts the validity of other faiths and world religions. Baha'is believe that Abraham, Moses, Zoroaster, Buddha, Krishna, Jesus and Muhammad are all equally authentic messengers of one God. The teachings of these divine messengers are seen as paths to salvation which contribute to the "carrying forward of an ever-advancing civilisation." But they also believe that this series of interventions by God through his messengers, has been progressive with relation to human history, each revelation from God evolving from the previous one, each more complex than those which preceded it, and each preparing the way for the next.

ORIGINS

Any discussion of the origins of the Baha'i Faith must begin with the mention of two great visionaries of Nineteenth Century Persia, as Iran was then called. The first of these was Mirza Ali Muhammed (1820-1850) who called himself as "The Bab", meaning "Gate", from a Shia Muslim concept. In 1844, The Bab announced to his few faithful followers that he was but the latest in a long line of spiritual leaders whose task it was to proclaim the advent of God's messenger upon this earth. He also spoke repeatedly of "He whom God shall make manifest", a Messiah whose coming had been proclaimed by all the world's scriptures. In his book, the *Bayán,* The Bab described the messianic figure as "the origin of all divine attributes", and stated that his command would be equivalent to God's command. The Bab stated further that once the messianic figure arrived, the perusal of just one of his verses would be greater than a thousand perusals of his own book, the *Bayan*. This prediction was widely recognised as being fulfilled by Baha'u'lla, the founder of the Baha'i Faith.

The Bab's open proclamations were perceived as a threat to state and clergy. His followers were persecuted and the Bab himself was arrested, tortured and eventually executed by the Persian authorities for heresay against Islam.

Baha'u'llah was born Mirza Husain Ali, in one of the most wealthy and influential families of Persia. (The Arabic word *Baha'* means 'glory' or 'splendour') His father was a wealthy government minister, Mirza Buzurg-i-Nuri. The family could trace its ancestry back to the great dynasties of Iran's imperial past. Baha'u'llah led a princely life as a young man, receiving an education that focused largely on calligraphy, horsemanship, classic poetry, and swordsmanship. His son and official biographer says of him:

From his earliest childhood he was distinguished among his relatives and friends.... in wisdom, intelligence and as a source of new knowledge, he was advanced beyond his age and superior to his surroundings. All who knew him were astonished at his precocity. It was usual for them to say, 'Such a child will not live,' for it is commonly believed that precocious children do not reach maturity.

In a letter Baha'u'llah recalled a childhood incident—that is, seeing an elaborate puppet show about war and intrigues in the court of a king and the riches of those in authority. After the performance, Baha'u'llah saw a man come out from behind the tent with a box under his arm. "What is this box?" Baha'u'llah asked him. "All this lavish display and these elaborate devices," the puppet master replied, "the king, the princes, and the ministers, their pomp and glory, their might and power, everything you saw, are now contained within this box." This taught the young boy that all the pomp and power of this world are transient; and that the Truth must be sought beyond these external trappings.

By the time he was fourteen, he was regarded as wise beyond his years. He could converse on any subject and solve any problem presented to Him. In large gatherings he would explain intricate religious questions to the *ulema* (clergy), and they were amazed by his perspicacity and his thorough knowledge of the scriptures.

The source of all evil is for man to turn away from his Lord and to set his heart on things ungodly. In all matters, moderation is desirable. If a thing is carried to excess, it will prove a source of evil.

When a thought of war comes, oppose it by a stronger thought of peace. A thought of war must be destroyed by a more powerful thought of love. Thoughts of war bring destruction to all harmony, well-being, restfulness and contentment.

Upon his father's death, a position in the ministry was offered to him, but he declined the offer politely. Instead, he chose a life of service and philanthropy, earning from the people the title, 'Father of the Poor'. He spent much of his time in communion with nature, saying, "The country is the world of the soul, the city is the world of bodies."

First a follower of the Bab, he hosted a gathering of the most eminent followers of the Bab, known as Babis. This gathering was significant as it served to establish an independent identity and character of the Babi religion. He too was imprisoned in one of the notorious dungeons of Persia known as "the dark pit". He refused to evade arrest with the help of his powerful friends, choosing instead to walk to the deadly prison where he was to be incarcerated. It is said that he was stoned and vilified by angry mobs as he was led away by the authorities.

He himself relates that in 1853, while incarcerated in the dungeon of the Síyáh-Chál in Tehran, he received the first intimations that he was the Messiah anticipated by the Bab. But it was only ten years later that he revealed to his followers that he had been sent by God to redeem the world, and to interpret God's Will for a new age.

Fortunately for the faithful, he escaped execution. But now began a saga of banishment from the land of his birth – the beginning of 40 years of exile, further imprisonment and persecution. He was forced to depart from his country even before recuperating from the ill health caused by being in the dungeon and from the wounds resulting from the weighty chains around his neck. He was sent first to Baghdad, where too, he attracted growing numbers of followers.

While he was in Baghdad, he withdrew to the mountainous wilderness of Kurdistan, where he lived alone for two years. He spent his time reflecting on the implications of the divine purpose to which he had been called. The Baha'is regard this period as the parallel of Moses' withdrawal to Mount Sinai, Jesu's forty days and nights in the desert, and Muhammad's retreat to the cave on Mount Hira. Baha'u'llah wrote some of his most renowned works in Baghdad, including the *Hidden Words*, *Seven Valleys*, and the *Book of Certitude* (*Kitab-i-Iqan*).

The Persian authorities used their influence to banish Baha'u'llah from Baghdad. In April 1863, before leaving for Constantinople (Istanbul), Baha'u'llah and his companions camped in a garden on the banks of the Tigris River for twelve days. It was here that

Baha'u'llah revealed to his close friends and followers that he was the Promised One foretold by the Bab, and indeed, in all the world's scriptures. Baha'is celebrate their most joyous festival, the holy Ridvan Festival, in commemoration of those twelve eventful days. Thus it was nearly ten years after the Revelation that Baha'u'llah proclaimed the truth to his people.

Persecution for him and his followers continued in Constantinople, from where he was banished to go to Adrianapole. He made no attempt to escape from his persecutors. Instead, he proclaimed to contemporary rulers and heads of state that he was God's redeemer, sent to heal the wounds of civilisation. This only ignited the wrath of the orthodox clergy. He and his family were subjected to inhuman treatment while at Adrianapole; this place was the farthest he would be forced to go from his native land. But even here, despite the extreme conditions under which he and the rest of the exiles lived, his teachings continued to spread. A greater flow of writings than ever before came from his pen and they were distributed by his followers to places as far away as Egypt and India.

Here in Adrianapole occurred one of the tragic incidents of the Messiah's life. Jealous of his ever growing popularity and the reverence which he attracted from people even in exile, Mírzá Yahyá, his half brother, hired people to poison him. Baha'u'llah became extremely ill, and it took him months to recuperate. The episode left him with a tremor that showed in his handwriting to the end of his life.

From 1867 onwards, Baha'u'llah wrote a series of letters to the kings and rulers of the world, including Emperor Napoleon III, Queen Victoria, Kaiser Wilhelm I, Tsar Alexander II and others. In these letters, he openly proclaimed His station as a Messenger of God. He urged the leaders to pursue justice and disarmament and exhorted them to band together into a commonwealth of nations, warning them of dire consequences should they fail to establish peace.

The gate leading to the Shrine of Baha'u'llah, the resting place of the founder of the Baha'i Faith

Lay not on any soul a load which ye would not wish to be laid upon you, and desire not for anyone the things ye would not desire for yourselves. This is my best counsel unto you, did ye but observe it.

He and his family were under orders to go to the prison city of Akka, but others accompanied him voluntarily. Baha'u'llah warned his companions that even greater trials awaited them and that if they wished to protect themselves, they should leave for other destinations immediately. It was a warning that the exiles chose to disregard. At that time, 'Akká (Acre) was regarded as 'the end of the world', a final destination for the most notorious murderers, highway robbers, and political enemies of the Ottoman regime. A walled city of filthy streets and damp, desolate houses, 'Akká had no source of fresh water, and the air was popularly described as being so foul that birds flying overhead would fall dead out of the sky. By banishing the Messiah with his family and followers to this wretched place, the authorities expected that they would soon perish.

But that was not to be. Here in this city at first, and later in its suburbs and environs, the Messiah was to live for over 24 years, till his death in 1892. Here he composed his most important work, the *Most Holy Book* (*Kitáb-i-Aqdas*). In it he outlined the vital precepts of the faith for his followers, and also laid the groundwork for Baha'i institutions, and articulates His vision for the development of human civilisation.

It was here, in April 1890 that Professor Edward Granville Browne of Cambridge University met Baha'u'llah in four successive interviews. Professor Browne wrote of his first meeting: "The face of him on whom I gazed I can never forget, though I cannot describe it. Those piercing eyes seemed to read one's very soul; power and authority sat on that ample brow.... no need to ask in whose presence I stood, as I bowed myself before one who is the object of a devotion and love which kings might envy and emperors sigh for in vain."

The Shrine of the Bab, Hai

In the early hours of May 29, 1892, Baha'u'llah passed away at the Mansion of Bahjí. Nine days later his will was unsealed. It designated 'Abdu'l-Bahá, his second son, as His successor and head of the Baha'i Faith. (His eldest son had died under tragic circumstances when the family had been imprisoned earlier at Akka.) It was for the first time in history that the founder of a world religion had made explicitly clear whom people should follow after his death. This declaration of a successor is the pivotal provision of what is known to Baha'is as the "Covenant of Baha'u'llah". It has enabled the Baha'i Faith to remain united around one central authority for over a century.

His followers grew in great numbers after his death. They established over 70,000 Baha'i centres worldwide.

THE TEACHINGS OF BAHA'U'LLAH

The Baha'is believe in one God as a single supernatural Being who created the universe and all creatures and forces within it. This Being, Whom we call God, has absolute control over His creation (omnipotence) as well as perfect and complete knowledge of it (omnipotence). They also believe that though people may pray to Him in different languages and call Him by different Names (such as Allah or Yehovah, God or Brahma), they are referring to the same unique Being.

Baha'u'llah taught that God is so far beyond His creation that human beings will never be able to grasp any clear image of Him; nor can they ever appreciate His majesty and power except in the most remote manner. The very terms we use to decribe God are indequate, as they relate to our limited human experiences and knowledge.

It is for this reason that the discipline of daily prayer, meditation, and study of the Baha'is. They feel that this disipline is one of the most important ways of growing closer to their Creator.

Baha'i notions of progressive religious revelation result in their accepting the validity of most of the world's religions, whose founders and central figures are seen as manifestations of God. Though their faith is sometimes described as syncretic combinations of earlier religions' beliefs, they describe their faith as an independent world religion, differing from the other traditions in its relative age and in the appropriateness of Baha'u'llah's teachings to the modern context.

Humanity is seen as essentially one, though highly varied; its diversity of race and culture are seen as worthy of appreciation and acceptance. Doctrines of racism, nationalism, caste, social class and gender-based hierarchy are seen as artificial impediments to unity. The Baha'i teachings state that the unification of humankind is the paramount issue of the present world.

Shoghi Effendi, the appointed head of the religion from 1921 to 1957, wrote the following summary of what he considered to be the distinguishing principles of Baha'u'llah's teachings, which, he said, together with the laws and ordinances of the *Kitáb-i-Aqdas*, constitute the bedrock of the Baha'i Faith:

The independent search after truth, unfettered by superstition or tradition; the oneness of the entire

My home is the home of peace. My home is the home of joy and delight. My home is the home of laughter and exultation. Whosoever enters through the portals of this home must go out with gladsome heart. This the home of light; whosoever enters here must become illumined.

human race, the pivotal principle and fundamental doctrine of the Faith; the basic unity of all religions; the condemnation of all forms of prejudice, whether religious, racial, class or national; the harmony which must exist between religion and science; the equality of men and women, the two wings on which the bird of humankind is able to soar; the introduction of compulsory education; the adoption of a universal auxiliary language; the abolition of the extremes of wealth and poverty; the institution of a world tribunal for the adjudication of disputes between nations; the exaltation of work, performed in the spirit of service, to the rank of worship; the glorification of justice as the ruling principle in human society, and of religion as a bulwark for the protection of all peoples and nations; and the establishment of a permanent and universal peace as the supreme goal of all mankind— these stand out as the essential elements which Baha'u'llah proclaimed.

The following principles are frequently listed as a quick summary of the Baha'i teachings. They are derived from transcripts of speeches given by 'Abdu'l-Bahá during his tour of Europe and North America in 1912.

- Unity of God
- Unity of religion
- Unity of humankind
- Equality between men and women
- Elimination of all forms of prejudice

- World peace
- Harmony of religion and science
- Independent investigation of truth
- Universal compulsory education
- Universal auxiliary language
- Obedience to government and non-involvement in partisan politics
- Elimination of extremes of wealth and poverty

With specific regard to the pursuit of world peace, Baha'u'llah prescribed a world-embracing collective security arrangement as necessary for the establishment of a lasting peace.

THE SACRED SCRIPTURES OF THE BAHA'I FAITH

The most holy text is the *Kitab-i-Aqbas*, written by Baha'u'llah. This text forms the book of laws in the Baha'i Faith. Other important texts include:

- *Gleanings from the Writings of Baha'u'llah*
- *Prayers and Meditations*
- *Epistle to the Son of Wolf*
- *The Seven Valleys and the Four Valleys*

Other sacred writings include those of the Bab and Abdul Baha'.

BAHA'I FESTIVALS

Ridvan: The twelve day period commemorating Baha'u'llah's announcement of his claim to prophethood and his departure from Baghdad in 1863, observed from sunset April 20 to sunset, May 2. The first, ninth and twelfth days of Ridvan are major Baha'i holy days on which work is suspended.

Most of the sacred festivals of this faith are associated with the Bab and the Messiah. These include:

A Baha'i Festival

Declaration of the Bab: celebrated in May

Ascension of Baha'u'llah: May 29

Martyrdom of the Bab: July 9

Birth of the Bab: October 20

Birth of Baha'u'llah: November 12

Day of the Covenant: November 26

Ascension of 'Abdu'l-Bahá: November 28

Ayyam-i-Ha : (i.e. Essence of God Festival) February 25 - March 1: This is celebrated through acts of love, fellowship, unity, charity and goodwill.

Naw-Ruz, the Baha'i new year, begins on March 21, the first day of spring. This is preceded by a period of fasting between March 2-March 20.

MARRIAGES IN THE BAHA'I FAITH

Baha'is understand that the family is the basic unit of society. Unless this all-important basic unit is healthy and stable, society itself cannot be healthy and unified. Monogamous marriage stands at the foundation of family life.

Baha'u'llah said of marriage that it is "a fortress for well-being and salvation." The Baha'i writings further state that married couples should strive to become "loving companions and comrades and at one with each other for time and eternity..."

Parental approval is considered essential for marriages. Baha'is believe that this requirement helps to preserve unity within the marriage – and within the extended family. This entails respect for parents from the children. It also ensures that parental support is always available to young couples during the crucial early years of their marriage.

Once parental permission is obtained, the marriage takes place, requiring only the simplest of ceremonies. In the presence of two witnesses designated by the local Baha'i governing council, the couple recites the following verse: "We will all, verily, abide by the will of God." For Baha'is, that simple commitment to live by God's will implies all of the commitments associated with marriage, including the promises to love, honour and cherish; to care for each other regardless of material health or wealth; and to share with and serve each other. As in most religions, the marriage vow is considered sacred in the Baha'i Faith. The partners are expected to be absolutely faithful to each other.

Beyond these simple requirements, Baha'is are free to celebrate their marriage according to their personal tastes, family resources, and cultural traditions, Baha'i ceremonies run the gamut from small to large, including all manner of music, dance, dress, food and festivity.

UNIQUE FEATURES OF THE BAHA'I FAITH

The central theme of Baha'u'llah's message is that humanity is one single race and that the day has come for its unification in one global society. One of the purposes of the Baha'i Faith is to help make this possible. A worldwide community of some five million Baha'is, representative of most of the nations, races and cultures on earth, is working to give Baha'u'llah's teachings a practical effect. Their experience will be a source of encouragement to all who share their vision of humanity as one global family and the earth as one homeland. In keeping with this philosophy Baha'is come from a wide range of ethnic and cultural backgrounds.

There is no clergy in the Baha'i Faith. Because the human race has entered upon the age of its maturity, each individual is able to explore the revelation of God and to decide on the issues of life through prayer, reflection, and consultation with others. To make this possible, the Baha'i scriptures have so far been translated into some 800 different languages.

The work of the Faith is entirely supported by voluntary contributions from the members. Giving to the Baha'i fund is regarded as one of the privileges of membership; the Faith does not accept outside contributions.

Life in this world, as Baha'u'llah presents it, is like the life of a child in the womb of its mother: the moral, intellectual, and spiritual powers which a human being develops here, with the help of God, will be the "limbs" and "organs" needed for the soul's progress in the worlds beyond this earthly one. The way of life which

Meditation is the key for opening the doors of mysteries. In that state man abstracts himself; in that state man withdraws himself from all outside objects; in that subjective mood he is immersed in the ocean of spiritual life and can unfold the secrets of things in themselves.

Baha'is seek to cultivate, therefore, is one that encourages personal development. Daily prayer and meditation free the soul from conditioned patterns and open it to new possibilities.

Under the unique *Consultative System* of this Faith, development projects have proliferated all over the world. They include tutorial schools, local clinics, classes in health care, agricultural projects, reforestation, alcoholism counselling, and children's hostels.

Throughout the critical first century of the Faith's existence the provisions laid down by Baha'u'llah have protected the Baha'i community from sectarianism, and have enabled it to adapt itself to the requirements of a rapidly evolving civilisation.

The Universal House of Justice, ordained by Baha'u'llah as the legislative authority in the Baha'i Faith, came into existence in 1963. It is a nine-member body elected at five-year intervals by the entire membership of the national governing institutions of the Baha'i world. The House of Justice directs the spiritual and administrative affairs of the Baha'i International Community. It serves, also, as a custodian and trustee of the Baha'i Holy Places and other properties in the Holy Land. Endowed by Baha'u'llah with the authority to legislate on all matters not specifically laid down in the Baha'i scriptures, the House of Justice is the institution that keeps the Baha'i community abreast of an ever-changing world.

The sufferings which their own fellow believers experienced as victims of religious persecution have particularly sensitised Baha'is to Baha'u'llah's teachings on human rights. The Baha'i International Community participates actively in United Nations consultations dealing with minority rights, the status of women, crime prevention, the control of narcotic drugs, the welfare of children and the family, and the movement towards disarmament.

The Baha'i Faith teaches that true religion promotes unity, and that unity is the fundamental prerequisite for the achievement of global peace. "The well-being of mankind," Baha'u'llah said, "its peace and security, are unattainable unless and until its unity is firmly established." Believing that the United Nations represents a major effort in the unification of the planet, Baha'is have supported its work in every way possible. The Baha'i International Community is accredited with consultative status with the United Nations Economic and Social Council (ECOSOC) and with the United Nations Children's Fund (UNICEF).

If love and agreement are manifest in a single family, the family will advance, become illumined and spiritual.

Buddhism is one of the great Indic religions, which was initiated in North India around the fifth century B.C. by Gautama Buddha. It is based entirely on the teachings of the Buddha, and may be said to have been founded by the Buddha himself.

BUDDHISM

A Buddha may be defined simply as 'an enlightened one' although some Pali scholars take the word to mean 'an awakened teacher'. Buddhism is a faith that encompasses a variety of traditions, beliefs and practices, largely based on teachings attributed to Gautama the Buddha.

Buddha in the Lotus Pose

Many Buddhists regard their faith as a philosophy rather than as a religion. But it is a definite system of beliefs and practices, and there are several sects or schools of Buddhism today, including the two major branches, *Theravada* ("The School of the Elders") and *Mahayana* ("The Great Vehicle"). Sub-sects include *Pure Land*, *Zen*, *Nichiren Buddhism*, *Tibetan Buddhism*, *Shingon*, *Tendai* and *Shinnyo-en*. There is also a third branch, *Vajrayana*, which is recognised by many. In recent times, scholars have seen the birth of several new offshoots of the old faith, which they classify as *Modern Buddhism*.

If there is one thing that is common to all the sects, it is the basic adherence to a traditional formula in which the practitioner takes refuge in *The Three Jewels*: the Buddha, the *Dhamma* (the teachings of the Buddha), and the *Sangha* (the Buddhist community). Buddhism is also practised by adherents alongside many other religious traditions — including Taoism, Confucianism, Shinto, traditional religions, Shamanism and Animism — throughout East and Southeast Asia. Modern influences have led to many new forms of Buddhism that significantly depart from traditional beliefs and practices.

ORIGINS

In a sense, Buddhism was one among numerous new ascetic religious and philosophical groups that broke with the Brahmanic tradition and rejected the authority of the Vedas and the Brahmins. These groups, whose members were known as *shramanas*, are now thought to belong to a non-Vedic strand of Indian thought distinct from Indo-Aryan faith.

The history of Buddhism as a religion begins with the life of Gautama Buddha, a historical figure whose life story is recorded in several early Buddhist texts. The foundation of Buddhism is indeed in the teachings of the Buddha, who lived the life of a wandering ascetic, spreading his message among the people as he moved among them. Starting in India, the cradle of all Indic faiths, Buddhism spread across Asia and is today established as a faith and a way of life virtually in every continent of the globe.

As it spread and grew over the centuries, Buddhism also became more diverse. Doctrinal divisions and the influence of many cultures have created a rich spectrum of philosophies, scriptures, art and iconography and practices.

He whose mind is not whetted by lust, he who is not affected by hatred, he who has discarded both good and evil - for such a vigilant one there is no fear.

ORIGINS

Gautama Buddha was born around 563 BC in Lumbini, near the present Indo-Nepal border. He was of royal descent; he was Prince Siddhartha, son of King Suddhodhana, leader of the Sakya clan. His mother Queen Maya, died shortly after his birth, and Siddhartha was brought up in royal luxury at the palace in Kapilavastu.

A wise man, who visited the palace, prophesied to the king that the young prince would grow up to be a great military conqueror or a universally respected spiritual teacher. The king was determined that his son should take over the kingdom in due course of time. To exclude all possibilities of the second option ever becoming a reality, he decided that the prince would be confined to the palace, completely shut out from the harsh realities of the world outside, and also shielded from any religious influences. Until he was 29, Prince Siddhartha lived a life of luxury and comfort, in the opulent palace of his father. He was married to Princess Yashodhara, a beautiful and virtuous maiden. They had a son named Rahula.

One should not pry into the faults of others, things left done and undone by others, but one's own deeds, done and undone.

This is what the Buddha was to say to his *bikkhus* later, about the kind of exclusive, luxurious, 'delicate' life that he led as a prince:

In my father's dwelling, lotus pools had been made – in one, blue lotuses, in another red, in another white – all for my sake. My dress was of Benaras cloth – my tunic, my robe and my cloak. And night and day, a white parasol was held over me that I should not be touched by cold or heat, by dust or weeds or dew. I had three palaces, one for the cold season, one for the hot, and one for the season of rains. Through the four rainy months, I stayed in the palace for the rainy season. I was entertained by female minstrels and I did not come down from the palace. I was delicate, O monks, extremely delicate, excessively delicate!

Everything seemed to be going according to the king's plan, but not for much longer.

A day came when he managed to venture into the outside world, perhaps by persuading his charioteer to take him on a series of rides around the countryside near the palace. In the course of these rides, he came across what are known in the Buddhist scriptures as *the four sights:* these were his first encounters with the sorrow and misery of the world, and he was deeply troubled by what he saw. He saw an old man, a sick man, a dead body and a *sanyasi* or renunciate: these sights changed the course of his life; indeed, they changed the course of history. He pondered constantly on the inescapable miseries of human life – illness, disease, pain and death. His life in the palace seemed superficial and vain. He could no longer continue to live in such utter indifference to people's misery in what seemed to him sheer ignorance and blindness. Soon after these encounters, the Prince decided to renounce the world and take up a life of spiritual quest, seeking a solution to the sorrows and sufferings of human life, which he could share with everyone afflicted by the pain of existence. He shaved his head, put on a mendicant's robe, and left his palace at the dead of night, to become a *jignasu*.

It is said that at first, the prince sought out teachers or gurus who could help him find answers to his questions. But their precepts and words did not satisfy him, nor were they able to provide him with answers to the questions which haunted him. Siddhartha then decided that he would follow the path of asceticism to attain to the truth he sought.

Since ancient times, India's sages and rishis have sought spiritual wisdom by retiring to the *tapobana* or the forest of meditation. Far from the madding crowds and the fret and fever of worldly life, they take to a life of asceticism and meditation to gain access to the ultimate truth about life. So it was with the prince. At first, he undertook a life of severe penance and asceticism, almost reducing himself to starvation and severe deprivation. It is said that he ate one grain of rice a day, and became so thin, that he was reduced to a bag of bones. He became weak and faint, and was close to death.

In a moment of epiphany, he saw a dancing girl and heard her sing a song which contained the message: *Tune the sitar neither low nor high...*

Siddhartha realised that he had resorted to the extreme: then and there he accepted a small bowl of sweetened milk and rice which a girl had brought to offer to the River-God, but offered instead to the emaciated ascetic whom she recognised as a holy man. Energised and revitalised by this encounter, he gave up his severe penances and self-destructive practices. He decided to beg for alms and take up serious meditation, instead of futile self-mortification. Five ascetics, who had been his companions until then, abandoned him at this point, as they thought that he had given up his spiritual quest; but they were mistaken! He was only now getting close to his goal. He took his yogic posture under the *bodhi* tree and vowed that he would not arise from meditation until he found the enlightenment he was seeking. Thus he had discovered for himself the Middle Path, the golden mean between self-indulgence and self-flagellation.

Under the Bodhi Tree

Not to do any evil, to cultivate good, to purify one's mind – this is the teaching of the Buddhas.

After several days, he awakened from his state of *samadhi*, an enlightened being, the Buddha, as he would be known henceforth. On achieving illumination, he wished at first, to withdraw from a world, darkened by sin and suffering. "Shall I teach to others what I have seen?" he asks himself. "If I teach, who shall understand? For men understand not, men wander after worldly things!" But he saw the world's great need: he saw men and women 'dimmed by dust'. He saw and had pity on them. And, filled with compassion, he moved out to give his message.

It was now his mission in life to teach this truth to the people so that they too, could be liberated from the vicious cycle of birth and death.

His first sermon was preached to just five disciples, the companions who had abandoned him a little earlier. This momentous discourse, referred to as the First Turning of the Wheel of Truth, was given at a Deer Park in Saranath, near Varanasi. This discourse forms the foundation and essence of all of the Buddha's teachings. It contained teachings on the Four Noble Truths and the Noble Eight-fold Path and forms the basis of Buddhist philosophy.

The Master spent his life in spreading this great message and in meditation and service. He spoke of five meditations: 1) The meditation of love: in this you send out your heart in love for the welfare of all creatures including birds and beasts, all beings including your enemies. 2) The meditation of pity: in this you send out vibrations of sympathy to all beings in distress, and you so discipline yourself as to call up in imagination their sorrows and anxieties. 3) The meditation of joy: in this you think of those who are happy and you feel happy in their happiness. 4) The meditation of fruitage of action: in this you think of the evil consequence of sin. How much men suffer for the pleasure of a moment! 5) The meditation of serenity: in this you rise above the dualism of like and dislike, wealth and want, and, in perfect tranquillity, contemplate yourself as the master of fate, the conqueror.

The Buddha spent the rest of his life travelling across North-Eastern India, spreading his message among the people. Many followers were drawn to him. Many disciples also joined the monastic order that he founded. Kings and princes embraced the faith that he offered, and chose to follow the path of awakening that he showed them. By the time he left his earthly

Conquer anger by love; conquer evil by good; conquer the stingy one by giving; conquer the liar by truth.

body at the age of eighty, there had developed around him a community or *Sangha* of monks and nuns, drawn from every tribe and caste, all of them devoted to practising the path that he taught them about. The Master passed away in 486 BC. His last words are said to be these:

"Behold, O' monks, this is my last advice to you. All component things in the world are changeable. They are not lasting. Work hard to gain your own salvation."

There are many legends and stories that have been built up around the life of Gautama the Buddha. According to author Michael Carrithers, a highly respected and widely published expert on Buddhism, the stories and legends may not be verifiable, but "the outline of the life must be true: birth, maturity, renunciation, search, awakening and liberation, teaching, death."

THE BUDDHA'S TEACHINGS

Soon after the passing away of the Buddha, his chief disciples and monks met at the first council at Rajagirha, under the leadership of Kashyapa. Upali recited the monastic code (*Vinaya*) even as he remembered the Master delivering it to him. Ananda, Buddha's cousin, friend and favourite disciple, recited Buddha's lessons (the *Sutras*). The monks put the teachings and sermons together after due discussions in a final accepted version. For the first two hundred years, Buddhist teachings remained an oral tradition.

THE THREE MARKS OF EXISTENCE

Impermanence is the characteristic feature of all aspects of life. All that we see, hear and experience are inconstant, unsteady and impermanent. All human beings reflect this flux in the process of ageing, disease and death. Because of this state of permanent flux, attachment to any form or experience can only lead to suffering.

Suffering or *dukkha* is another aspect of existence. *Dukkha* has been variously interpreted as pain, misery, disquietude or disharmony.

The self is actually *anatta* or non-self. The *atman* is not an unchanging, permanent essence, but like all else in existence, changeable. *Anatta* is not a metaphysical concept, but an approach to liberation from suffering.

THE MIDDLE PATH

This is one of the vital guiding principles of Buddhist teaching. It is a path that avoids the two extremes of self-indulgence or excessive sensuality, as well as drastic asceticism and self-mortification. Both the extremes lead only to an imbalance in life and thought. Neither can release us from suffering.

SPECULATION AND DIRECT EXPERIENCE

Dharma or truth is "beyond reasoning"; it transcends logic. In other words, truth cannot be discussed, analysed or imbibed through words and concepts. Intellectual activity cannot lead us to enlightenment. All insight must come from the aspirant's experience, critical investigation and reasoning instead of by blind faith. The Buddha once said:

Do not accept anything by mere tradition ... Do not accept anything just because it accords with your scriptures ... Do not accept anything merely because it agrees with your pre-conceived notions ... But when you know for yourselves—these things are moral, these things are blameless, these things are praised by the wise, these things, when performed and undertaken, conduce to well-being and happiness—then do you live acting accordingly.

Hatred never ceaseth by hatred in this world; by love alone doth hatred cease. This is an ancient law.

For a state that is not pleasant or delightful to me must also be to him also; and a state that is not pleasing or delightful to me, how could I inflict that upon another?

THE BUDDHIST CONCEPT OF KARMA

In Buddhism, Karma refers to those actions (physical, verbal, mental or intellectual) that arise out of one's deliberate intention. Each of these actions bring about a result or fruit. It is the intention, rather than the outward aspect of the action which brings about the effect of the action.

Some schools of Buddhism claim that there can be no such thing as divine grace or mercy that can negate one's bad karma; but others claim that the reading, reciting or hearing of certain scriptures can clear people of their heavy karmic loads.

NIRVANA

Literally translated, *nirvana* means extinction or cessation. However, in Buddhist thought, it refers to the cessation of the cycle of birth-death-rebirth. It is also the extinction of the vicious circle of craving-desire-suffering. Another meaning of *nirvana* is 'quietened' or 'calmed'. Buddhists believe that anyone who has attained *nirvana* is, in effect, a *buddha*.

Bodhi literally means 'awakening' or 'enlightenment'. It implies the extinction of *raga, dwesha and moha* (greed, hate and delusion).

In one sense, *nirvana* is also that which is unchanging and permanent, beyond the flux and change of human existence. Not wishing to give it a material name, the Buddha called it *nirvana* or extinction – the unchanging reality beyond all changes.

The term, *parinirvana*, generally refers to the final or perfect *nirvana* attained by an enlightened one at the moment of death, when the physical body ceases to exist.

BODHISATTVAS

This term too, is interpreted in different ways by different schools of thought. In Mahayana Buddhism, a *bodhisattva* is one who has attained enlightenment, but refrains from seeking *nirvana* out of compassion for other suffering men. In Theravada Buddhism, it refers to one who is on the way to enlightenment.

As a mother with her own life guards the life of her own child, let all-embracing thoughts for all that lives be thine.

THE FOUR NOBLE TRUTHS

1. All of human existence, from birth till death, is *dukha*, suffering.

2. The cause of suffering is attachment, craving or *tanha*, desire.

3. Suffering ceases when desires cease.

4. Enlightenment and release from suffering (*nirvana*) can be attained by following the Noble Eight-fold Path (*dhamma*).

These truths are not just concepts to memorise, but deep and profound insights into the nature of life, suffering, death and liberation. They are not just meant to be 'taught' but imbibed through experiential wisdom.

THE NOBLE EIGHT-FOLD PATH

The Eight-fold Path is the way to attain liberation, enlightenment or *bodhi*. Dr. C. George Boeree sums it up thus:

1. Right view is the true understanding of the four noble truths.

2. Right aspiration is the true desire to free oneself from attachment, ignorance and hatefulness.

(These two are referred to as *prajña* or wisdom).

The great compassionate heart is the essence of Buddhahood.

---

3. Right speech involves abstaining from lying, gossiping or hurtful talk.

4. Right action involves abstaining from hurtful behaviours, such as killing, stealing and careless sex.

5. Right livelihood means making your living in such a way as to avoid dishonesty and hurting others, including animals.

   (These three are referred to as *shila* or morality).

6. Right effort is a matter of exerting oneself in regards to the content of one's mind. Bad qualities should be abandoned and prevented from arising again; Good qualities should be enacted and nurtured.

7. Right mindfulness is the focusing of one's attention on one's body, feelings, thoughts and consciousness in such a way as to overcome craving, hatred and ignorance.

8. Right concentration is meditating in such a way as to progressively realise a true understanding of imperfection, impermanence and non-separateness.

   (The last three are known as *samadhi*, or meditation.)

Thus the Noble Eight-fold path counsels wisdom, ethical conduct and mental discipline to achieve release from the cycle of birth and death. The focus is on practice rather than belief. Following the path, we can realise the truth for ourselves.

The Eight-fold Path may be understood in two ways: as a holistic, simultaneous development in which all the virtues are practised in parallel; or as a progressive series of stages through which the practitioner moves, the culmination of each stage leading to the beginning of another.

THE FOUR INTOXICATIONS

1. Sensuality
2. Pride
3. Ignorance
4. Idle speculation

FIVE HINDRANCES WHICH IMPEDE VIRTUE

1. *Kamachandra* or sensual desire
2. *Vyapada* or aversion
3. *Uddhacca-kukkucca* or restlessness

4. *Thina-middha* or sloth and unconsciousness

5. *Vicikiccha* or doubt

The fundamental teachings of Buddhism are summarised by Shakyamuni in the *Dhammapada:*

Not to do any evil,

To cultivate good,

To purify one's mind,

This is the teaching of the Buddhas.

THE TEN PRECEPTS OF BUDDHISM

1. Refrain from taking lives

2. Refrain from taking what is not given

3. Refrain from un-chastity

4. Refrain from speaking false speeches

5. Refrain from taking intoxicants

6. Refrain from taking food at inappropriate time

7. Refrain from dancing, singing, playing music and watching entertainment programs

8. Refrain from using perfume, cosmetics, wearing of garland

9. Refrain from using high chairs and sleeping on luxurious beds

10. Refrain from accepting gold and silver (money)

Of the above, the first five are for all Buddhists, including laymen. The last five are for monks.

THE THREE JEWELS OF BUDDHISM

Every convert or new entrant to Buddhism is required to take the refuge prayer:

Buddham sarnam gacchâmi.
Dhamam sarnam gacchâmi.
Sangham sarnam gacchâmi.

I take refuge in the Buddha.
I take refuge in the Dharma.
I take refuge in the Sangha.

Do not believe on the faith of the sages of the past. Do not believe what you yourself have imagined, persuading yourself that a God inspires you. Believe nothing on the sole authority of your masters and priests. After examination, believe what you yourself have tested and found to be reasonable, and conform your conduct thereto.

The Buddha himself, the *dharma* (the truth or wisdom as enunciated by Buddha) and the *sangha* (the community of Buddhist monks and nuns) are the three jewels of Buddhism.

THE SACRED SCRIPTURES OF BUDDHISM

Buddhist scriptures and religious texts are very many in number, and each sect has its own sacred texts. These are commonly divided into two categories, canonical and non-canonical. The former, called the *Sutras* (Sanskrit) or *Suttas* (Pali) are believed to be the teachings of the Buddha in his own words. The latter are the various commentaries on these canonical texts, other treatises on the Dharma, and collections of quotes, histories, grammars, etc.

The Tripitaka (Tripitaka in Pali) is the earliest collection of Buddhist teachings and the only text recognised as canonical by Theravada Buddhists. *Tripitaka* means "three baskets," from the way in which it was originally recorded. The text was written on long, narrow leaves, which were sewn at the edges then grouped into bunches and stored in baskets. Typically, they comprise three sections:

- *Sutras* (discourses)

Health, contentment and trust are your greatest possessions, and freedom your greatest joy.

- *vinaya* (relating to the rules of monastic discipline)
- *abhidharma* (analytical texts)

The collection is also referred to as the Pali Canon, after the language in which it was first written.

Mahayana Buddhism too, reveres the *Tripitaka* as a sacred text, but adds to it the *Sutras*, which reflect distinctively Mahayana concepts. Most of the Mahayana *Sutras*, which number over two thousand, were written between 200 BC and 200 AD, the period in which Mahayana Buddhism developed. Different divisions of Mahayana Buddhism emphasise different *Sutras*, but some texts, like the *Lotus Sutra* and *Heart Sutra*, are important to most branches of Mahayana. Some 600 Mahayana *Sutras* have survived in Sanskrit, or in Chinese and/or Tibetan translation.

Non-canonical texts include the *Visuddhimagga*, or Path of Purification, by Buddhaghosa, which is a collection of Theravada teachings that include quotes from the Pali Canon. The *Milinda Pañha* is a popular condensation of the *Dharma* in the form of a dialogue between the Buddhist sage Nâgasena and the Indo-Greek King Menander.

Shantideva's *Bodhicaryavatara* has always been an influential text in both Mahayana and Vajrayana traditions. His *Shikshasamucaya* is especially valuable as it contains references to texts which are no longer extant in any other form.

Some Tibetan Buddhist texts are regarded as a unique and special class of texts called *terma*. These texts are held to have been either composed or hidden by *tantric* masters and/or elementally secreted or encoded in the elements and retrieved, accessed or rediscovered by other *tantric* masters when appropriate.

MISCELLANEOUS TEXTS

- The *Dhammapada*: a collection of sayings and aphorisms.

- The *Udana*: a collection of inspired sayings in verse usually with a prose introduction that sets a context of sorts for the saying.

- The *Sutta Nipata*: parts of the Sutta Nipata, are thought to represent the earliest strata of the written canon.

- *Theragâthâ* and *Therîgâthâ* are two collections of biographical verse related to the disciples of the Buddha (male and female respectively).

- *Jataka:* which recount former lives of the Buddha. These remain popular in many forms of Buddhism.

Many of these texts are available in translation as well as in the original language. The Dhammapada, for instance, has a Pali version, three Chinese version, a Tibetan version and a Khotanese version.

One of his students asked Buddha, "Are you the messiah?"
"No", answered Buddha.
"Then are you a healer?"
"No", Buddha replied.
"Then are you a teacher?" the student persisted.
"No, I am not a teacher."
"Then what are you?" asked the student, exasperated.
"I am awake", Buddha replied.

UNIQUE FEATURES OF BUDDHISM

Five hundred millions, in their noblest moments, turn to Gautama Buddha as the light of life. His influence has gone among the nations. Buddha, the Awakened One, is today a world-force.

The Buddha's message has been a shaping power of civilisation through the centuries. In its emphasis on understanding, the message of the Buddha has a fascination for modern consciousness. The Buddha taught that truth was greater than tradition. The Buddha showed the weakness of ritualism. The Buddha shifted the centre of life from the sentimental to the mental. "Think for yourselves!" was his word to his disciples on the last day of his earth-life.

Live in joy, in love,
Even among those who hate.
Live in joy, in health,
Even among the afflicted.
Live in joy, in peace,
Even among the troubled.
Look within. Be still.
Free from fear and attachment,
Know the sweet joy of living in the way.

Buddham Sharanam Gacchami

The Buddha's message is a message of hope and courage. Strive with desires! Conquer *trisna!* Be a hero in the strife! And who are the real heroes of humanity? They who, like Ashoka, turn from war to peace. When he accepted Buddha, Ashoka turned his back on war and sent missionaries of peace, far and wide; and Mahinda, Ashoka's son, went to Lanka and laid there the foundation of a new civilisation of brotherhood and peace.

Buddhism is not a pessimistic faith that dwells on suffering and misery; rather, it insists that zest is essential to overcome suffering and attain liberation. It teaches us to empower ourselves to eradicate suffering through wisdom and right actions.

Buddhist teaching is rational and practical. It encourages us to test and verify its truths through our own experiences, instead of relying on blind faith.

There is no fire like greed,
No crime like hatred,
No sorrow like separation,
No sickness like hunger of heart,
And no joy like the joy of freedom.

Persecution and fanaticism are totally alien to Buddhism. Aldous Huxley writes: "Alone of all the great world religions Buddhism made its way without persecution, censorship or inquisition."

Lord Russell remarks: "Of the great religions of history, I prefer Buddhism, especially in its earliest forms; because it has had the smallest element of persecution."

A Buddhist scholar, Narada Mahathera, says with pride: "To the unique credit of Buddhism it must be said that throughout its peaceful march of 2500 years no drop of blood was shed in the name of the Buddha, no mighty monarch wielded his powerful sword to propagate the Dhamma, and no conversion was made either by force or by repulsive methods. Yet, the Buddha was the first and the greatest missionary that lived on earth."

According to Mahathera, it was the Buddha who first vehemently protested against the degrading caste system which was prevalent in India. In the words of the Buddha it is not by mere birth one becomes an outcast or a noble, but by one's actions. Thus fishermen, scavengers, courtesans, as well as kings, warriors and brahmins, were freely admitted to the Order and enjoyed equal privileges and were also given positions of rank. Upali, the barber, for instance, was made the chief in matters pertaining to Vinaya discipline. The timid Sunita, the scavenger, was admitted by the Buddha Himself into the Order. Angulimala, the robber and criminal, was converted to a compassionate saint. The fierce Alavaka sought refuge in the Buddha and became a saint. The courtesan Ambapali entered the Order and attained salvation. Thus the welcoming portals of Buddhism were wide open to all, irrespective of caste, colour or rank.

Buddha gave the message of hope that the *bodhi,* wisdom was open to all. He blessed the lowly and the lost. He gave love to the sweeper and the barber. Little wonder, that the lowly flocked to him in answer to his call, "Follow me"!

Buddhism encourages the spirit of free enquiry and complete tolerance. There are no commandments, no imperatives in the Buddha's teachings. He exhorts, persuades, rather than commands. Thus Buddhism is regarded as "the teaching of the open mind and the sympathetic heart".

Buddhist meditation techniques are used by several teachers as well as experts to develop traits like mindfulness, concentration, tranquility and insight. These techniques are well preserved in ancient texts and are extensively used by psychologists and psychiatrists as healing practices to help alleviate a variety of health conditions such as anxiety and depression.

Many new adherents in the West are attracted to Buddhism as they see it as a liberal, progressive and deeply intellectual, philosophical system; whereas in the East, Buddhism is still regarded as familiar and traditional. In many countries of Asia, Buddhism is recognised as an official religion and receives state support. In the West, Buddhism is recognised as one of the growing spiritual influences.

Overall, we may say that there is a diversity of recent forms and practices of Buddhism in modern times.

Buddhism, as a church, disappeared from India: but the gracious life and the noble message of the Buddha transformed the life of India. Through Buddha and his order of *bhikkhus* the wisdom of the Rishis, was scatterd to the millions. Buddha's message unified the people and initiated new forces of unification and reflection which brought out the birth of a new Hinduism. A new love for the poor and for the bird and beast was born. The *rishi*-conception of the king as a servant of the poor came to life again in Ashoka, the People's King. And outside India, in Burma and Sri Lanka, in Thailand and Java, in China and Japan, in Asian lands, the message of Buddha has shaped culture and civilisation.

In the world's history, ancient or modern, there has not appeared another who received, in his own life-time, the reverent homage of millions, as did this *"yogi who practised the yoga of the self."* This man, with a begging bowl in his hand, was yet called a *chakravarti:* he was a true "ruler of men"; he came to be revered as a "teacher of men and the gods". Princes deemed it as a proud privilege to pay homage to him. His was a life of singular purity and singular love. He had the simplicity of a child and the humility of a saint.

BUDDHISM AND *AHIMSA*

In Hindu, Jain and Buddhist traditions the concept of nonviolence is translated into the practice of the following virtues:

* non-injury to all living beings

* not causing pain and suffering to others including plants and animals

Look within. Be still.
Free from fear and attachment, know the
sweet joy of living in the way.
We are what we think.

- compassion towards all living creatures

- abstaining from animal and human sacrifices

- cultivation of forgiveness, universal love and friendliness

- non-violent reaction to violent thoughts, words and actions

- mental and verbal nonviolence towards self and towards others

- abstaining from meat eating

- abstaining from hunting, animal fights and similar practices in which animals are subjected to cruelty and suffering

In all three traditions, *ahimsa* is linked with the idea that all violence entails negative karmic consequences.

It is only Jainism that insists on vegetariarism and rejects ritual sacrifices. In most Buddhist traditions, however, vegetarianism is not mandatory. Monks and lay persons may eat meat and fish on condition that the animal was not killed specifically for them.

Although nonviolence is one of the key precepts of Buddhism, many Buddhists including monks do not refrain from eating meat.

All that we are arises with our thoughts.
With our thoughts, we make our world.

BUDDHIST FESTIVALS

There are many special or holy days celebrated by devout Buddhists throughout the year. Some of these days celebrate the birthdays of Bodhisattvas in the Mahayana tradition or other significant dates in the Buddhist calendar. Some holy days are specific to a particular Buddhist tradition or ethnic group, as in Japan, Thailand, Korea or Sri Lanka.

Buddha Purnima or *Buddha Jayanti* ("Buddha Day") is the most important Buddhist festival of the year as

Buddha Purnima Celebrations

it celebrates the three momentous events – the birth, enlightenment and death of the Buddha on the one day, which is the first full moon day in May.

BUDDHIST NEW YEAR

In Theravadin countries, such as Thailand, Burma, Sri Lanka, Cambodia and Laos, the new year is celebrated for three days from the first full moon day in April. In Mahayana countries the new year starts on the first full moon day in January. (This depends also on the lunar or solar calendar used by different countries.)

A major festival of the Tibetan Buddhists is the Losar Festival or Monpa Festival, which marks the Tibetan New year.

Hemis Gompa

This festival is one of the most auspicious occasions for the Buddhist community in India. The Hemis fair is celebrated with great jubilance to mark the birth of Guru Padmasambhava or Guru Rimpoche, the revered incarnation of Lord Buddha. The main festivities are marked by a grand two-day fair at the Hemis Gompa which is the biggest Buddhist monastery located near Leh in Ladakh.

Magha Puja Day (Four-fold Assembly or "Sangha Day")

This commemorates the occasion of the great Four-fold Assembly, an important event in the teaching life of the Buddha. It is so-called because of its four important factors: (1) All the 1250 monks who assembled to hear the Master at that time were *Arahats* or realised souls; (2) All of them were ordained by the Buddha himself; (3) They assembled by themselves without any prior call; (4) It was the full moon day of Magha month (March).

Asalha Puja Day ("Dhamma Day")

This festival marks the first sermon delivered by the Buddha, known as the First Turning of the Wheel.

Pavarana Day

This day marks the conclusion of the Rains retreat (*vassa*). It is followed by the *kathina* ceremony in which the laity gather to make formal offerings of robe cloth and other requisites to the *Sangha*.

Ullambana

This festival is celebrated with much popularity in many Buddhist countries. On the occasion of Ullambana, it is believed that the 'Gates of Hell' are opened and the dead ones pay a visit to their loved ones. Therefore, offerings are made to the spirits of the dead and to the hungry ghosts for good fortune and luck. It falls on the 15th day of the 7th lunar month.

Buddhist Festivals are both pious and joyful occasions. Typically on a festival day, lay people visit the local temple or monastery and offer food to the monks. They take the Five Precepts and listen to a Dharma talk. They distribute food to the poor, and in the evening perform the ceremony of circumambulation of a stupa three time as a sign of respect to the Buddha, Dhamma, Sangha.

BUDDHIST MARRIAGES

In Buddhism, marriage is considered as personal and individual concern, and not as a religious duty. Buddhist marriages have been considered as secular matters in many Buddhist countries. The parties take a blessing from monks at the local temple after the civil registration formalities have been completed. Although Buddhist monks do not solemnise a marriage ceremony, they do perform religious services in order to bless the couples. Buddhism does not regard marriage as a religious duty nor as a sacrament that is ordained in heaven. However, it does offer some guidelines for marriages. While Buddhist practice varies considerably among its various schools, scriptures such as the *Digha Nikaya* describes the respect that one is expected to give to one's spouse.

TIBETAN BUDDHISM

Special mention must be made of Tibetan Buddhism, which follows the Mahayana tradition. Following the occupation by China, Tibetan diaspora, under the charismatic leadership of their spiritual head, the Dalai Lama, has made their version of Buddhism easily accessible to people all over the world. The Dalai Lama himself has become a symbol and a focus of Tibetan cultural identity. As a Tibetan scholar observes, "The Dalai Lama is regarded as an incarnation of the *bodhisattva* of compassion and patron deity of Tibet. In that role the Dalai Lama has chosen to use peace and compassion in his treatment of his own people

Buddhist holy flags

and his oppressors. In this sense the Dalai Lama is the embodiment of an ideal of Tibetan values and a cornerstone of Tibetan identity and culture."

The goal of spiritual development in Tibetan Buddhism is to achieve enlightenment (Buddhahood); but this is meant to most efficiently help all other sentient beings attain this state.

The Kagyu, or "practice" lineage, contributed greatly to the Tibetan tradition, through the teachings of its extraordinary practitioners, such as Marpa Lotsawa, the great translator and Jetsun Milarepa, Tibet's greatest yogi. This tradition continues unbroken to the present day, and the teachings of enlightened Kagyu masters are considered among the most precious jewels of spiritual insight and practical guidance in the world.

Thousands of candles can be lighted from a single candle,
and the life of the candle will not be shortened.
Happiness never decreases by being shared.

Christianity is the world's most popular religion, in terms of sheer numbers. Over 30% of the world's population is Christian by faith; as many as 75% of Americans, Canadians and Europeans identify themselves as Christian, although these people belong to 1500 different denominations of Christianity. The Christian concept of salvation tells us that God sent his son among men to be a guide and saviour. It was from Jesus Christ that Christianity derives its origin and its name.

CHRISTIANITY

Jesus: The Messiah

From the grandeur and ritual splendour of St. Peter's Basilica in Rome to the makeshift shacks on the wayside where newly converted Christians congregate in rural India, from the intellectual complexity of St. Thomas Aquinas to the simple and selfless service of the Little Sisters of the Poor, from idealistic reformers like Martin Luther to twenty-first century Prophets of the poor like Mother Teresa, from the Roman Catholic church to the Eastern Orthodox Faith, from Quakers and Unitarians to Anglicans and Christian Scientists, from Seventh Day Adventists to the Syrian Orthodox Church, there are over two billion people who share the basic tenets of Christianity – i.e. belief in Jesus Christ as the Saviour, belief in the Bible as the word of God, and the firm belief that theirs is the true Christian faith, among all others.

A Christian scholar once remarked: "Christianity today, is not the religion of Jesus; it is the religion about Jesus." What he means is that people today repose more faith in Jesus as God, than in his teachings. Indeed, Jesus is the one binding factor in all the sects of Christianity. One of the reasons for the many differences within the Christian faith is simple: because the world changes, religions also change and evolve. It changes people; and it is itself changed in this process.

The Saviour is born

Give and it shall be given to you. For whatever measure you deal out to others, it will be dealt to you in return.

Given this kind of diversity in belief and practice, it is not easy to give a brief introduction to Christianity. Mainstream Christians tend to be inclusive; they regard everyone who believes in Christ as a true Christian. Liberal Christians are engaged in reinterpreting their religion for the third millennium, and encourage serious dialogue with other faiths in an attempt to understand and appreciate the value of non-Christian religions. At the other end of the scale, we have more fundamentalist and evangelical denominations who dismiss other religions and other notions of God as being false, and indeed 'damned' in Christian terms. Protestants believe in a unique personal and individual approach to their God and their faith; Roman Catholics insist on the intermediation of the Church as their approach and access to God. This wide diversity of beliefs and practices is a characteristic of the larger Christian umbrella of sects and churches in the world today.

Who is a Christian? There are many answers to this question: to some believers, one has to be 'born again', to be a true Christian; to others, one has to be baptised to take such a description; there is no consensus on who is a true Christian among the various Christian denominations. But, in a broad world view, we must accept as a Christian any individual who seriously regards himself to be Christian.

The term Christ appears in English and most European languages, owing to the Greek usage of

Khristós (meaning 'anointed' or 'covered in oil'). In Hebrew, the original term used in the Bible was the equivalent of 'messiah'. The apostle Peter tells Jesus, "You are the Christ, the Son of the living God".

The name Jesus is spelled IESUS in the 1611 King James Version of the Bible. Yeshua, in Hebrew was a common name among Jews of the Second Temple Period, and is thought to be the Hebrew or Aramaic name for Jesus. In modern Hebrew, Yeshu and Yeshua are in fact the common transcriptions for Jesus.

Christian views of Jesus say that Jesus is divine, that he is the Messiah whose coming was prophesied in the Old Testament, and that he was resurrected after his crucifixion. Many Christians do believe that Jesus is the "Son of God" (generally meaning that he is God the Son, the second person in the Trinity) who came to provide salvation and reconciliation with God by his death for their sins. Other Christian beliefs include Jesus' birth through Immaculate Conception (virgin birth), performance of miracles, ascension into Heaven, and a future Second Coming. While the doctrine of the Trinity is accepted by most Christians, a few groups reject the doctrine of the Trinity, wholly or partly, as non-scriptural.

In Islam, Jesus (transliterated as *Isa*) is considered one of God's important prophets and a worker of miracles. Jesus is also called "Messiah", but Islam does not teach that he was divine.

ORIGINS

Jesus Christ is the central figure of Christianity. The principal sources of information regarding Jesus' life and teachings are the four canonical gospels – that is, the New Testament versions according to Matthew, Mark, Luke and John. The following details are considered to be historical and accurate: that he was a Jew who was regarded widely as a teacher and healer; he was baptised by John the Baptist, and was crucified in Jerusalem on the orders of the Roman Prefect of Judaea, Pontius Pilate, on the charge of sedition against the Roman Empire.

Further details available in the Gospel are: Jesus was born between 7–2 BC and died 26–36 AD. The reason for assigning these dates is as follows: The Gospel of Matthew places Jesus' birth under the reign of Herod the Great, who died in 4 BC, while the Gospel of Luke describes the birth as taking place during the first census of the Roman provinces of Syria and Judaea in 6 AD. Scholars therefore generally assume a date of birth between 4 BC and 6 AD.

Our love must not be a thing of words and fine talk. It must be a thing of action and sincerity.

According to some sources, December 25 was chosen as the "birth-day" of Jesus because it coincided with the Roman festivity of *Sol Invictus* ("The undefeated sun") which was still being celebrated in the 3rd century, and the Church wanted to associate the day with the birth of the Son of God rather than the birth of the Sun. The common Western standard for numbering years, in which the current year is 2009, is based on an early medieval attempt to count the years from Jesus' birth.

According to the Gospels, the death of Jesus took place during the time that Pontius Pilate was the Roman Prefect of Judea, i.e. between 26 and 36 AD. Many early historians agree that it was Pilate who passed the order to execute Jesus.

Put together, the four gospels give us a beautiful account of the life of Jesus, though some details vary. Jesus was born to a devout Jewess named Mary and a carpenter named Joseph. According to the Gospels of Matthew and Luke, Jesus was born of Immaculate Conception, to a Virgin Mother, conceived by a miracle of the Holy Spirit before the couple had had any relationship. Matthew and Luke also tell us that Jesus was born in Bethlehem, the ancestral hometown of Joseph, to which the couple had travelled, to register themselves for the census ordered by the Roman Governor. Mark and John do not discuss Jesus' birth; they begin their narratives with Jesus' adulthood.

All the Gospels are virtually silent when it comes to Jesus' early life, but some information can be inferred from them and other sources. Jesus was from a small town called Nazareth in the province of Galilee, where he trained as a carpenter under his father. He probably spoke Aramaic, a Semitic language related to Hebrew. The Gospel of Luke offers us one very interesting event from this early period: 12-year old Jesus wanders off from his parents in Jerusalem to discuss religion in the temple. When his frantic parents finally find him, Jesus asks, "Didn't you know I would be in my Father's house?" [Luke 2:41-51.]

The Gospels resume with the life of Jesus when he is about thirty years old. All four gospels say that Jesus' first act at this time was to be baptised by John the Baptist, a charismatic and ascetic figure, probably related to him, who called people to repentance and baptised those who responded. This event marks the beginning of Jesus' life of teaching and healing, or 'public ministry' as it is referred to. Many Christians believe, that Jesus became Divine at this point.

If ye have faith as a grain of mustard seed, ye shall say unto this mountain, remove hence to younder place; and it shall remove; and nothing shall be impossible to you.

We may infer from the Gospels, that Jesus spent the next few years (one to three years) teaching people his profoundly new and 'radical' doctrines of love, charity, compassion and forgiveness towards one's enemies, as against the so-called Old Testament doctrine of revenge and retribution, and working miracles among his disciples and before large crowds. His recorded miracles included turning water to wine, walking on water, cursing a fig tree so that it becomes withered, healing the sick, multiplying a small meal to feed a crowd, casting out demons, and even raising a man from the dead.

These are 'facts of the life' as we may gather from the Gospels. But there are profoundly moving incidents such as the rising of Lazarus from the dead; the devotion of Mary Magdalene; the betrayal by Judas Iscariot – and so many events that have captured the imagination of the world, and become part of the people's religious psyche.

THE TEACHINGS OF JESUS

Any one who reads the Gospel, including non-Christians, are profoundly moved by the depth, profundity and the intense conviction with which Jesus taught his followers. He did not refer to external powers, but spoke with the quiet conviction of his own authority. He often preached through the form of parables – disarmingly simple stories from nature,

Basilica of the Annunciation at Nazereth

After the baptism, Jesus travelled through the regions of Galilee, Samaria, and Judea, teaching in the synagogues and speaking to the crowds of people who followed him wherever he went. From among them, he selected twelve disciples, who become known later as the Twelve Apostles. Two of them, Matthew and John, are the traditional authors of the Gospels that carry their name.

The name of the LORD is a strong tower;
the righteous run to it
and are safe.

agriculture and the life of the common people, which nevertheless carried profound and difficult teachings. It is said that his teachings left people baffled and tongue-tied, shaken out of their complacency and self-righteousness. He spoke of loving God above all other things, caring about all other people as much as we care about ourselves, the coming kingdom of God and eternal life.

Jesus taught that God was like a loving father to all of us: God knows and loves each of us personally, as parents know and love their children. God will give good things to those who ask: "For everyone who asks receives, and he who seeks finds, and to him who knocks it shall be opened." God is loving and merciful, and always ready to forgive repentant sinners. In a conversation with the skeptical Pharisee, Nicodemus, Jesus revealed his own divinity: God loved the people He had created so much that He sent Jesus, his own son, to save them from the forces of evil and their sinful ways. Those who put their trust in Jesus and His teachings could be saved and reach God's spiritual kingdom:

Naked, and ye clothed me: I was sick, and ye visited me: I was in prison, and ye came unto me.

"For God so loved the world, that He gave His only begotten Son, that whoever believes in Him should not perish, but have eternal life. God did not send the Son into the world to judge the world, but that the world should be saved through Him." [John 3:16-17]

Time and again, Jesus refers to God as "the Father" or "our heavenly Father". "The kingdom of God" that he talks about is not an earthly kingdom, but a spiritual realm. It is the kingdom of people's hearts and souls. People who seek worldly power cannot find this kingdom; only those who choose to love God and serve Him, can inherit this kingdom. In a beautiful parable of the sower and the seed, Jesus tells us that three things are needed to belong to God's kingdom: awareness, understanding, devotion to God and commitment to the faith. The seed that falls on the hard path, symbolises a person who does not understand the Word of God and the Commandments; he will fall into the temptation of evil and lose sight of God's kingdom. The seed that falls on the shallow, rocky soil, is like a person lacking a strong commitment; he will drift away from faith because of social pressure, inconvenience, embarrassment or persecution. The seed that falls among thistles, refers to the faith of a person who is not totally devoted and succumbs to the pettiness of worldly life and the desires for worldly wealth, power and status. The seed that falls on good ground represents the heart of a man who listens to the message and understands it and goes out and brings thirty, sixty, or even a hundred others into the kingdom. And this kingdom of God is not far to seek: "It is within you," Jesus emphasised. Entry to this kingdom is not through one's right or privilege, but through God's grace and mercy.

Once a man asked Jesus, "Of all the commandments, which is the most important?" "The most important one," answered Jesus, is this: 'Hear, O Israel, the Lord our God, the Lord is one. Love the Lord your God with all your heart and with all your soul and with all your mind and with all your strength.' [Mark 12:28-30]

Christian scholars interpret 'loving God' to include the following:

• Know and obey God's Commandments

• Trust in God and Jesus

• Put God above all else

• Be committed

• Be humble before God and men

• Make time for prayer

In the Parable of The Wise and Foolish Builders [Luke 6:46-49], Jesus compares a man who hears His words and puts them into practice to a house built on a solid foundation or rock; it will weather any storm.

On the other hand, a man who hears His words and does not put them into practice is like a house built without a foundation; the first storm will cause it to collapse and be destroyed. Thus obeying the Will of God is of paramount importance. As the Bible says, "Faith without works is dead."

Jesus also tells us: "Do not let your hearts be troubled. Trust in God; trust also in me." Significantly, he adds, "The work of God is this: to believe in the one he has sent." (i.e, Jesus himself)

Jesus taught that serving God and serving wealth are incompatible goals. "No servant can serve two masters. Either he will hate the one and love the other, or he will be devoted to the one and despise the other. You cannot serve both God and Money."[Luke 16:13]

Jesus emphasised humility above all else. Once the disciples came to Jesus and asked, "Who is the greatest in the kingdom of heaven?" He called a little child and had him stand among them. And he said: "I tell you the truth, unless you change and become like little children, you will never enter the kingdom of heaven.

Beloved, follow not that which is evil, but that which is good. He that doeth good is of God: but he that doeth evil hath not seen God.

Therefore, whoever humbles himself like this child is the greatest in the kingdom of heaven." And again, "He who is greatest among you will be your servant. For whoever exalts himself will be humbled, and whoever humbles himself will be exalted." [Matthew 23:11-12]

Prayer, as a loving communication with God, is vital for all men: thus Jesus tells us, "Ask, and it shall be given to you; seek, and you shall find; knock, and it shall be opened to you... For everyone who asks receives, and he who seeks finds, and to him who knocks it shall be opened... If you then, being evil, know how to give good gifts to your children, how much more shall your Father who is in heaven give what is good to those who ask Him!"

We can see from the Gospels that Jesus spent a lot of time praying, especially at difficult times in His ministry. The famous Lord's Prayer is Jesus' model of the perfect prayer:

Our father, who art in heaven, hallowed be thy name, thy kingdom come; thy will be done on earth as it is in heaven; give us this day our daily bread and forgive us our trespasses; as we forgive those who trespass against us; and lead us not into temptation, but deliver us from evil.

Commit to the LORD whatever you do, and your plans will succeed.

Jesus also insisted that all his followers should love their neighbours even as they loved themselves: "A new command I give you: Love one another. As I have loved you, so you must love one another. By this all men will know that you are my disciples, if you love one another." [John 13:34-35]

By 'neighbours' Jesus literally meant all mankind, even our enemies! Jesus told His famous parable of the Good Samaritan to make this clear, that neighbour meant all persons, everywhere – not just our friends, allies, countrymen, but even strangers, other social groups and even our enemies. "Love your enemies! Pray for those who persecute you! In that way you will be acting as true sons of your Father in heaven. For he gives his sunlight to both the evil and the good, and sends rain on the just and on the unjust too. If you love only those who love you, what good is that? Even scoundrels do that much. If you are friendly only to your friends, how are you different from anyone else? Even the heathen do that. But you are to be perfect, even as your Father in heaven is perfect." [Matthew 5:43-48]

"Forgive and forget," was Jesus's counsel to all men. We should always be willing to forgive others, even when they don't ask for forgiveness. Holding a grudge, or seeking revenge should have no place in the lives of those who truly love their neighbours. Jesus constantly beseeches us to remember that we are all God's children. Just as He loves all His people and is willing to forgive their sins, we should be willing to forgive also.

The Old Testament law specified revenge for all wrongs: "an eye for an eye, a tooth for a tooth" (Exodus 21:23-25, Leviticus 24:19-20.) But this rule was too harsh for the kingdom of the spirit. In His Sermon on the Mount, Jesus says:

"You have heard that it was said, 'An eye for an eye, and a tooth for a tooth.' But I say to you, do not resist him who is evil; but whoever slaps you on your right cheek, turn to him the other also."[Matthew 5:38-39]

Loving our neighbours is not just an abstract concept or theory: it means serving others selflessly; it means feeding the hungry, clothing the poor, and serving the sick and the lonely. "Whatsoever you do to the least of my people, that you do unto Me." [Matthew 25:31-46] Nor will such kindness go unrewarded in the eyes of God; what we give, we will also get. Which brings us to The Golden Rule uttered by Jesus: "So in everything, do unto others what you would have them do unto you, for this sums up the Law and the Prophets."[Matthew 7:12]

Jesus's simple, remarkable, unique and profound teachings are summed up in the Eight Beatitudes which he gave to his followers in The Sermon on the Mount:

Blessed are the poor in spirit,

for theirs is the kingdom of heaven.

Blessed are they who mourn,

for they shall be comforted.

Blessed are the meek,

for they shall inherit the earth.

Blessed are they who hunger and thirst for righteousness,

for they shall be satisfied.

Blessed are the merciful,

for they shall obtain mercy.

Blessed are the pure of heart,

for they shall see God.

Blessed are the peacemakers,

for they shall be called children of God.

Blessed are they who are persecuted for the sake of righteousness,

for theirs is the kingdom of heaven."

[Gospel of St. Matthew 5:3-10]

St. Augustine described the Beatitudes as "the ideal for every Christian life".

Father, forgive them: for they know not what they do…

A gentle answer turns away wrath, but a harsh word stirs up anger.

THE CRUCIFIXION OF JESUS

Jesus's teachings stirred the hearts of the masses, and both orthodox Jews and the Roman occupiers feared that this would undermine their authority. Jesus prophesied very accurately, the events that would follow: He taught his disciples about the will of God and about the "new covenant" God will bring to humanity through Him. The purpose of this "new covenant" is to restore those who accept it into a renewed fellowship of forgiveness and love with God. What is this new covenant? Jesus, the Son of God who was born as a man, would himself pay for the sins of all humanity by being crucified unjustly on a Roman cross. Three days later, He would rise to life, having conquered death, to give hope to a hopeless world. It happened exactly as Jesus taught, and His disciples were witnesses to an amazing miracle. Their teacher, Jesus of Nazareth, died and three days later rose again to become their Messiah.

HISTORY OF THE CHURCH

Upon His resurrection, Jesus commanded His disciples to spread his teachings to all the world. The doctrines of the apostles brought the early Church into conflict with some Jewish religious authorities. This eventually led to their expulsion from the synagogues, and also brought about the first martyrdoms of St. Stephen and St. James the Great. From now on, Christianity acquired an identity distinct from Rabbinic Judaism, out of which it was born.

According to Biblical accounts, Simon Peter was one of the Twelve Apostles, chosen by Jesus from his first disciples. He was a fisherman assigned a leadership role by Jesus and was with Jesus during events witnessed by only a few apostles, such as the Transfiguration. Peter is revered by all Christians to this very day, as the founder of the Church. This claim is based on a passage in Matthew 16. In this passage, Jesus asks his disciples who they think he is. Peter answers, "You are the Christ, the Son of the Living God." Jesus replies: "Blessed are you, Simon son of Jonah, for this was not revealed to you by man, but by my Father in heaven. And I tell you that you are Peter, and on this rock I will build my church."

The Gospel of John also corroborates this, for in this scripture, the resurrected Jesus commands Peter: "Feed my sheep."

In the early history of Christianity, five cities emerged as important centres of Christianity: Rome, Jerusalem, Antioch, Alexandria and Constantinople. But by the fifth century AD, Rome began to claim its supremacy over all other cities, and the 'Bishop of Rome' eventually became the Pope, the head of the Church and the spiritual authority of all Christians.

The Church is thought to have been 'undivided' till about the eleventh century. Then the Eastern Orthodox Church of Constantinople broke away from the Roman Catholic Church, which insisted on its own spiritual supremacy. The Eastern Orthodox Church comprises the churches of Russia, Greece, eastern Europe and other Mediterranean nations (formerly part of the Byzantine empire), which are governed by an Ecumenical Council. In 1517, the Protestant movement led by Martin Luther further split the church in two.

Church of the Holy Sepulchre, Jerusalem

Today, Rome is identified with the Roman Catholic Church – perhaps the leading Christian sect among more than 1500 different denominations of Christianity. Other leading sects are: Protestants, Anglicans, Presbyterians, Methodists, Unitarians and several more.

There is no fear in love; but perfect love casteth out fear...

According to the *Encyclopaedia Britannica Book of the Year*, Christianity is the most widespread religion in the world. They have established "significant" communities, in 254 countries and territories. This leads the Baha'i faith at 205 locations and Islam at 172.

The percentage of the world's population that regard themselves as Christians appears to be remarkably constant. It has risen only from 33.7% in 1970 to 33.9% in 1996. Its current annual growth rate is about 2.3% which is approximately equal to the growth rate of the world's population.

CHRISTIAN RITUALS AND PRACTICES

Christian rituals and religious practices vary according to denominations, but some of them are common to all forms of Christianity.

Most Christians attend worship services at church on Sundays, which generally include singing, prayer and a sermon. At home, most practicing Christians pray regularly and many read the Bible.

Nearly all Christians will have been baptised, either as an infant or as an adult, and regularly participate in communion (also called the Lord's Supper and the Eucharist). Baptism and communion are considered sacraments – sacred rituals instituted by Christ himself.

The Catholic Church recognises five additional sacraments, as well as many other distinctive practices that are known as "sacramentals" or "devotions" and include praying the rosary and going on pilgrimages. Both Catholic and Orthodox Churches have religious orders. The most distinctive practice of Orthodoxy is the emphasis on icons, although Catholics use them as well.

General Christian practices include:

- Baptism
- Confirmation
- Communion
- Sunday Services
- Prayer
- Bible Study

Love your enemies and pray for those who persecute you. For if you love those who love you, what reward have you? Do not even the tax collectors do the same?

- Evangelism and Missions
- Ordination
- Marriage
- Funerals

PROTESTANT RITUALS:

- The Altar Call (Evangelical)
- Speaking in Tongues (Pentecostal)
- Spirit-Led Worship (Quaker)

SPECIFICALLY ROMAN CATHOLIC RITUALS:

- Mass
- Confession
- Penance
- Last Rites
- Canonization and Veneration of Saints
- Devotion to Mary
- Praying the Rosary
- Pilgrimages
- Stations of the Cross
- Icons

- Ordination to Religious Orders
- Monastic Life
- Holy Water
- Exorcism

Do not resist one who is evil. But if anyone strikes you on the right cheek, turn to him the other also.

THE SACRED TEXTS OF CHRISTIANITY

The primary sacred text of Christianity is the Bible. Its name is derived from the Latin word *biblia,* which simply means "books". The Christian Bible is made of two parts: the Old Testament, which is almost identical to the Jewish Bible; and the New Testament, a collection of Christian writings that includes biographies of Jesus and the Apostles (the Gospels and The Book of Apostles), letters to new churches, (Epistles) and an apocalyptic work (the Book of Revelations).

The word Testament means "covenant," so the notion of old and new Testaments reflects the Christian perspective that the Church is the successor to the nation of Israel as God's chosen people. The Old Testament, which is the sacred text of the Jews, is viewed by all Christians as foundational, authoritative, and relevant; but it is also regarded as having been superceded and fulfilled by the New Testament (covenant) God has made with the Church, through Jesus and his apostles.

HOLY DAYS AND FESTIVALS OF CHRISTIANITY

Like all Abrahamaic religions, holy days, feasts and fasts are a significant part of Christian religious practice. The feast days celebrate joyous events, such as the birth and resurrection of Christ, while the fast days provide a special opportunity to focus on introspection, self-denial and repentance. Some Christian holidays such as Christmas and New Year have come to have a considerable impact on western culture and traditions.

Advent (adventus, "coming") marks the beginning of the church year and the approach of Christmas.

Christmas marks the celebration of the birth of Jesus. The English word "Christmas" derives from the old English *Christes maesse*, or "Christ's mass."

The celebration of *Epiphany* (*epiphaneia*, "manifestation") recalls the visit of the Magi, symbolising Christ's manifestation to Gentiles.

Made famous by the Shakespearean play, *Twelfth Night* marks the end of the Christmas season.

Lent is a 40-day period of fasting and repentance in preparation for Easter.

Ash Wednesday is the first day of Lent, a period of fasting that leads up to Easter. Its central ritual is placing of ashes on the forehead.

Palm Sunday is the sixth Sunday of Lent and the last Sunday before Easter. It commemorates the entry of Jesus into Jerusalem, just before his trial and crucifixion.

Good Friday marks the day on which Jesus was crucified.

Jingle bells – the spirit of Merry Christmas

Easter is the most holy of Christian festivals. *Easter Sunday* marks the solemn and joyous occasion of Christ's resurrection.

Thanksgiving Day is a holiday celebrated primarily in Canada and the United States. It is essentially a harvest festival, which is celebrated on the second Monday of October in Canada and on the fourth Thursday of November in the United States. Families get together for a traditional Thanksgiving dinner, in memory of the Pilgrim Fathers who made pioneering efforts to settle in the 'new world' as it was then called. Historically, it was religious in origin, meant to offer thanks to God; but now it is primarily identified as a national holiday.

CHRISTIAN MARRIAGES

Christians regard marriage as a sacrament, instituted and ordained by God for the lifelong relationship between one man as husband and one woman as wife, and is to be "held in honour among all..." Marriages have social as well as religious significance for Christians. While civil ceremonies have become increasingly prevalent in the West, most practicing Christians still prefer to conduct their weddings in their Church, under the direction of their priest or pastor. A Christian bride traditionally wears a white gown, as white represents purity. Her head is covered with a white veil and she wears a coronet of white flowers. The groom wears a black suit with a tie. Both the groom and the bride accept each other in front of the priest.

Christian weddings are beautiful and elegant. The bride, dressed in white, enters the church on the arm of her father, and she is accompanied by bridesmaids who hold her veil and flowers. The groom is accompanied by his close friend, called the best man. The father walks down the aisle with the bride, while the bridesmaids and ushers follow her.

Actual marriage rituals commence when the groom and his bride come up before the altar. As they come forward, the priest talks to them about the sanctity of marriage and the joy it gives to all the people who are present in church to witness the solemnisation of the wedding. In the meanwhile, hymns are sung by the choir. This is followed by special readings from the Bible. Two witnesses come forward from each side, in whose presence the groom and the bride proclaim that they want to take each other as man and wife.

No one can serve two masters; for either he will hate the one and love the other, or he will be devoted to the one and despise the other. You cannot serve God and mammon.

They declare the wedding vows after this. The priest blesses the rings and gives them to the couple. The boy and the girl exchange the rings. Subsequently, the priest declares them to be man and wife. The holy process ends with the sealing of their vows as the priest asks the groom to kiss his bride. The brief religious ceremony is followed by a grand wedding feast.

UNIQUE FEATURES OF CHRISTIANITY

Christianity is the world's most popular monotheistic religion. Christians believe that Jesus, their saviour, is the visible manifestation of their invisible God.

Many Christian sects revere the doctrine of the Holy Trinity – that is, the triple manifestation of God as the Father, the Son and the Holy Spirit.

The Church is venerated as a mediator between man and God, although some Protestant sects reject this concept.

The most distinctive teaching of Christianity is that Jesus died to expiate for the sins of humanity. His sacrificial death opened up the gates of paradise which had been shut by Adam and Eve's transgression. Thus the concept of Original Sin is peculiar to Christianity: it avers that all men are born sinners. It is only his faith and the grace of God that can save him and grant him salvation.

According to the Bible, God created man in his own image, but man's sin corrupted him.

Christianity shares many beliefs with Judaism and Islam, including resurrection of the dead, the day of judgement as well as heaven and hell as literal destinations for the virtuous and the vicious.

For Christianity, the world and this life on earth are real; they can be improved by man's good deeds.

Popular Christianity accepts the existence of devils, angels and evil spirits.

Christianity emphasises the humanitarian values of simplicity, humility, love, charity, compassion and forgiveness above all else. These values are emphasised in beautiful parables like The Prodigal Son.

Do not be anxious about your life, what you shall eat or what you shall drink, nor about your body, what you shall put on. Is not life more than food and the body more than clothing?

The power and influence of Christ opened a new era in world history, emphasising the typically Christian virtues of humility, charity, piety and compassion. Christ's own life and teachings reflected these virtues, which are still regarded as the hallmarks of true Christians.

God is not only the Father, but the Saviour and Redeemer in the form of Christ. Good Christians are enjoined to imitate God and strive to be perfect like Him.

God's love signifies service in all humility. This is exemplified by Jesus Christ in the Last Supper, when he washed the feet of his disciples. It also signifies sacrifice, for God allowed His only son to die on the cross, for the redemption of mankind. Therefore, all suffering is regarded by Christians, as redemptive, corrective and purifying.

All sects of Christianity believe in proselytization and conversion. In fact, many sects regard this as their sacred duty and obligation.

Monasticism came into the early church, leading to the establishment of many Monastic Orders such as the Franciscans, the Jesuits, the Carmelites and others. Equally, there are convents or orders for nuns, women who give up worldly life to serve God through a life of poverty, chastity and obedience to His will. The Roman Catholic Church still has celibate clergy, who are committed to the vows of chastity; Protestant churches do not insist on celibacy.

Many Christian sects are remarkable for their missionary zeal; not only have these missionaries established schools, colleges, hospitals and orphanages throughout the world, but are also actively engaged in spreading the word of God, as they call it.

Look at the birds of the air: they neither sow nor reap nor gather into barns, and yet your heavenly Father feeds them. Are you not of more value than they?

*Indians are the proud inheritors of a rich heritage –
the heritage of what people call "Hinduism". May I
tell you, I do not like to use the word Hinduism –
for the Hindu faith, I believe, is not an "ism" – it is
not a creed or a dogma.*

Lord Krishna with the magical flute

THE HINDU FAITH

Among all the great religions of the world, Hinduism occupies a unique position. It is the only religion that has not been founded by a person or persons. It has existed eternally without a founder. It does not rest on any beliefs or dogmas or on the words of a Prophet but on universal and eternal spiritual principles. Unlike other religions, which are organised institutions, Hinduism is not an organised religion but a self-evolved one. Other religions have their protectors and propagandists. Hinduism is scientific in its approach and is based on the reasoning and realisations (in superconscious states) of great spiritual geniuses called *rishis*.

THE ETERNAL RELIGION

There are many religions in the world today. Each of them has a name of its own. Each of them was founded by a single person, at a certain point in time, at a certain stage in the history of the world. These founders were undoubtedly great men – each one a seer, a sage, a prophet, an incarnation of God. As we know, Christianity was founded by Jesus Christ 2000 years ago. Islam was founded by Prophet Mohammed in the 7th century AD. Here in India, Buddhism was founded by Gautama, the Buddha, 2500 years ago. A little earlier, Jainism had been founded by Mahavira. Each religion has a name of its own, a founder, and a definite period in which it was founded.

The Hindu faith, by contrast, has no name, no founder. No one knows when this religion began, or where its roots lie, although speculations abound. But one thing is certain: the Hindu faith is rooted in the oldest scriptures of the world, the Vedas.

The attainment of one-pointedness of the mind and the senses is the best of austerities. It is superior to all other duties and religious austerities.

I love to think of Hinduism as a faith without beginning or end. It has been existing from the very remote past. Therefore, if it is necessary to call it by a name, that name must be *Sanatana Dharma* – the Eternal Religion. The term *Sanatana Dharma* has also been translated as *Righteousness Forever* or *That which has no beginning or end.*

UNIQUE FEATURES OF THE HINDU FAITH

Scholars and historians everywhere agree that the *Sanatana Dharma* is unique in several respects:

It is the only non-prophetic religion in the world. While all other major religions are rooted firmly in history with one person as the founder and his teaching as one doctrine to follow, Hinduism does not take its origin in the life or teaching or spiritual experiences of any one individual. Rather, it is based on certain universal, timeless values and ideals. By its insistence on these *eternal truths*, embedded in the Vedas, Hinduism implicitly postulates that these truths, first received by the *rishis,* can be found out by *anyone* who seeks them through devout and relentless pursuit.

It is definitely the oldest religion in the world. It is said to be as old as civilisation itself – some would even say, as old as the world.

He is the Sun illumining all!
His countenance is radiant in all places,
Yea, in the cave of the heart He shines!
Ageless is the Atman - the Ancient of
days!
In Him is no darkness!
In Him is neither day nor night!
They who know and love Him,
They come to immortality!

There have been several ancient religions which we read about in world history – the Greek religion with its vast pantheon of Gods; the Egyptian religion, with its animistic faith; the Inca faith of American Indians of which very little is known to us. But these religions have all been superceded by others; these faiths have failed to survive; while Hinduism, older than all of these and other contemporary religions, has survived the test of time.

Hinduism gives us the greatest possible freedom to practice our faith – for, in the words of my Beloved Master, Sadhu Vaswani, "the goal is one, but the paths are many". Hinduism has always recognised this fact, and emphasised that man's journey to eternity is essentially an inner journey. God-realisation is thus open to all – the family man as well as the ascetic. Hinduism also teaches us that all forms of worship are acceptable to God. We may use idols; we may go to temples; we may recite set prayers; we may offer a simple form of worship with flowers and a lamp; or we may perform an elaborate *puja* with set rituals; we may sing *bhajans* or join a *kirtan* session; or we can just close our eyes and meditate upon the light within us. Each and every one of these forms of worship is acceptable – so are many others, like selfless service; or absolute faith; or the dedicated performance of one's duty, in the spirit of worship; or selfless sacrifice. Hinduism tells us that God accepts any kind of worship, any type of prayer that comes from the heart. The language, the rituals, the location of worship is not important.

Hinduism has always been the most open minded of faiths. Debates and discussions (*tarka*) were always encouraged. In the ancient *ashramas*, disciples were encouraged to question their *gurus* until concepts were made clear to them — a process called *prashneya*.

This holds good even today. No Hindu teacher will resort to dogma or try to retreat behind difficult Sanskrit statements. There is no authority, no set text, no hierarchical organisation to govern the Hindu conduct and belief. "Do's" and "Don't's" — *THOU SHALL* and *THOU SHALL NOT* are alien to Hinduism.

He is not born,
Nor can He ever die!
He came not into being,
Nor ceaseth He to be!
Birthless, deathless, changeless still,
Abideth he forever!
Death toucheth Him not,
Dead though his house - the body - seems!

There is no aspect of life, no ideology which is not discussed in Hindu scriptures. If its *Advaita* philosophy is abstract and ascetic, its *Charvaka* philosophy is materialistic and atheistic.

While Hindus worship a hundred different idols, in the words of Max Muller, "The religion of the Vedas knows no idols." In fact, one does not even need to know Sanskrit to be a practising Hindu — for truly, the great Hindu scriptures and elaborate commentaries on them are available in several languages.

Our ancient sages and seers understood very well indeed that people would come from different backgrounds, have different tastes, different notions and different abilities. That is why they did not impose a unitary ritual or unitary form of worship on different individuals with different temperaments. Thus some of us celebrate sacred days with feasts and lots of good food to eat; while others observe a strict fast on those very days. Some spiritual aspirants gather together to listen to discourses; yet others sit in silent meditation. Some people break coconuts before the deity; others light lamps; some simply repeat the Name Divine.

In its essence, Hinduism is essentially monotheistic – but it is misunderstood by many people as polytheistic. Our sages declare in the Upanishads: *Ekam sat viprah bahuda vadanti* – "The Truth is one, it is spoken under various names."

Further, it is said:
Aaakasaat patitam toyam yadha gachchati sagaram
Sarva deva namaskaram Keshavam prati gachchati

"Just as rain water which falls from the sky, irrespective of where it falls, ultimately reaches the ocean, so too, the worship offered to all deities reaches the Supreme Reality that is Keshava."

While the uninitiated of other religions, as well as the ill-informed Hindus may mistake this for polytheism; it must be stressed that God is only One; He is all-knowing, all-powerful and present everywhere; thus it is that He has countless aspects and countless names. Whatever form and whatever name we bestow upon Him, we call upon the One God, the Supreme Reality. As we evolve, as we grow in wisdom and piety, we will reach the beautiful state of God-realisation where we will discover the Nameless and Formless One.

Therefore, it would be true to say that the evolved Hindu, who has truly understood his religion, does not worship multiple gods – but believes in various aspects of the One behind the many. As the *Ishopanishad* tells us so beautifully, *Ishavasyam idam sarvam* - "All that is, is a vesture of the Lord".

Hinduism does not force its teachings or doctrines upon anyone. There are no set dogmas to be followed by Hindus. Rather, you are given complete freedom to think for yourself - not to accept anything on authority or hearsay, but to verify the truth of what is told to you before you accept it. You are not told to

---

Do thou the deed with thy heart fixed on the Lord:
Renounce attachment to the fruit: so be thou still the same in failure and in success!
Equilibrium, at-one-ment, that is yoga!

---

believe something which cannot be proved or verified. Hinduism asks you to do what you consider to be true. There is no place in true Hinduism for sophistry and dogmatic fiat, or superstition and baseless beliefs. Man is given full freedom to investigate into the validity of the beliefs placed before him. It is no sin even to doubt the very existence of God.

Hinduism has never been sectarian or bound by creed. It has a place for everyone. As was said earlier, it even allows space for those who do not believe in God. You may be an agnostic, even an atheist, and yet be a Hindu.

Thus nihilism, atheism, agnosticism and other such attitudes have their due place in the Hindu's search for truth. Freedom, the first condition for growth – mental, moral and spiritual – is granted absolutely and unconditionally to the Hindu.

The main note of Hinduism is one of respect and goodwill for other creeds. Hinduism does not believe in proselytisation or conversion. The Hindus never went out to conquer or convert. They have always been worshippers of truth and believe that the ultimate victory belongs to truth.

Hinduism has been rightly regarded as the mother of all religions. Therefore, all religions have thrived in India. No religion has ever been persecuted here. Thanks to the predominant influence of Hinduism,

India has always stood for religious harmony and understanding. Thus has India become the land of many religions, where every religion is respected.

Unlike some religions, Hinduism does not operate on a fear-psychosis. For instance, some creeds will lay it down that God sits in judgement if you do not follow a particular creed. In Hinduism, we are taught not to be afraid of God, but to think of God as the all-loving father or mother – whom you may approach anytime and at any place. The Hindu has a personal relationship with God – as a father, mother, brother, friend or beloved. Some saints like Surdas have even regarded the Lord as their child.

Hinduism has always been eclectic – choosing the best out of other systems and absorbing the best therefrom. This is what has made Hinduism a growing religion – a religion, which, like the Sun, is ever ancient, ever new.

Unlike other religions which are organised institutions, Hinduism is a self-evolving one. Other

From the unreal lead me to the Real!
From darkness lead me into Light!
From death lead me to the Life Immortal!

religions have their protectors and propagandists. Hinduism is scientific in its approach, and is based on the reasoning and realisations (in super conscious states) of great spiritual geniuses called rishis. Some of them – like The Buddha, Shankaracharya and Chaitanya Mahaprabhu – are considered divine incarnations. As for Sri Krishna, singer of the Song Celestial which we know as the Bhagavad Gita – He was God Himself, who, wearing a human form, visited the earth to give salvation to millions.

In the Gita, after Lord Krishna has passed on many truths concerning life to his dear devoted disciple Arjuna, He finally tells him: "I have declared the truths to you; you must go and reflect upon these teachings and Do As You Choose."

Hinduism uses no compulsion. You are free to enquire into its principles; you must be convinced of their truth, before you accept them. The laws of life are inviolable; they need no defenders, no patrons, no protectors. Each one of us must reach the highest by his own free choice. There has never been any indoctrination in Hinduism.

This fact has been beautifully expressed by Dr. S. Radhakrishnan: "Hinduism is wholly free from the strange obsession of some faiths that the acceptance of a particular religious metaphysics is necessary for salvation, and non-acceptance thereof is a heinous sin meriting eternal punishment in Hell."

Yes, chant the Name!

Sing on the sacred word: Hari! Hari!

Radiant are your faces

With beauty supernal:

Blessed, indeed, are you!

Sing still the Name

And pour into mine ears

Hari's Name, Hari's Name,

O ye cowherd!

Hinduism does not believe in propagation, proselytisation or conversion—for it is essentially a way of life, rather than a religion. Hinduism is renowned for its tolerance of all religions. St. Thomas, one of Jesus Christ's twelve apostles, came to Madras soon after the death of Christ. No one stopped him from propagating the Christian faith. When Christian missionaries, Buddhist monks from China and Muslim pirs came into our country, they were greeted and welcomed as honoured visitors. Members of the orthodox Syrian Church, Zoroastrians and Jews have all been proud to call India their home.

Perhaps the greatest example of Hindu tolerance and open mindedness is that of Emperor Ashoka, a Hindu king who converted to Buddhism and subsequently, actively propagated The Buddhist faith.

Even today, Hindu scholars devote themselves to the study and understanding of various religions – for their Faith enjoins them to seek Truth in all its forms, from all its sources. Thus, the *Srimad Bhagavata* tells us: "Like the honey bee gathering trickles of honey from different flowers, the wise man assimilates the essence of different scriptures and sees only the good in all religions."

Hinduism has neither hierarchy, nor established authority. There is no persecution, no excommunication for dissenters within Hinduism. We must not forget that Mahavira and Buddha were born Hindus but chose to deviate from the authority of the Vedas.

As Swami Vivekananda said: "I am proud to belong to a religion which has taught the world both tolerance and universal acceptance. We believe not only in universal toleration, but we accept all religions as true. As different streams from different sources, all mingle their waters in the sea, so different paths which men take … all lead to God."

The *Sanatana Dharma* includes a number of sects and cults, allied to one another, yet having many differences. It is more like a league of religions than a single religion with a definite creed. It is a fellowship of faiths, a federation of philosophies. It accommodates all types of people; it provides spiritual food for every soul – from the highest to the lowest – for their growth and evolution. There is nothing in any one of the world's religions which we do not already have in the *Sanatana Dharma*; for it is truly a synthesis of all types of religious experiences. It is a synthesis of mysticism, asceticism, pantheism, polytheism and transcendentalism. It is a whole and complete view of life. It is characterised by wide tolerance, high spiritual purpose and deep humanity.

I am neither ears nor tongue,
Nor senses of smell and sight,
Nor hands, nor feet:
Nor am I ether, fire, water, air!
I am pure Knowledge:
I am unbroken Bliss!
I am Shiva! I am Shiva!
I have no form or fancy:
All pervading am I, the Atman:
And beyond the senses am I!
Pure Knowledge and Bliss am I!
I am Shiva! I am Shiva!

In India, almost everyone – literate or illiterate, rich or poor – knows something of philosophy and religion. The cowherd who tends the cattle, the peasant who ploughs the field, the boatman who sails over rivers and seas, the labourer who works in the factory, the office assistant, the executive, the businessman and the industrialist – each one will quote passages replete with psychological truths. Even the barber repeats a sacred formula before he takes up the razor.

The *Guru-shishya parampara* is an ancient Hindu tradition, a great lineage of the Hindu faith. It refers to the unique relationship that exists between a Master who transmits teachings to his chosen disciples. This refers specifically to the tradition of imparting spiritual knowledge, which Hindus trace back to the origins of the created Universe. The Guru is not just a formal teacher, but a spiritual preceptor – a reservoir and a transmitter of spiritual knowledge, spiritual power and energy, which he passes on to his disciples. Perhaps the underlying principle of this relationship is that subtle, advanced, spiritual knowledge is best transmitted through an ideal relationship based on: 1) the *Guru's* great wisdom, compassion, magnanimity and detached and dispassionate love for all humanity; and 2) the *shishya's* dedication, devotion, capability for sacrifice and service, veneration for the Guru and disinterested pursuit of knowledge. Thus the *Guru-shishya parampara* venerates the Guru as the human embodiment of God, and promotes the spirit of reverence for *atma-vidya*, the science of the spirit.

For that which is born, death is certain, and for the dead, birth is certain. Therefore grieve not over that which is unavoidable.

The *Guru-shishya* lineage traces its divine origins to the Creator God of the Holy Trinity, Lord Brahma. Lord Brahma is described as *Swayambhu* (self-created) for He was created directly by God, and was the direct recipient of vedic knowledge from Godhead. From Him begins the great tradition of the *Guru-shishya* lineage. However, this lineage also assumes that Lord Vishnu is the first Guru as he taught the Vedas to Brahma. Lord Shiva is also worshipped as Dakshinamurthy or the *Adi Guru*.

Hinduism places before us four goals of life, pertaining to all aspects of human existence. They are known as the *purusharthas* – i.e. human purpose. These are:

- *Dharma* — righteousness, duty, morality, virtue, ethics, encompassing notions such as *ahimsa* (non-violence) and *satya* (truth)

- *Artha* — wealth, prosperity, glory

- *Kâma* — wish, desire

- *Moksha* — liberation, i.e. liberation from *Samsara*, the cycle of birth-death-rebirth-reincarnation

As we can see, the four *purusharthas* represent a holistic approach to the fulfillment of man's spiritual, ethical, material and emotional needs.

Dharma is a unique concept of Hinduism, which governs all aspects of a devout Hindu's life. The *Atharva Veda* describes *dharma* thus: *Prithivim dharmana dhritam*; i.e. "This world is upheld by *dharma*".

Dharma can also be taken to mean righteousness; it is a code of conduct that enjoins all Hindus to live their lives according to the laws laid down in the scriptures. It is the very foundation of Hindu life and thought. *Dharma* is a cosmic law that emphasises right action, right attitude and right thought towards all beings, all of creation, indeed, towards the whole Universe. Anything that helps a human being to reach God is *dharma* and anything that hinders a human being from reaching God is *adharma*.

Dharma is defined in the *Vaiseshika* philosophy as "that which confers worldly joys and leads to supreme happiness". Thus *dharma* ensures that we live a joyous, peaceful, righteous life here on earth, as well as assuring us of eventual union with the Supreme.

It is obvious that while *artha* and *kama* are inescapable aspects of human life, our pursuit of these goals must be governed by *dharma* – right thinking and right conduct or in short, ethical principles.

By an interesting correlation, the four *purusharthas* also correspond to the four stages of human life as enumerated in the *shastras* – i.e. the four *ashramas* as they are called: *Brahmacharya* (the stage of the student or disciple), *Grihastha* (the stage of the householder or married man/woman), *Vanaprastha* (life of retirement and contemplation) and *Sannyasa* (renunciation).

Brahmacharya (literally, walking with God) is essentially a life of self-discipline and self-control; for this is a prerequisite for the disciple who wishes to attain true knowledge. *Grihastha ashrama* is a sacred institution for all lay people, for it is the foundation of family life and social stability and progress. *Vanaprastha* is a stage where the man approaching old age prepares himself through a life of seclusion and contemplation for the final stage of *Sannyasa* – renunciation. I would define *sannyasa* as a stage in which the aspirant finally realises that the whole universe is his home, and doing good is his religion.

The central ideal of the *Vedanta* (literal meaning: the end of the Vedas) is the concept of Oneness. The forms of this Universe are many; but there is only One life which animates all these forms. All life is sacred; and all creation is an aspect of God. The Lord lives in the divine spark that is man's soul, even as He lives in the stone, the grass, the plant, the river, the bird and the animal. Therefore, the ideal of Vedanta enjoins us not to eat the flesh of animals and other living creatures: for animals and birds are our brothers and sisters in the One Family of Creation.

All life is sacred – and there is no death for the *atman*– the soul. According to the Gita, the *atman* is imperishable: waters cannot drown it, fire cannot burn it, weapons cannot cleave it, nor can it be dried by air. Bodies perish; but the body is only a garment man has worn in this birth. The soul will leave its mortal vesture, and move on to a higher plane, until it assumes another form, another shape, another birth, which is a fruit of its previous *karma*.

India, the home of the Hindu Faith, has had a long history of wars and invasions. Perhaps no other country in the world has been invaded, attacked and looted more often than this land. So many invaders and conquerors tried to impose their faith on Hindus– some, by forcible conversion, yet others through

He (the brahmachari) should look upon his Guru as God. Verily is the Guru the embodiment of Divinity. Accordingly the student must serve Him and please Him in every way.

propaganda. Despite these invasions and these attempts at religious conversions, India has remained predominantly Hindu in faith. How has this been possible? What makes the Hindu faith so firm and strong, so vital and long-lived?

The Hindu Faith lives on, despite the ravages of time, for it has a message to give the modern world– that there can be no true freedom without spirituality. The emphasis of the Hindu faith has always been on the unfolding of the inner powers, the *atmashakti*. It is precisely because of this *atmashakti,* this inner soul power, that India has been able to ride many a storm and quell many a tempest. When all other ancient civilisations have perished, when all other ancient religions have been wiped away without a trace, India lives on, and the Hindu faith is still vibrant and vital!

HINDU BELIEFS

The Light of the *atman*, the Light of the self, the Light of the spirit — it was around this that the glorious culture of ancient India was built! This culture was known as *atmavidya* — the science of the spirit. For spirituality too, is a science, it concerns the discovery of the one self in all.

Spirituality makes us raise the fundamental question: What is man? Or, to put it more personally, what am

I am the origin and also the dissolution of the entire universe.

I? It is this self-knowledge that Hinduism leads us to seek.

There are five Laws of this *Atma vidya* — the science of the self — five laws which every individual and every nation must obey, if we are to reach the goal of life.

The very first law is what I would describe as the law of the seed.

What is the law of the seed? Ask any farmer, ask any peasant, ask the simple village folk who live by the land — and they will tell you the law of the seed: as you sow, so shall you reap.

As you sow, so shall you reap. Each one of us has been given a plot — the field of our life. In this field of life, we are sowing seeds everyday. Every thought I think, every word I utter, every deed I perform, every emotion that I arouse within my heart, every feeling, every fancy, every wish — all these are seeds I am sowing in the field of my life.

The law of *Karma*, simply stated, is the law of cause and effect. It is a scientific law. It is a universal law. It is built up of these two aspects: as you sow, so shall you reap: as you think, so you become. You cannot sow thorns and reap apples.

The second law, is the law of the wheel.

There are some questions that have always troubled seekers on the path: Why is there so much suffering in this world? Why is it that even good people suffer? Why does God allow evil and injustice? What happens to us when we die?

The law of the wheel, which is the law of rebirth or reincarnation, emphasises a cardinal Hindu doctrine—the body dies; but the soul does not die. Is this not the great truth that Lord Krishna avouches to Arjuna in the Bhagavad Gita?

The *atman* is not born, nor can it ever die. It never came into being, nor ceaseth to be! Birthless, deathless, changeless, still, abiding and ancient is the *atman*! It is not slain, even though the body is slain!

The *Chandogya Upanishad* too, expresses the same truth: "Verily, indeed, when life hath left it, this body dies. But Life does not die."

The highest Yoga is the control of the mind.

The body is a garment worn by man as long as he needs it; it is cast off when it is old and worn out; the soul then wears another garment. The garment, the body, is *not* the self. The body dies, but the soul does not. The soul brings with it the impressions, the essence of its experiences in this earthly life. These experiences together form the *karma* of the *jiva*.

Each birth into which the soul enters here upon earth, is but a step in its evolution to perfection. Until this goal of perfection is reached, the soul enters another body, assumes another earthly existence and is re-born. The cycle of birth and death is repeated until the goal of perfection is ultimately attained.

Many of the doubts and anxieties that haunt us about life, are miraculously cleared when we understand the Law of Rebirth and Reincarnation.

There are seeds we have sown in past existence, which we are reaping now. The present is thus the effect of the past. Therefore, it follows logically, that the past and the present together will determine the future. Thus, it is wrong to look upon *karma* as destiny which we cannot escape. Rather, we are the architects of our own destiny — for, by accumulating good *karma* — thinking good thoughts, cultivating good feelings, speaking good words and performing good actions — we can actually change our future!

We who live in the world, still attached to karmas, can overcome the world by grace alone.

When we accept the second law — the Law of the Wheel — the question arises: how long shall we keep whirling in this wheel of birth and death? How may we seek liberation from this wheel?

The third law is the law of assimilation.

The ancient *rishis* referred to three stages — *shravana*, *manana* and *nidhyasana*. The first stage is *shravana* — which means hearing. We must hear good things; we must hear good teachings; we must hear spiritual discourses. But hearing is not enough. We must not stop there. *Shravana* in modern language also refers to reading. Many of us recite from the scriptures. Some people actually know the Bhagavad Gita by heart! They recite the whole of the Gita. But mechanical recitation of the scripture will not take us very far.

Therefore, the *rishis* talk of the second step, which is *manana*. *Manana* means reflection; it means thinking upon what we have heard and read. When you ponder upon what you have heard, doubts are likely to awaken within your heart. These doubts should be placed at the feet of a spiritual elder or a Guru. He may be able to clear these doubts and show you the way. But *manana* is a vital stage — you must reflect upon the teachings.

The third step is the most essential — for you cannot stop with reflection. The third step must be taken by everyone who wishes to tread the path of the seeker — this third or crucial step is *nidhyasana* or assimilation. You must assimilate the teachings you have been given into your daily life. Your life must bear witness to the great teachings you have heard, reflected upon and finally, absorbed. You must become the very picture of the great truths that you have assimilated.

The fourth law is the law of reverence.

This is the law of *Shraddha*. The essence of the *Vedas* — what we call *Vedanta* — is one of the fundamental principles of Hindusim. *Vedanta* teaches us that there is but One Life in all!

The One Life permeates the entire Universe and all of creation. The One Life sleeps in the mineral and the stone, stirs in the vegetable and the plant, dreams in birds and animals, it wakes up in man. Therefore, let us respect, revere life in all forms.

It must be emphasised that, reverence has three aspects: reverence for what is above us, reverence for what is around us and reverence for what is beneath us.

The fifth and final law is the Law of *yagna*, the law of sacrifice.

The Lord says to his dear, devoted disciple Arjuna: "Whatever you do, whatever you give in charity, whatever austerity you practise — do it as an offering unto Me!" This is true *yagna*: to make of your entire life, an offering to the Lord. Sacrifice your ego-self; sacrifice your desire — and do whatever you will, but do it for the love of God.

Whatever you do — do it for the love of God. Make your entire life an offering unto God; and when you arrive at this stage, you will find that there is but one aspiration in your heart: you ask for nothing, neither power, nor possessions. The one aspiration of your heart is: unto Thee be all the glory, O Lord! Not mine, but Thine be the glory, O Lord!

Based on these wonderful laws, in that ancient period of India's history, India built a civilisation of Light— a civilisation which made India a teacher of the nations of East and West. The message of that great civilisation, the message of Hindu faith, the message of our *rishis*, still continues to inspire countless people all over the globe.

SACRED SCRIPTURES OF THE HINDU FAITH

The great Hindu scriptures are usually classified under six spiritual categories:

1) *The Shrutis* reveal knowledge on the *Vedas*. To this we add the *Upanishads* too.

2) *The Smrutis* are the ancient law codes of the Hindus, also known as the *Dharma Shastras*. Based on the *Vedas*, they are second only to the *Vedas* in order of importance.

Of the various kinds of penances in the form of action or austerity, the constant remembrance of Krishna is the best.

The singing of His name is the best means for the dissolution of various sins, as fire is the best dissolver of metals.

The most heinous sins of men disappear immediately if they remember the Lord even for a moment.

3) *The Itihasas* or the great epics i.e The Ramayana and the Mahabharata, which reveal great truths even to the common people, the lay believers. *The Bhagavad Gita,* which is actually a part of the Mahabharata, but is in itself, a "Scripture Universal", as Sadhu Vaswani puts it.

4) *The Puranas* are ancient legends and myths which crystallise the teachings of the *Vedas* for the benefit of laymen. They are stories and parables which are absorbing — and they helped to take Hinduism to the hearts of the common folk.

5) *The Agamas* may be described as "operating instructions" for Hindu worship in the three main sects of Hinduism — the *Vaishnava, Shaiva* and *Shakti* sects.

6) *The Darshanas* are the six basic philosophical expositions relating to Hinduism.

India's ancient Rishis, who were the scientists of spiritual knowledge or *atma-vidya,* received the knowledge of eternal truths through a process of deep meditation. This *received* or *revealed* knowledge is enshrined in the *Vedas,* which form the very basis of Hinduism.

The fountainhead of this spirituality, the very source of the Hindu life-force are the *Vedas* — perhaps the earliest records of humanity that have come down to us. We look upon the *Vedas* as revealed knowledge — divine, infallible knowledge revealed to the ancient

Illness is not cured by saying the word "medicine," but by taking medicine. Enlightenment is not achieved by repeating the word "God" but by directly experiencing God.

inhabitants of this glorious land, through the grace of God. The purpose of this divine revelation was simple, but wonderful – to enable man to live a truly happy and purposeful life, to be aware of his own innate divinity, and to attain his ultimate goal – Eternal Bliss.

The Vedas are referred to as *Shruti* — meaning, that which is heard. For indeed, this divine revealed knowledge has not come down to us through the written text — but memorised and passed on by verbal repetition. Some scholars also interpret *Shruti* to mean – not composed, but *heard* by the ancient rishis from a divine source. Thus the Vedas are also described as *apaursheya* — not of human endeavour. Scholars estimate that the *Vedas* were compiled over six thousand years ago — and characteristically, the compiler's name is not mentioned at all. Devotional legends in the Indian tradition attribute the compilation to Sage Vyasa, who is, on account of this connection, known as Ved Vyas.

The word *Veda* is derived from the Sanskrit *Vid* meaning "to know". Thus *Veda* means knowledge – and the divine compilation comprises true knowledge that was revealed by God Himself to the *rishis,* who were men of pure minds, pure thoughts and pure action. The knowledge, transmitted from the *rishis* down to generations of devout disciples is thus not mere book-knowledge, but eternal knowledge revealed by God — knowledge of the Changeless and the Unchangeable One — the Supreme Reality.

THE SMRUTIS

The ancient, sacred law codes of Hindu society were composed by the great law givers — Manu, Yajnavalkya, Parasara and Gautama. These codified texts are also known as *Dharma Shastras* or the *dharma sutras* of Hinduism. Like all great Hindu texts, these are also based on the teachings of the *Vedas,* and are second in authority only to the *Vedas.*

Any society or civilisation, can only flourish when it follows certain well laid laws or rules which govern man's conduct, and help him to maintain such manners and customs which will help to protect and preserve his culture. This is what the *smrutis* do — they give us clear directions on how every class or group of men should lead their lives and perform their duties. Rules are also laid down for individuals in daily life, as well as for communities and nations. They also tell us how men should conduct themselves at different ages and different stages of life. The rights, privileges and duties of kings are spoken of in details. The duties, the obligations and the status of women are discussed. Judicial, social issues are dealt with, as also are rituals of purification and other *samskaras.*

THE BHAGAVAD GITA

Though it is textually a part of the *Mahabharata,* the value of the Gita as a sacred Hindu scripture is inestimable. It is a world-scripture with a world message. Nor is this message meant for India alone: The Gita, in the words of my Beloved Master, Sadhu Vaswani, is "a Bible of Humanity".

The Gita, the song of the Lord, is essentially a Song of Life. It shows how a man (the *jiva*), who lives a life of separation, may be united with the Source. Man has been separated from the Eternal in whom is his Home — hence his restlessness. Travelling across millenniums comes the word of the Lord:

Just as a fire is covered by smoke and a mirror is obscured by dust, just as the embryo rests deep within the womb, wisdom is hidden by selfish desire.

Lord Krishna, the charioteer with his friend and disciple, Arjuna

This be my Word Supreme, to Thee, O Arjuna!
Let go the rites and writ duties:
Come to Me for single refuge!

Bring thy heart to Me!
Fix thy thoughts on Me!
Serve Me! Worship Me!
Cling in faith and love and reverence to Me!
So shalt thou come to Me!
And I shall free thee
From the bondage of Sin!

Three important terms in the Gita are to be noted. The first is the *Atman*, the spirit, our true Home. The second is *Prakriti*, the cosmos in which we find ourselves. And the third is *Yoga*, the way walking which the *jiva* may return to the true homeland.

The *jiva* is in exile here. We are all in exile. Our Home is elsewhere: and this Home is calling us. Coming into this world of name and form, entering into dimensions of space and time, the *jiva* has got entangled. There is the play between the *Purusha* and *Prakriti*, according to the *Gita*. The play goes on! And the *jiva* is entangled in this play. How may the *jiva* get disentangled and reach his Home? How? By yoga, says the Gita. It is the way of union, re-union, the way which we may tread to be re-united with the Source.

The *Gita* speaks of three ways, three *margas* – the *karma marga*, way of selfless action; the *gnana marga*, way of wisdom; and the *bhakti marga*, the way of devotion. The ways are many: the Goal is One. The ways are as many as are the souls of men, and the Gita teaches that all the ways lead the seeker to the One Supreme. "On whatever path men approach Me," says Sri Krishna, "on that I go to meet them, for all the paths are Mine, verily Mine!"

Truly wise is he who is unstirred by praise or blame, by love or hatred. He is not moved by the opposites of life. Verily, does he delight in the blissful Self.

The Gita has seven hundred *shlokas*, in eighteen chapters. It is in the form of a *samvada*, a dialogue between Sri Krishna and his dear devoted disciple, Arjuna. These 700 verses, even today, guide myriad souls to weather the storms of life and move on ever onward, forward, inward, upward, Godward.

THE *ITIHASAS*: THE RAMAYANA AND THE MAHABHARATA

The *Itihasas* are the ancient historical epics of the Hindus. The word *itihasa* in sanskrit (*iti - ha - asa*) literally means it so happened. Scholars of semantics may quarrel over whether the *itihasas* are history, myth or legend. But for the devout Hindu, these epics bring home to us, the very essence of Vedic truth. Children love them as stories. Adults realise the valuable lessons they teach us on the art of right living. Sages and savants perceive the eternal truths that are embedded therein.

The *Itihasas* are the stories of great men and women whose lives, words and actions will help us to realise the four *purusharthas* — *Dharma*, *Artha*, *Kama* and *Moksha*. Our two well known epics are the *Ramayana* and the *Mahabharata*.

The Ramayana literally means, "The wanderings of Rama". It is thought to be the first epic poem ever written. It consists of 24,000 stanzas in seven cantos.

It was composed by Rishi Valmiki — through divine grace and revelation from the Lord Himself.

At the centre of the epic is the Divine figure of Lord Rama — an *avatara* of Sri Vishnu, who took birth on this earth, in the guise of a human being to show us

SITA-RAMA
HERO AND HEROINE OF THE RAMAYANA

Lord Rama: An Immortal of History

the ideal we should all aspire to — the ideal son, brother, disciple, husband and ruler.

The *Mahabharata* is the longest epic poem in the world. Scholars tell us that it is more than eight times the size of Homer's *Iliad* and *Odyssey* put together. It contains over 100,000 stanzas, and is therefore called *Satasahasni*. It consists of 18 *Parvas* or chapters, with a 19th section which forms a sort of appendix to the whole. It is the world's longest poem; and its unique feature is that it contains within itself, the Bhagavad Gita which is regarded by many as the ultimate world scripture.

Written by Rishi Ved Vyas who is thought to have compiled the Vedas, the *Mahabharata* is often referred to as the Fifth Veda — for its myriad stories and incidents bring out every truth that is embedded in the Vedas. *Yata Dharma Stato Jaya* where there is righteousness, there is victory — may be said to be the central theme of this encyclopedic epic. It celebrates the ultimate and unfailing triumph of good over evil, and the story brings home to us eternal, universal truths that can teach us to aspire to the best life here and here after.

PURANAS

The *Puranas* have been described as the *Vedas* of the common folk – for they are a fascinating, collection of myths and parables which embody the great *Vedic* truths, and enable every one of us to assimilate these eternal truths.

The word *purana* means ancient. As the renowned French scholar and Indologist, Louis Renou puts it, the *Puranas* are indeed, venerable antiquities. Each one of them is devoted to a description of the characteristics and exploits of a deity or divinity. Details of creation, the genealogy of the Gods and royal dynasties are woven into the fabric of the *puranas* which are also embellished with secular, religious and philosophical speculations.

There are eighteen *Mahapuranas* divided into three categories of six each:

1. The *Brahma Puranas* — *Brahma, Brahmananda, Brahma-Vaivarta, Markanandeya, Bhavishya* and *Vamana Purana*.

He who, at the time of death, thinking of Me alone, goes forth, leaving the body, he attains unto my Being. There is no doubt in this.

2. The *Vaishnava Puranas* — *Vishnu, Narada, Srimad Bhagavad, Garuda, Padma* and *Varaha Purana*.

3. The *Saiva Puranas* — *Matsya, Kurma, Linga, Vayu, Skanda* and *Agni*.

Apart from these, there are also about 27 minor *puranas* or *upa puranas*.

Undoubtedly the best known and perhaps the most beloved among the *puranas* is the *Srimad Bhagavatam* (consisting of 18,000 stanzas divided into 12 chapters). This great text is in the form of a conversation between Rishi Sukha, son of Ved Vyas and King Parikshit, the son of Abhimanyu and the only surviving heir to the Pandavas. The circumstances of the conversation are truly fascinating — for King Parikshit was doomed to die in 7 days, and during these last days of his earthly existence, sage Sukha narrated to him the entire story of the *Dashavatar*, or the ten *avatars* of Lord Vishnu. At the end of the narrative, on the 7th day the king was killed by a serpent's sting. The symbolic significance of this context cannot be lost on us – for we are all like the doomed king, left with very little time upon this earth. The best thing we can do here, is to seek God-realisation and in this endeavour, scriptures like the *Bhagavatam* are a great help.

THE *AGAMAS*

The *agamas* give us practical guidelines on various Hindu forms of worship. From them, people still derive instructions on how temples should be built; how festivals are to be observed; how to sit in meditation and how to perform various ceremonies.

Like the Upanishads, there are many *agamas*. They are divided into three main groups, according to the Deity whose worship they are devoted to — *Vishnu, Shiva* or *Shakti* — the *Vaishanva agamas*, the *Saiva agamas* and the *Shakti agamas*.

Each *agama* consists of four sections — the philosophy behind the system; the mental discipline required; the rules for construction of temples; and religious practices.

The *agamas* do not relate directly to the *Vedas* — but they do not go against *Vedic* teachings.

THE DARSHANAS

Hindu philosophy is expanded in the *Darshanas*. There are essentially six systems of philosophy — each

One should not behave towards others in a way which is disagreeable to oneself. This is the essence of morality. All other activities are due to selfish desire.

putting forth a different method of perceiving the truth. The six systems of philosophy are:

1. The *Nyaya* of Rishi Gautama. This is concerned with the logical analysis of the world.

2. The *Vaiseshika* of Rishi Kashyapa. This is the system of particularities — the nine elements of which the Universe is composed: earth, water, fire, air, ether, soul, mind, time and space.

3. The *Sankhya* of Rishi Kapila is perhaps the most ancient philosophical system in the world. Recognising no personal God, this school of thought only sees forces of *Purusha* (spirit) and *Prakriti* (matter).

4. The *Rajayoga* of Maharishi Patanjali is based on the idea of dualism — subject and object. It prescribes certain practices — *Raja yoga* and *Hatha yoga* — through which union with the One might be achieved.

5. The *Mimamsa* of Rishi Jamini which advocates the avoidance of rebirth.

6. The *Vedanta* of Rishi Ved Vyas describes the true nature of *Brahman*.

SOME MISUNDERSTANDINGS AND MISREPRESENTATIONS

Many people regard the vexed caste system as 'the curse' of Hindu society.

Let it be stated that prejudice, intolerance and class divisions are not the monopoly of Hindu society alone.

As my Beloved Master, Sadhu Vaswani explains, the classification of ancient Hindu social order is based *not* on birthright, but the natural qualities of a man. If a nation is to be built and developed on the right lines, each one of the four orders must bring its

What sort of religion can it be without compassion?
You need to show compassion to all
living beings.
Compassion is the root of all
religious faiths.

contributions to the common weal. There is nothing great or small to him who would be a helper of the state. All work is noble: all efforts are useful. Differences make harmony. He who tills the soil or rears the cattle or carries on trade or digs the earth is as useful as he who fights for the State or governs it, or meditates in a quiet corner. A healthy, progressive society aims at a harmony, an integration of all orders.

THE HINDU DEITIES

When Christians, Muslims or Jews first encounter Hinduism they are likely to be struck by the profusion of gods and goddesses vividly represented in paintings, sculpture and other art forms. After a visit to India,

Mark Twain wrote: "India has two million gods, and worships them all. In religion all other countries are paupers; India is the only millionaire."

As Sri Ramakrishna, the great mystic, explained, there can be as many spiritual paths as there are spiritual aspirants and similarly there can be as many gods as there are moods, feelings and emotions within the individual believer. One of the fundamental concepts of Hinduism is expressed in the following words:

Ekam Sat Vipra Bahuda Vadanti

i.e. God is One: wise men know Him by different names.

The Vedas refer to the One Supreme Spirit — the Formless and Changeless One — as *Brahman*. He is constantly referred to as *TAT* — That. He is That

In the beginning was only Being,
One without a second.
Out of Himself he brought forth the cosmos
And entered into everything in it.
There is nothing that does not come from Him.
Of everything He is the inmost Self.
He is the truth; He is the Self supreme.
You are that, Shvetaketu; you are that.

which cannot be defined or described. As Gurudev Sadhu Vaswani used to say, "To define God is to deny Him." A very similar notion is expressed in the Tao saying: "That which can be described by man is not Tao."

Brahman is regarded as the aspect of creation in the Supreme Spirit.

Vishnu is the sustaining, preserving, protecting aspect of the Supreme Spirit.

Shiva represents the aspect of dissolution in the Supreme Spirit.

The three Deities, Brahma, Vishnu and Shiva may be described as the Holy Trinity of the Hindu faith. Their spouses are also worshipped by the devotees for they are symbolical representations of the energy or the *Shakti* of the Divinity. The *Devis* or goddesses of Hinduism project the Female or Mother aspect which we naturally perceive as kind, compassionate, approachable, all-giving and all-forgiving.

Saraswati or Vidya is the goddess of knowledge and learning. She is the consort of Brahma.

Lakshmi is the consort of Vishnu. She is the goddess of prosperity and plenty, the deity of all the material and spiritual wealth that sustain us during life here and here-after.

Parvati is the consort of Shiva — the *Shakti* aspect of the Lord. She is also worshipped as Kali and Durga — she who destroys evil, she who helps us conquer the demons or "animals" which constitute our lower qualities, and awakens the higher virtues of love, compassion, truth and purity.

Lord Ganesha is the God of power and wisdom and goodness. Depicted as an elephant-headed deity riding on a mouse, He symbolises strength and humility. It is Ganesha who is invoked first; it is His name that all Hindus repeat at the beginning of any form of worship.

The multiplicity of Gods and deities should not mislead us into dismissing Hinduism as mere idol-

Birth ceases when all attachments are severed;
Otherwise, one beholds unceasingly the transitoriness of life.
Attach yourself to Him who is free from all attachments.
Bind yourself to that bond in order that all other bonds may be broken.

worship. The *murthis* or idols in our temples are but symbols that help us to focus our devotion on God— though some of us fail to look beyond the symbol, into Infinity which it represents. As an English commentator puts it, "An idol is nothing but a window overlooking Eternity." Thus all "gods" are representatives of the One God.

The differences between Hinduism and the western, monotheistic religions are indeed subtle. Historian Arnold Toynbee once wrote:

There may or may not be only one single absolute truth and only one single ultimate way of salvation. We do not know. But we do know that there are more approaches to truth than one, and more means of salvation than one. ... This is a hard saying for adherents of ... Judaism, Christianity, and Islam, but it is a truism for Hindus. The spirit of mutual good-will, esteem, and veritable love ... is the traditional spirit of the religions of the Indian family. This is one of India's gifts to the world.

THE GREAT ACHARYAS OF THE HINDU FAITH

No account of Hinduism would be complete without a reference to the great Acharyas. The word *acharya* in Sanskrit means a Holy teacher, a spiritual guide or preceptor. The Acharyas became the founders of distinct sects of Hinduism, which still follow their precepts and teachings. However, it must be emphasised that all the great Acharyas recognise the fundamental authority of the main Hindu scripture – the Vedanta Sutras, the Upanishads and the Bhagavad Gita.

The great Acharyas were recognised as *avatara purushas* (divine souls) in their own time.

Sri Shankaracharya or **Adi Shankara** as he was known, expounded the *Advaita* (non-dualism) philosophy in its clearest and most beautiful form. Advaita philosophy is rigorous in insisting that Brahman alone is real. All the differences and pluralities we perceive are illusory and unreal.

Sri Ramanujacharya was the founder of *Visishtadvaita* philosphy – so called because it combines *advaita* (non dualism) with *visesha* (attributes). Scholars therefore regard this as "qualified Monism". God alone is; all that we see, hear and touch are His manifestations.

Sri Madhavacharya's *Dvaita* philosophy may be described as unqualified dualism. It is thus called *adhyanta beda-darsana* (the doctrine of absolute differences). God is the only independent Reality. God is the efficient cause of the world – but not its material cause. Thus the world is a distinct reality from God.

Sri Vallabhacharya propounded the philosophy of *Shuddha advaita* or pure monism. It views the world of men and matters as real – for God has created it. The soul of man is a subtle form of Brahman; it remains unchanged by the influence of *maya*.

The great Acharyas and the systems of philosophy they evolved are landmarks in the evolution of the Hindu Faith through the ages. We must also bear in mind, that despite their differences, they all explore the vital relationship between God, the world and the soul. They are, ultimately, different attempts to discover the truth.

HINDU FESTIVALS

India has been described as the Land of Festivals. The many sacred feasts, *pujas* and holy days that dot the Hindu calendar, are not merely days for fun and feasting. Rather, they are vital, social, cultural and religious celebrations that bring people together, and remind them of their great and glorious heritage as inhabitants of an ancient and still vibrant civilisation.

Guru Purnima

The full moon day of the month of *Ashad* (July-August) is the sacred Guru Purnima day. This day is sacred to the memory of the great sage, Ved Vyasa, who has rendered great service to all humanity for all times by compiling the four Vedas, the eighteen Puranas, The Mahabharata and the Bhagavata. He is revered by many as the Adi Guru of Humanity.

On the sacred Guru Purnima Day, Vyas *puja* is performed and disciples worship their Gurus (spiritual teachers). Saints and men of God are honoured on this day.

Makar Sankranti

Sankramana in Sanskrit means, "to begin to move". The day on which the sun begins to move in *makara*

Three men went into the jungle on different occasions and saw a chameleon. "A chameleon is red," said the first man. "No, a chameleon is green," said the second man. "Nonsense, a chameleon is brown," said the third man. Those who disagree about the nature of God are like these three men.

rasi is called *Makar Sankranti*. It falls on the 13th or 14th of January.

It is said that on this sacred day of *Makar Sankranti*, Bhishma Pitamaha (the grandfather of the Pandavas) – the man of resolve, gave up his body on a bed of arrows on the battlefield of Kurukshetra.

In Maharashtra, people distribute multicoloured sweets, called *Til-gul*, symbolising sweetness in our dealings with each other.

In South India this day is observed as the Pongal festival. To the farmer this day is a day of rejoicing. He offers his first harvest of the year to the Almighty– in the form of the Sun God. Sweets are prepared in every home. The pot in which the rice and milk are cooked is specially decorated.

The Makar Sankranti is one of India's most important festivals, which have a great value for national integration. In the North and South all Indians celebrate this festival with great enthusiasm. The Makar Sankranti is also one of the greatest bathing days in India. There is an old saying that a bath at Prayag on the Makar Sankranti, at Kashi during an eclipse, and at Ayodhya on Ramanavmi are the holiest. The essential undercurrent of the festival is to keep the unity of the nation.

Janmashtami

The sacred day of *Janmashtami* falls on the 8th day of the dark half of the month of *Bhadra* (August-September). It heralds the birth of Lord Sri Krishna– the *Avatara* of Vishnu. Sri Krishna was born at 12 midnight. A total fast is observed by the devotees on His birthday. Butter, Krishna's favourite food is kept open in the house in the hope that Krishna Himself will come and eat it. The women of South India decorate their houses. From the doorway to their puja room, the floor is decorated with footprints of a small child using flour paste. This signifies that Lord Krishna will Himself come and eat their butter – to bless their devotion. Krishna's many *leelas* (divine acts and miracles) are enacted with great joy and enthusiasm on this day.

Sri Ramanavmi

This scared day commemorates the birthday of Lord Rama, an *avatara* of Lord Vishnu. It falls on the ninth day of the month of *Chaitra* (March-April). Temples are adorned with images of Lord Rama. In South India, a 9-day festivity is observed. *Kathas* on the stories of Sri Rama are narrated and the repetition of *kirtans* of Sri Rama reverberate in every lane. The holy Ramayana is read in many temples and homes.

Shivratri

It falls on the 13th or 14th day of the dark half of *Phalguna* (February – March). *Shivratri* means the great night of Shiva. A whole night vigil is observed in honour of Lord Shiva. A strict fast is observed on this day. The *Shiva linga* is worshipped and offerings of milk, curd and rosewater are made to the Lord. *Shiva Mahima stotras* and *Shiva Tandava stotras* are recited with great fervour. Shiva temples are flocked with endless queues of devotees.

Shiva: The Compassionate One

Deepavali

Deepavali literally means a row of lights. It falls on the last days of the dark half of *Kartik* (October—November). Some celebrate it as a 3-day festival:

*   *Dhanteras:* The 13th day of the dark half of Kartik

*   *Narak Chaudas:* The *Chaturdashi*

*   *Deepavali:* The return of Sri Rama to Ayodhya after defeating Ravana

Deepavali is one of the most important festivals in the Indian Calendar. The Deepavali lights are symbolic of the light of love, hope and faith, which are meant to dispel the darkness of ignorance and despair in our lives.

Kindle the Light

On the sacred Deepavali Day families exchange sweetmeats. Fire works are let off in every household. On this day it is also believed that Lakshmi was united with Lord Vishnu. Therefore in every household, Lakshmi Puja is performed on this day to propitiate the Goddess of Wealth.

It is also believed that on this day, Lord Krishna killed the demon Narakasura. In South India, people wear new clothes after an early morning bath which is considered equivalent to *Ganga Snan* on this auspicious day. In Northern India, businessmen begin their new account books on this day. Houses are cleansed and earthen lamps decorate and illumine each home.

Ganesh Chaturthi

One of the most popular of Hindu festivals, it signifies the birthday of Lord Ganesha. It is observed on the 4th day of *Bhadrapad* (August-September). Clay statues of Ganapathi are made and worshiped for 10 days, after which the idols are immersed into water. Ganapathi as He is affectionately known, is perhaps the most popular deity worshipped by millions of Hindus all over India. Ganapathi is worshipped and evoked at the beginning of every function or ceremony in the Hindu household – at the inauguration of factories and offices, at marriages and at the start of journeys. Ganesha is also known as Vignavinayak, the Lord who removes all obstacles. His favourite food is

modaka (sweet balls of rice flour) which is offered to him on this auspicious occasion. Maharashtra observes Ganesh Chaturthi as an important religious, cultural and social festival for 10 days. This tradition was inaugurated by Lokmanya Tilak, who saw the festival as a unifying and integrating factor towards communal harmony.

Lord Ganesh: The Remover of Obstacles

MANY PATHS: ONE GOAL

Durga Puja or Navratri

This festival is observed twice a year, once in *Chaitra* and *Aswayuja.* It lasts for 9 days in honour of the nine manifestations of Goddess Durga. People observe fast during these nine days, offer prayers and feed the poor. The beginning of summer and winter are two important climatic junctions. They are taken as opportunities to commence worship. These are indicated by *Ramanavmi* in *Chaitra* and Durga Puja in *Aswayuja.*

The celebration of Durga Puja reflects the splendid cultural diversity of India. However, the common aim everywhere is to propitiate the Goddess to bestow wealth, prosperity, knowledge and good health. *Durga Puja* commences on the first day and ends on the 10th day of the bright half of *Aswayuja* (September-October). The 10th day is observed as *Dussehra* or *Vijay Dashmi.* It is believed that Goddess Durga is permitted by Lord Shiva to visit her mother during these nine days. The festival celebrates her visit to her maternal home and concludes on the 10th day when she returns back to her husband.

In West Bengal, Durga Puja is celebrated with great gusto, as also in Assam and Meghalaya. In South India, Navratri, as it is called, is celebrated as the festival of dolls meant exclusively for women and girls. The Dussehra festival is observed with grandeur and pomp at the Royal Palace in Mysore. Durga Puja

Durga: The Divine Mother

is one of those unique festivals in which the Almighty is adored as "The Mother". There are many people who love to look upon God as their Mother and turn to Her for every thing they need. It is said that

The Dussehra is therefore India's annual day of victory. It celebrates the victory of forces of light over forces of darkness.

MARRIAGES IN THE HINDU FAITH

In Hindu *dharma*, marriage is viewed as a sacrament and not a contract. A Hindu marriage joins a man and a woman for life, so that they can pursue *dharma* (duty), *artha* (possessions), *kama* (physical desires) and *moksa* (ultimate liberation) together.

The *Grihastha Ashrama* (the householder stage), or the second of the four stages of life begins when a man and a woman marry and start their family and household. For a Hindu, marriage is a sacred obligation, for it is the only way to continue the lineage and thereby repay his debt to his ancestors.

The basis of a happy and fulfilling married life is the sense of unity, intimacy and love between husband and wife. Therefore, marriage is not for self-indulgence but meant to be a lifelong social and spiritual responsibility. Married life offers the young couple an opportunity to evolve into ideal soul mates.

A Hindu wedding ceremony is essentially a Vedic *yagna* (a fire-sacrifice). The primary witness of a Hindu marriage is *Agni* (or the Sacred Fire). *Agni sakshi* or the witness of *agni,* consecrates the sacred union, and this is deemed to be more binding than a legal contract or a civil registration of marriage. By law (The Hindu Marriage Act) and tradition, no Hindu marriage is deemed complete unless it is solemnised in the presence of the Sacred Fire, and seven encirclements (*saptapadi*) have been made around it by the bride and the groom together.

Giving the bride away (*kanyaadaan*) and accepting the bride (*paanigrahan*) are both considered to be auspicious rituals ensuring good *karma* for both the families involved.

When they are brought before the sacred fire, the hands of the bride and groom are tied together – which is *Panigrahana Hathleva*. This is followed by *Gathabandhan*, wherein ends of the clothing worn by the bride and groom are tied together in a knot, signifying the sacred wedlock.

The rituals of the *Laja Homa* and *Parikrama* or *saat pheras* denote the actual core of the wedding ceremony, circling the holy fire seven times, making seven promises to be fulfilled in married life. After this the couple is officially married to each other.

Vidaai, the most emotional ritual, is the one where the bride bids farewell to her parents and family and makes her way to her husband's home.

At the groom's house, there is the *Griha Pravesh*, where the mother-in-law welcomes the bride with the traditional *aarti*. At the entrance the bride places her feet in a paste of vermillion powder, symbolising the arrival of good fortune and purity. Then she kicks over a vessel filled with rice and coins to denote the arrival of fertility and wealth in her marital home. There are several other rituals associated with weddings, in different communities, which are too numerous to mention here.

The Hindu wedding ceremony is traditionally conducted in Sanskrit. Hindus attach a lot of importance to marriages and there are very many social and religious ceremonies that are very colourful and extend for many days, involving family, friends and neighbours.

Smaller than a grain of rice, smaller than a grain of barley, smaller than a mustard seed, smaller than a grain of millet, smaller even than the kernel of a grain of millet is the Self. This is the Self dwelling in my heart, greater than the earth, greater than the sky, greater than all the worlds.

Islam is one of the major religions of the world.
The Muslim population of the world today is
estimated at more than one billion, covering
four continents and many different areas of the
world. It is the dominant religion of North
Africa, the Middle East, and certain areas of
Asia and Europe.

The sacred Ka'bah

ISLAM

The word, Islam, is derived from the Arabic word *salaam*, which is often interpreted as meaning "peace". Etymology tells us that *Islam* is derived from *sin-lam-mim*, which carries the basic meaning of safety and peace. Other root meanings of the word also connote "submission" or "surrender". Modern scholars translate the term to mean "losing oneself for the sake of God and surrendering one's own pleasure for the pleasure of God". The message of Islam was revealed to the Holy Prophet Muhammad, 1400 years ago. It was revealed through the angel Gabriel and was preserved in the Holy Qur'an. A Muslim is a follower of Islam. "Muslim" is an Arabic word that refers to a person who submits himself to the Will of God.

Reza Aslan, a writer and scholar of comparative religions, tells us that Islam is a religion firmly rooted in the prophetic traditions of the Jewish and Christian scriptures. While religious historians view Islam as having been founded in 622 CE by Muhammad the Prophet, many Muslims believe that Islam existed from the dawn of creation, and that Prophet Muhammad was the last and by far the greatest of a series of Prophets. In fact, there is a theory that the Biblical Prophet Abraham was blessed with two sons, the younger of whom, Issac, founded Israel and Judaism, while the older son, Ishmael, became the founding father of the Arab nation and the ancient religion of Islam. Thus both Jews and Palestinian Arabs claim that the nation known to them as 'Israel' or 'Palestine' is their promised and sacred land. 'The covenant of Abraham' is acknowledged by both faiths, but its interpretation differs. Nor does the link between the two religions end there; the three religions regard the first five books of the Bible (Old Testament) as their sacred scriptures. Jews revere this as the Torah; Muslims call the Torah the *Tawrat* and consider it the word of Allah given to Moses; Christians call this the Pentateuch. However, Muslims also believe that this original revelation was corrupted by earlier scholars, and the true and authentic version was revealed to Muhammad later, so that it might be propagated in its right form. A number of verses from the Qur'an refer to Muhammad as the promised prophet mentioned in the Torah. The *Tawrat*, as it is called, is always mentioned with respect in Islam. The Muslims' belief in the *Tawrat*, as well as the Prophethood of Moses, is one of the fundamental tenets of Islam. In recent times, peace-loving scholars of all three faiths have begun to emphasise these commonalities, rather than focus on the differences, in order to foster mutual understanding and tolerance.

ORIGINS

As we said earlier, many Muslims believe that true Islam dates back to the creation of the world, and look upon Adam as one of their earliest prophets, followed by Abraham, Moses, Jesus (Isa) and Prophet Muhammad, the last in the line. But for the purpose of history, many regard Prophet Muhammad as the Founder of Islam. It was to him that

The holy Qur'an

God chose to reveal the Qur'an, and it was he who was responsible for establishing the faith as we know it today. Unlike the Founders of the other great faiths of the world, Prophet Muhammad was born relatively recently, in the late 6th century AD, about the year 570. Omid Safi, Professor of Religion and Philosophy, observes that Muhammad was probably the first religious leader to rise up in the full glare of modern history.

Many details are available to us about the life of the Prophet, who is held in such great reverence by the followers of Islam, that he is never ever mentioned without the prayer *Peace be upon him* or *PBUH* in short. Muhammad, son of Abdullah, of the tribe of Quraysh, was born in Mecca (Makkah) fifty-three years before the *Hijrah* (literally, migration; in historical terms, the date of Muhammad's flight to Medina, and also the time at which Islam becomes an established religion). His father died before he was born, and he was protected first by his grandfather, Abdul Muttalib, and after his grandfather's death, by his uncle Abu Talib.

The Grand Mosque at Mecca

As a young boy he travelled with his uncle in the merchants' caravan to Syria, and some years later made the same journey in the service of a wealthy widow named Khadija. So faithfully did he transact her business, and so excellent was the report of his behaviour, that she soon afterwards married her young agent; and the marriage proved a very happy one, though she was fifteen years older than he was. Throughout the twenty-six years of their life together he remained devoted to her; and after her death, when he took other wives he always mentioned her with the greatest love and reverence. This marriage gave him rank among the notables of Mecca, while his conduct earned for him the surname *Al-Amin*, the "trustworthy".

Even in those days, Mecca was the holy city of the Arabs and a pilgrim centre for all Arabs. Several travellers visited the city from surrounding provinces, making Mecca a busy and flourishing centre of trade. The people of Mecca regarded themselves as direct descendants of the Prophet Abraham. They believed that their temple, the Ka'bah, had been built by Abraham for the worship of the One God. It was still called the House of Allah, but the chief objects of worship here were a number of idols, which were called "daughters" of Allah and intercessors. The religion

A man said to the prophet, "Give me a command." He said, "Do not get angry." The man repeated the question several times, and he said, "Do not angry."

most of them followed at that time was a blend of animism and polytheism. Despite the efforts of travelling missionaries and traders, neither Christianity nor Judaism had managed to take roots in the inhospitable desert land. However, not all the faithful of Mecca were happy about this kind of idol worship; some of them longed for a return to the original Abrahamaic or monotheistic faith, turning away in sorrow and anger from contemporary heresies. These people were known as the *Hunafa* (literally, those who turn away). They were non-conformist, but made no attempt to form a community. Instead, each of them sought the truth by the light of his inner consciousness. Muhammad soon became one of them.

In those days, Muhammad was in the habit of retiring to the solitude of a cave in the mountains near Mecca, in order to seek solitude for reflection and meditation. He did this especially during the month of Ramadan, or the hot month. It was here in the cave of Hira, in the Mountain of Light, as it is called, that Revelation came to him, when he was about forty years old. He heard an awe-inspiring voice say: "O Muhammad! Thou art Allah's messenger, and I am Jibril (Gabriel)." He raised his eyes and saw the divine form of the angel; again and again. He turned his eyes away, but wherever he turned, the angel confronted him. When at last the angel vanished, he returned to Mecca, greatly disturbed, and shared his experience with his dear and devoted wife. Khadija comforted him, assuring him that God would never let harm come to

a good man like him. Together, they consulted an elderly relative, a scholar of the ancient scriptures. The old man assured them that the angel who came to Muhammad was the same divine messenger who had earlier come to Moses; and that Muhammad was the one chosen to be the Prophet of God among his people.

A quiet, humble and sensitive man, Muhammad was at first reluctant to accept such a tremendous role and onerous responsibility. However, the continuation of the revelations and the moral support he received from his wife, made him accept the responsibility with utter devotion and piety. Thus he earned the title, "the slave of Allah".

In repeated revelations and mystic communications the truth of Islam was revealed to Muhammad. These revelations were heard and memorised with reverence, and recorded meticulously. Thus the Qur'an came into being, the Word of God as revealed to the Prophet Muhammad.

For the first three years after his revelation, the Prophet preached his message only to the members of his immediate family. It is said that his wife Khadija became the first of his followers or converts; the second

Whoso believeth in his Lord, he feareth neither loss nor oppression.

was his cousin Ali; the third his servant Zayd, a former slave. His old friend Abu Bakr also was among those early converts.

At the end of the third year, the angel commanded him to "arise and warn" the general public. Faithful and obedient as ever, he began to preach his message to the people, warning them against the folly of idolatry and belief in false gods. The essence of his teaching might be expressed in these words: "There is no God but Allah, and Muhammad is His prophet."

The people of Mecca were divided; while vested interests preferred to cling to their idolatry, some people began to convert to the new faith. Muhammad preached strongly against the idolatrous worship of the Ka'bah. This incensed the Quraysh clan, inciting them to malign him and denigrate his followers. However, Muhammad persisted with his preaching, against all odds. It is thought that his bloodthirsty enemies did not kill him, for fear of reprisal from his powerful family and clan. In the meanwhile, ever increasing numbers of humble folk converted to the new faith, and this began to alarm the Quraysh. They ostracised the prophet, his family and his followers; they ordered him not to preach; they drew up a document to this effect, and placed it in the shrine of the Ka'bah. But when this document was brought out a few months later, it was found to have been eaten up by white ants; all that remained of the lengthy document were the words: *Bismik Allahumma* ("In Thy Name, O Allah").

In the meanwhile, a delegation from the city of Yathrib (al-Medinah) arrived in Mecca, having heard that a prophet of God lived there. They eagerly acknowledged Muhammad as God's messenger, and swore allegiance to him. This is known as the first pact of al-'Aqabah. The pilgrims returned to Yathrib accompanied by a Muslim teacher from Mecca. Before long, almost every family in Yathrib had converted to the new faith.

Next year, more Muslims arrived from Yathrib, to swear their allegiance to the prophet and his faith. They invited him to go to their city with them, promising that they would defend him as one of their own. Thus began the first Hijrah, or the flight to Medina, as it is called.

The Quraysh became aware of what was going to happen, as Muslims began to sell their property in Mecca, to start moving to Medinah. The new faith and its followers were a threat to the very prosperity

Consult thy heart, and thou wilt hear the secret ordinance of God proclaimed by the heart's inward knowledge, which is real faith and divinity.

of Mecca and its chief tribe; for the recent developments threatened the flourishing trade and the constant influx of pilgrims to the city. They did not want to let Muhammad escape from their control. So they cast lots to choose one member from each clan, who, together, would kill the Prophet, so that the heinous crime would be blamed on the whole tribe of Quraysh. We are told that it was at this point in time that the Prophet received the first revelation ordering him to make war upon his persecutors "until persecution is no more and religion is for Allah only."

The last of the Muslims to remain in Mecca were Abu Bakr, Ali and the Prophet himself. Abu Bakr, a wealthy trader, had arranged for two riding camels and a guide in readiness for the flight. The Prophet only waited for God's command. It came at last. On the very day appointed for his murder, the Prophet left Mecca, taking refuge in the mountain caves, with the murderous enemies in pursuit. Abu Bakr was terrified; but the Prophet assured him that Allah was with them, and they had nothing to fear. It was after a considerable delay, and an exhausting journey that they finally reached Medinah. Here, a warm welcome awaited him. What is more important, a fresh start and a new lease of life was given to his faith. His followers renamed Yathrib *Medinah al Nabi* – The City of the Prophet. The first Muslim state in the world was established in Medinah.

Till that time, the *Qiblah* (the place toward which the Muslims turn their face in prayer) had been Jerusalem. The Jews of Medinah imagined that the choice implied a leaning toward Judaism and that the Prophet would ally with them. He now received command to change the *Qiblah* from Jerusalem to the Ka'bah at Mecca.

For thirteen years the Prophet and his followers had been strict pacifists; now, they were constrained to go out in expeditions, to ensure that their people were not attacked or persecuted, for such was the command from God. The battle at Badr was the first of these campaigns, and it brought triumph to the Muslims against an attack from their old enemies, the Quraysh. This was only the first of many such campaigns. In the years that followed, the faith was consolidated by the persistent efforts of the Prophet and his devoted followers. Through religious discussion, persuasion, military activity and political negotiation, the Prophet became the most powerful leader in Arabia, and Islam was firmly established throughout the area.

He will not enter hell, who hath faith equal to a single grain of mustard seed in his heart.

Muhammad passed away when he was sixty-three years old. His followers refused to believe that he was no more. The Prophet's close friend and early convert, Abu Bakr, said to them in memorable words: "O People! If Muhammad is the sole object of your adoration, then know that he is dead. But if it is Allah (The One God) you worshipped, then know that He does not die."

The Prophet's actions and words were remembered and later recorded (known as Hadith), so that Muslims in future generations to the end of time could try to act and speak and live as he did. He has served as an example for all Muslims in all periods to modern times. Being the virtual ruler and military leader of the whole of Arabia, he still remained a humble, modest, simple man, always gentle, always soft-spoken, always kind to the least of his people. He will remain a model example for all of humanity.

He had nominated Abu Bakr to lead the prayers when he had fallen ill. After his death, Abu Bakr became the first *Caliph*, which means, *The Shadow of God on Earth*. Caliph Abu Bakr sent his armies to Syria, Persia and North Africa to spread Islam. When he died, his successors continued the holy wars, as they were called.

Within a hundred years of the Prophet's death, Islam had spread to Syria and Jordan in the North; to Egypt, Tunisia and Algeria on the African continent; to Persia in the West, and beyond the Khyber pass, to the Indian subcontinent.

The spread of Islam continued for many years. It was no longer the unified religion of the Arabs, but a faith adopted by many races and nations, and divided into different sects according to their practices.

Today, Islam is a major world religion, with over 1 billion followers worldwide. It is also the fastest growing religion in the world.

There are two basic sects in Islam: Shia and Sunni. Both follow all the fundamental tenets of Islam; they differ only on the concept of leadership.

The division between *Shia* and *Sunni* dates back to the death of the Prophet; this was when Abu Bakr, the prophet's close friend and follower was nominated to lead the faith and became the first Caliph. Sunni Muslims agree with the position taken by many of the Prophet's companions, that the new leader should be elected from among those who were capable of

O son of man, were you to come to Me with almost an earthful of sins, and then you met Me without joining anything with Me in the Godhead, then would I come to you with an earthful of forgiveness.

Verily in the remembrance of Allah, do hearts find rest.

leadership. The word "Sunni" in Arabic comes from a word meaning "one who follows the traditions of the Prophet."

On the other hand, some Muslims share the belief that leadership should have stayed within the Prophet's own family, among those specifically appointed by him or among Imams appointed by God Himself. This is the position taken by the Shia Muslims, who believe that leadership should have passed directly to his cousin/son-in-law, Ali. Throughout history, Shia Muslims have not recognised the authority of elected Muslim leaders, choosing instead to follow a line of Imams which they believe have been appointed by the Prophet Muhammad or God Himself. The word "Shia" in Arabic means a group or supportive party of people.

Shia Muslims believe that the Imam is sinless by nature, and that his authority is infallible as it comes directly from God. Therefore, Shia Muslims often venerate the Imams as saints and perform pilgrimages to their tombs and shrines in the hope of divine intercession.

Sunni Muslims make up the majority (85%) of Muslims all over the world. Significant populations of Shia Muslims can be found in Iran and Iraq, and large minority communities in Yemen, Bahrain, Syria and Lebanon.

THE FUNDAMENTAL PRECEPTS

Allah is the proper name for Almighty God, and is often translated merely as "God." Allah has other names that are used to describe His characteristics: the Creator, the Sustainer, the Merciful, the Compassionate, etc.

Muslims believe that since Allah alone is the Creator, it is He alone who deserves to be worshipped; Islam is strictly monotheistic. Any worship and prayers directed at saints, prophets, other human beings or nature is considered idolatry.

Lo! The God-fearing are in a state secure,
Amid gardens and watersprings,
Attired in silk and gold brocade facing one another:
Thus: and We shall wed them to houris with wide lovely eyes.

In the Qur'an, we read that Allah is Compassionate and Merciful. He is Kind, Loving and Wise. He is the Creator, the Sustainer, the Healer. He is the One who Guides, the One who Protects, the One who Forgives. There are traditionally ninety-nine names, or attributes that Muslims use to describe Allah's nature.

The fundamental pillar of faith in Islam is to declare that "there is no deity worthy of worship except the One True Almighty God" (in Arabic: *La ilaha ill Allah*").

Muslims pray directly to God, with no intermediary, and seek guidance from Him alone, because "...Allah knows well the secrets of your hearts". (Qur'an 5:7)

According to Islam, God has four fundamental functions: creation, sustenance, guidance and judgment. The overall purpose of humanity is to serve Allah, to worship Him alone and to adopt a moral lifestyle.

Islam believes in the continued revelations of God to the prophets. It also demands complete submission and surrender to the Will of God; it is an important principle of Islam that all Muslims are members of the *ummah,* or community of believers. There are not supposed to be any distinctions based upon race, class, income, ethnicity, nationality, or any other of those superficial distinctions. Being a Muslim is all that really counts.

The concept of purity is central to Islamic belief. There are different aspects of   purity to be maintained by the faithful. One is through the avoidance of using drugs and alcohol or engaging in gambling. Another is through not eating certain foods, like pork. And finally, there is the matter of maintaining a measure of ritual cleanliness.

Muslim beliefs are often summed up in the following seven principles:

1. *Tawheed* – the unity of God

2. *Risallah* – acceptance of the Prophethood of Muhammad, a messenger of God

3. *Mala'ikah* – belief in angels

4. *Kutubullah* – belief in God's books (like the Qur'an and the Psalms of David)

5. *Yawmuddin* – belief in a Day of Judgment

6. *Al-Qadr* – acceptance of pre-destination

7. *Akhriah* – faith in a resurrection after death

So remember the name of thy Lord and devote thyself with a complete devotion.

THE FIVE PILLARS OF FAITH

As a Muslim, each member must carry out five essential duties, called The Five Pillars of Faith. They are:

1. A Muslim must acknowledge that "There is no God but Allah and Muhammad is his Prophet."

2. A Muslim must pray five times daily facing Mecca: at dawn, at noon, in the mid-afternoon, at dusk, and after dark.

3. Each Muslim must pay a *zakat* to the government.

4. A Muslim must fast for the month of *Ramadan*. During the fasting month, one must refrain from eating, drinking, smoking and sexual intercourse from dawn until sunset.

5. A Muslim must make a pilgrimage to Mecca. Every adult Muslim who is physically and financially able to do so must make this pilgrimage at least once in his or her lifetime.

These practices may be described as the cornerstones of Islam. These are obligations which are required of every Muslim. They are known as: *shahadah* (statement of faith), *salat* (prayers), *zakat* (alms), *sawm* (fasting) and *hajj* (pilgrimage).

Often called a "way of life", Islam offers guidance and discipline with reference to all aspects of daily life,

Time for prayer

from birth and death rites, to courtship and marriage relationships, as well as in education and business dealings.

Islam lays great emphasis on education. The Prophet Muhammad once said that Muslims should "seek knowledge, from the cradle to the grave." Education is a life-long endeavor, and Muslim parents have many choices with regards to their children's education. In addition, most Muslims try to learn at least the basics of the Arabic language, although only 15% of Muslims speak Arabic as a native tongue.

Muslims follow a set of dietary laws which are outlined in the Qur'an. Everything is permitted (*halal*), except what God specifically prohibited (*haram*).

Islam has set minimum standards for personal modesty, which are reflected in the various styles of clothing worn among Muslims. Muslims view these values of public decency as timeless.

Islam has given detailed regulations for the economic life of the people, which is required to be balanced and fair. Muslims recognise that wealth, earnings and material goods are the property of God, and that men are merely His trustees.

Jihad, is believed to be a religious duty of Muslims. In Arabic, the word *jihad* means "struggle". It appears frequently in the Qur'an and may be translated as an idiomatic expression meaning "striving in the way of Allah" (*al-jihad fi sabil Allah*). A person engaged in *jihad* is called a *mujahid*, while the plural is *mujahideen*. Some scholars refer to this duty as the sixth pillar of Islam.

The scholar John Esposito argues that *jihad* requires Muslims to "struggle in the way of God" or "to struggle to improve one's self and/or society". There are four major categories of *jihad* that are recognised: *jihad* against one's self (*jihad al-nafs*), *jihad* of the tongue (*jihad al-lisan*), *jihad* of the hand (*jihad al-yad*) and *jihad* of the sword (*jihad al-sayf*).

The noblest speech is the invocation of Allah.

Prophet Muhammad is said to have regarded the inner struggle for faith as the "greater *jihad*", giving it priority over physical warfare. Muslim scholar Mahmoud Ayoub states, "The goal of true *jihad* is to attain a harmony between *Islam* (submission), *iman* (faith) and *ihsan* (righteous living)." Greater *jihad* is thus similar to what Christians describe as the struggle to resist sin in all forms. i.e. fighting temptation, doubt, disbelief or despair.

However, it must also be stated that some Muslim traditionalists see *jihad* differently: they believe that the world is divided into two houses: the House of Islamic Peace (*Dar al-Salam*), in which Muslim governments rule and Muslim law prevails; and the House of War (*Dar al-Harb*), the rest of the world, inhabited by non-believers. They say that the duty of *jihad* will continue, perhaps interrupted by periodic truces, until all the world either adopts the Muslim faith or submits to Muslim rule. Those who fight in the *jihad* are believed to gain in both worlds — treasures in this one, paradise in the next.

Many scholars continue to distinguish *jihad*, (legitimate struggle) from *fasad*, (illegitimate violence), and argue that terrorism should be called *fasad*, not *jihad*. The faithful are appalled by the term Islamic terrorism, which they denounce as a reprehensible contradiction in terms, for Islam basically means "peace".

THE SACRED SCRIPTURES

The Qur'an or the Koran as it is known to many, is the central religious text of Islam. Muslims believe the Qur'an to be the book of divine guidance and direction for mankind, and consider the original Arabic text to be the final revelation of God. The faithful hold the belief that the Qur'an was revealed to Muhammad by the angel Jibril (Gabriel) over a period of approximately twenty-three years, beginning in 610 AD, when he was forty, and concluding in 632 AD, the year of his death. Although its primary transmission was oral, it was carefully written down by the Prophet's early followers.

The Qur'an is referred to by many other names, within the sacred text. Thus we have terms like *al-furqan* ("discernment"), *al-huda* ("the guide"), *dhikrallah* ("the remembrance of God"), *al-hikmah* ("the wisdom") and *kalamallah* ("the word of God"). Another term is *al-kitab* ("the book"), though it is also used in the Arabic language for other scriptures.

The Qur'an consists of 114 chapters of varying lengths, each known as a *sura*. These are classified as Meccan or Medinan, depending on where the verses were revealed. The title of each chapter is derived from a name or quality discussed in the text, or from the first letters or words of the *sura*. Muslims believe that Muhammad, on God's command, gave the chapters their names. The chapter arrangement is not thought to be connected to the sequence of revelation. Thus longer chapters are placed first and shorter chapters follow.

Tafsir (interpretation) is the Arabic term that denotes commentary of the Qur'an. The Prophet himself commented on the meaning or virtues of particular verses of the Qur'an, and those statements have been passed down to us in the *Hadith*. The *Sahabah*, or companions of Muhammad, also interpreted and taught the Qur'an. Many pious Muslims believe that it is prohibited to attempt Qur'anic interpretation solely on an individual's own opinion.

Though at first *Tafsir* was almost always written in Arabic, during the 20th century many Muslims felt the need for commentaries in their own languages so that those who do not know Arabic could still have access to the meaning of the Qur'an. Thus commentaries began to be published in several

Whenever men gather together to invoke Allah, they are surrounded by Angels, the Divine Favour envelops them, and Peace (as –sakinah) descends upon them, and Allah remembers them in His assembly.

languages including Urdu, Bengali, French and English.

Few religions hold their scripture in such awe and reverence as Muslims offer to the Qur'an. As one scholar puts it, "If Christ is the Word of God made flesh, the Qur'an is the Word of God made text, and questioning its sanctity or authority is thus considered an outright attack on Islam."

HOLY DAYS AND FESTIVALS

Muslims have two major religious observances each year, *Ramadan* and *Hajj*, and corresponding holidays connected with each one. All Islamic holidays are observed according to the lunar-based Islamic calendar.

Ramadan is an entire month that Muslims spend in daytime fasting. It corresponds to the days when the Prophet retired to the mountain cave to meditate in solitude.

Towards the end of *Ramadan*, Muslims observe *Lalyat al-Qadr* or the "Night of Power", which is when the first verses of the Qur'an were revealed to Muhammad.

Eid al-Fitr or "The Festival of Fast-Breaking" concludes the month of *Ramadan*.

Remember Allah, standing, sitting and reclining.

During the 12th month of the Islamic calendar in each year, millions of Muslims undertake the annual pilgrimage to Mecca (now in Saudi Arabia) called *Hajj*. This is one of the five pillars of the faith, devoutly followed by many Muslims.

During one day of the *Hajj*, pilgrims gather at the Plain of Arafat to seek God's mercy, and Muslims elsewhere fast for the day. This is known as the *Day of Arafat*.

Eid Al Fitr celebrations

At the end of the *Hajj*, Muslims throughout the world celebrate the holiday of *Eid al-Adha* (Festival of Sacrifice). This commemorates the trials and triumphs of the Prophet Abraham, and his willingness to sacrifice his own son to obey the will of God.

There are other historical events and annual observances observed by some Muslims (e.g. Muharram) but these are not universal Muslim holy days.

MARRIAGES

In Islam, marriage is a social and legal relationship intended to strengthen and extend family relationships. Islamic marriage begins with a search for an appropriate partner, and ends with an agreement of marriage, the contract and the wedding party.

The choice of a marriage partner is one of the most important decisions a person will make in his or her lifetime. Muslims approach this decision with prayer, careful investigation and family involvement. Friends and family are involved in the search and selection of a suitable bride/groom.

And whenever you give your word, say the truth.

All people are a single nation.

Muslims view marriage as the foundation of society and family life. In a practical aspect, Islamic marriage is thus structured through legally-enforceable rights and duties of both parties. In an atmosphere of love and respect, these rights and duties provide a framework for the balance of family life and the fulfillment of both partners.

A Muslim marriage is not merely a sacrament, but a covenant, solidified by either verbal agreement (oral contract) or signing a written contract. Whether oral or written, the marriage contract (*nikkah*) is legally binding, and at a minimum should be based on:

- the couple's consent to marry
- the approval of the bride's guardian
- the presence of two Muslim witnesses
- the specification of a *mehr,* or gift to the bride.

In Islam, marriage is considered both a social agreement and a legal contract. In modern times, the marriage contract is signed in the presence of an Islamic judge, *imam* or trusted community elder who is familiar with Islamic law. The process of signing the contract is usually a private affair, involving only the immediate families of the bride and groom. Both the groom and the bride must consent to the marriage, verbally and in writing. This is done through a formal proposal of marriage (*ijab*) and acceptance of the proposal (*qabul*). The bride has a right to receive a gift from the groom (*mehr*) which remains her own property as security in the marriage. The gift is payable directly to the bride and remains her sole property, even in case of later divorce. The *mehr* can be in the form of cash, jewelery, property, or any other valuable asset. Two adult witnesses are required to verify and validate the marriage contract.

After a couple signs the Islamic marriage contract, families usually hold a public wedding party (*walima*). A wedding is always a happy time for families to celebrate. In the Muslim world, there are colourful, cultural variations from place to place. The various wedding traditions reflect the diversity of the Muslim world.

UNIQUE FEATURES

While other religions are named after their founders, such as Christianity and Buddhism; after a tribe or ethnic group, such as Judaism; Islam (Peace, submission, surrender to the will of God) is unique because its name represents its outlook on life and reflects its universal nature.

Your God is one God; there is no God but He, Most Gracious, Most Merciful.

From the very beginning of the mission of Prophet Muhammad, his followers came from a wide spectrum of individuals — there was Bilal, the African slave; Suhaib, the Byzantine Roman; Ibn Sailam, the Jewish Rabbi and Salman, the Persian. This has continued down the annals of history, with people from all regions and all races embracing the faith.

In other religions, even monotheistic faiths, people are exhorted to approach God through an intermediary, such as a saint or an angel or a Prophet or teacher. However, it is only in Islam that a person is required to pray to God directly.

The teachings of Islam, even though they do cover religious rituals and morality, also extend to all other aspects of life. The Prophet Muhammad's mission encompassed not only spiritual and religious teachings, but also included guidance for such things as social reform, economics, politics, warfare and family life.

To GOD belongs the east and the west; wherever you go there will be the presence of GOD. GOD is Omnipresent, Omniscient.

By maintaining a balance between man's spiritual and physical needs, the teachings of Islam suit the needs of society as a whole.

Islam is unique as a religion without any mythology. The oneness of God, the prophethood of Muhammad and the concept of life after death are the basic articles of its faith. All of the teachings of Islam flow from those basic beliefs and are simple and straightforward. There is no hierarchy of priests, no abstractions, no complicated rites or rituals.

Islam does not believe in asceticism. It does not ask man to avoid material things. It holds that spiritual elevation is to be achieved by living piously in the rough and tumble of life, not by renouncing the world. It urges moderation in everything, and condemns indulgence.

Islam has always regarded knowledge and education as religious pursuits. Thus great Muslim leaders and kings were patrons of education. In the words of Gurudev Sadhu Vaswani, "Not a mosque but had a school. Knowledge and prayer joined hands together. Muslims made contributions to Algebra, Chemistry,

A place for prayer

Logic, Philosophy, Theology, Medicine and Literature."

Islam is also a great gospel of social equality, and love and compassion for the poor, a corrective to both the excesses of capitalism and the emptiness of Communism. As the Prophet put it so eloquently, "That person is not a perfect Muslim who eats his fill and leaves his neighbour hungry."

Indeed, those who submit themselves absolutely to GOD alone, while leading a righteous life, will receive their recompense from their Lord. They have nothing to fear, nor will they grieve.

While all Prophets and Founders of the various faiths warned against idolising or iconising, it is only Prophet Muhammad who has successfully resisted deification even after his death. "I am a man," the Prophet asserted again and again. "Call me a servant of Allah!" Thus the earlier English appellation, "Mohammadan" was rejected outright by all Muslims, and has completely disappeared from current usage.

Not one of you is a believer until he loves for his brother what he loves for himself.

Like Hinduism, Jainism is also one of the ancient religions of India, dating back to the pre-historic age. As a formal, institutionalised faith, it is thought to have been established in India in the Seventh Century B.C. This was a time of great religious upheaval in India, directed against the excessive ritualism of the Hindu faith as it was practised at that time.

Mahavira: The Great Victor

JAINISM

A *Jain* literally means the follower of the *Jinas* or 'conquerors', highly evolved and spiritually elevated beings, who had mastered the self through discipline, austerity and complete control of the senses. Jinas attained enlightenment through their own personal efforts, and became *tirthankaras* or the great 'ford makers' who showed their followers the way to salvation that they had discovered through their austerity and self-discipline. In all, there were twenty-four *tirthankaras*, who at various times refreshed and revitalised the faith. The last and most famous among them was Vardhamana Mahavira, the founder of the religion which we call Jainism today.

ORIGINS

Jains identify Lord Rishabhdeva or *Adinath* (First Lord) as the first *Tirthankara* who lived prior to the Indus valley civilisation. He is referred to with great respect in Hindu scriptures such as the *Rig Veda* and the *Srimad Bhagavad* as an *avatara* or divine incarnation. Lord Rishabha, according to Jain tradition, was a king of the Ikshvaku clan, who contributed greatly to the progress of society, at a time when civilisation was progressing from the primitive to the complex, i.e. from the stone age to the agricultural age. He is credited with having taught his people various occupations and professions like agriculture, animal husbandry, architecture, etc. in order that they might earn their living. He is also credited with establishing the basic Jain *dharma* of compassion. At a certain stage in his life, he chose the way of renunciation and asceticism to seek enlightenment. He lived up to the age of one hundred; he is said to be the founder of the *shramanic* tradition (the tradition of continence and austerity) and was

Anger is not for the wise or the religious. They will endure persecution and not be angry. Only the ignorant and sinful will give way to anger.

Be fair and impartial to all. Treat all men as brothers at all times. As one treats men, so should he treat all animals. They are also our brothers.

responsible for the propagation of the basic principles of Jainism.

It is thought that his eldest son Bharata, became the first emperor of ancient India, although he too, eventually renounced the world to attain salvation, becoming a *siddha*. Many ancient scriptures say that India was named *Bharatavarsha* after him. Another son, according to Jain traditions, was Prince Dravid, who was the founder of the clan of Indian Dravidians.

Not much is known in historical terms of the twenty-one *tirthankaras* who followed Adinath; however, it is said that the twenty-second *tirthankara*, Arishtanemi or Neminatha is referred to in the Rigveda and the Yajurveda , and is described as being a cousin of Lord Sri Krishna. The twenty-third *tirthankara* was Parsvanath, who was the predecessor of Mahavira.

It is thought that Parsvanath gave a new identity to Jainism, and actually set up an order of ascetics who influenced Lord Mahavira to embrace the faith. Some sects actually claim that it was Parsvanath who was the founder of Jainism. In fact, they also believe that Lord Mahavira's parents were actually followers of Parsvanath. The latter remained a popular and revered figure even during Mahavira's lifetime. It was only when Mahavira attained liberation and established his own ascetic order, that many of Parsvanath's followers left their own sect to join him. Some historians believe that each of these groups continued to keep their individual identity as *shwetambaras* (white robed ascetics, who were the followers of Parsvanath) and *digambaras* (naked ascetics who were the followers of Mahavira). However history credits Mahavira with being the official founder of the religion as it is known today.

Lord Mahavira was born as Prince Vardhamana, son of King Siddhartha and Queen Trishala. The young prince married Yashodha, and lived the life of a householder until he was thirty years old. Not much is known of his life as a youth. But Pali scriptures tell us that he was a man of great physical and moral courage, patient and wise, enduring hardships and

A man may conquer thousands and thousands of invincible foes, but that is of no consequence. His greatest victory is when he conquers only his own self through indomitable courage.

The good show the way to the others by their good acts. Each day passes never to return. Therefore, do good at all times, for you can never call back a day to perform a good deed that was not done.

calamities, indifferent to pleasure and pain alike, rich in self-control and gifted with fortitude, and was therefore given the name Mahavira. After the death of his parents, he renounced the world and became a wandering ascetic, undertaking severe austerities and penances, until he attained enlightenment, around the age of forty-two. For about thirty years after this, he moved from place to place, preaching his message to the people. His most outstanding teachings are the gospel of *Ahimsa* (non-violence), *Aparigraha* (non-possession), *Anekantavada* (the multi-dimensional theory of perception), *Kriyavada* (the doctrine of action) and *Sakahara* (vegetarianism). He also tried

Sattvic food

121

to address the evils of society such as the problems of slavery, status of women in family, caste system, untouchability, exploitation, economic inequality, violent sacrifices and basic human weaknesses such as the desires and passions of the flesh, etc.

His personal charisma and his profound wisdom attracted many followers from all walks of life, including royal personages, who willingly embraced his faith. He also founded the order of naked ascetics known as *digambara jains*, who swore permanent allegiance to his path and also committed themselves to preserving his teachings for posterity. When Lord Mahavira passed away at the age of seventy-two, he had over 14,000 monks in his order. They took up the task of compiling his teachings and his sermons into the *Agamas*, which still remain as the sacred scriptures of Jainism for his many followers.

It is obvious that the life of Mahavira closely resembles the life of the Buddha. Both were renowned *kshatriya* princes; both were born and brought up in luxury; both were happily married with children and eventually, both renounced their family lives to become wandering ascetics, until they attained enlightenment. In fact, many of their teachings too, are alike. And yet, the faiths they established are very different from each other. According to some scholars, Mahavira was actually a senior contemporary of Gautama the Buddha, and the two great *avatara purushas* actually held serious dialogues on their beliefs, but parted ways amicably due to doctrinal differences.

A wise man discovers his duty and does it at all costs. It is the duty of all to be impartial and to abstain from causing injury to all living things.

JAIN PHILOSOPHY

Jainism denies that there was or is a God, an omnipotent or superior power that created the world. Mahavira did not believe in castes or in idol-worship. He also said that prayers and sacrifices had no value whatsoever.

All souls are unborn, uncreated, eternal and equal. All living things, animate and inanimate, trees, water and fire, are credited with having souls. Each soul is capable of evolution and liberation through its own effort. When a soul becomes heavy with sin, it sinks down; when it is good and pure, it rises in evolutionary progress, until it attains *nirvana* or liberation. This liberation depends entirely on personal effort; no divine intervention can help the soul in this process. Thus good actions, good intentions and good convictions are the basis of good *karma*. This is one of the reasons why Jainism appeals to modern intellectuals. Jainism is a religion which emphasises self-reliance. It does not have any place for the grace of a guru or teacher; even the great *tirthankaras* are venerated only because they were pure, enlightened souls who are not really worshipped; but gratitude is expressed to them for the valuable teachings they left behind.

Jainism postulates that the entire world is possessed of life and soul, including plants, trees, birds, animals, water and fire. It is man's prime duty to protect all this. We are to treat others, as we want to be treated, and this refers not only to other people but also to the whole of the earth. One is therefore expected to respect the planet and its natural beauty. Jainism does this philosophically by accepting the principle of the interdependent existence of all living beings, including man, animals and inanimate aspects of nature.

The cardinal principle of Jainism is *ahimsa* or non-violence. It is said that when Mahavira was on his deathbed, he called his close disciples to preach his last sermon to them. One of them asked him, "O master, which of your teachings is the most important for us to observe?"

"Of all my teachings," Lord Mahavira replied, "the first of my five commandments is the most important:

"Do not kill animals for food; do not hunt or fish, or even kill the tiniest creature at any time. Do not kill the insects that bite you or sting you. Do not go to war. Do not use violence against those who attack you. Do not step upon the tiniest creature or worm on the roadside, for it too, has a soul."

EXISTENTIAL SUFFERING

Mahavira taught that human life was essentially one of suffering. Birth, illness, unfulfilled desires, loss of loved ones, death – all, all aspects of life are intrinsically suffering.

Where does this suffering come from? People suffer, and are unhappy because they are never satisfied; they want more and more and more. Thus desire is the root cause of all suffering.

How may we escape from this suffering? By giving up all desires. When a man rises above all desire, his soul is prepared to ascend the tough path to *nirvana*, which is the greatest happiness of the soul.

The temporal world is constantly afflicted by sorrow and suffering. One must make the most strenuous and dedicated efforts to transcend the eternal cycle of transmigration, birth and rebirth, in order to escape from the vicious cycle of sorrow and suffering.

Avoid all evil. One may commit evil by doing something wrong or by approving another's evil act. Do not cause others to sin.

THE WAY TO NIRVANA

The way to liberation, to the greatest happiness of the soul, is through what Mahavira called, "the three jewels of the soul": 1) Right conviction; 2) Right knowledge; 3) Right conduct.

Right conduct is essential for *nirvana*; and the five commandments of right conduct are:

1. Do not kill any living thing, or hurt any living thing by word, thought or deed

2. Do not steal

3. Do not lie

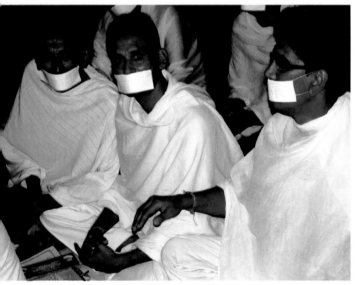

Harm no one!

The man of faith has chosen the right pathway. He should practice his faith at all times.

4. Do not live an unchaste life or become intoxicated

5. Do not desire or covet anything

Once, his bewildered followers asked Mahavira a question: "You do not believe in the order and duty of the castes; You say that there is no Supreme Power that created this world; You do not believe in saying prayers, worshipping idols or in offering sacrifice to the gods. How then can we attain to *nirvana*?"

Mahavira's answer to them was significant: "Not in prayer, nor in sacrifice, nor in idol-worship will you find the way to *nirvana*. Only by doing good can you reach *nirvana*. Within you lies your own salvation!"

KARMA

The concept of *karma* is as important to Jainism as it is to Hinduism. All of us have to reap what we sow; and the seeds we sow are not merely our deeds, but also our thoughts and words and intentions. All of these affect our future births and determine our condition in the ages to come. The Jain theory of

Karma, and also its Buddhist version, has no place for God as the creator, supporter or protector and destroyer of the world. Nor does Jainism believe in the principles of reward, judgement, incarnation and forgiveness. One will have to bear the result of one's own deeds. They cannot be extinguished by the mercy of God or Guru.

THE *TATTVAS* OR CONCEPTS OF JAINISM

All Jains believe in seven fundamental concepts:

1. *Jiva* – souls and living things

2. *Ajiva* – non-living things

3. *Asrava* – the influx of karma

4. *Bandha* – the bonds of karma

5. *Samvara* – the breaking of the bonds of karma

6. *Nirjara* – the gradual shedding of the weight of karma

7. *Moksha* – salvation or liberation

To these are added two other vital concepts – that of *punya* (merit) and *papa* (demerit) through one's own actions.

Devout Jains explicate these *tattvas* with a simple story: A man rows a boat to cross a river. The man is *jiva*, the boat is *ajiva*. During the journey, midway upon the river, the boat springs a leak and water starts to flow in: the incoming waters are a potential threat and represent *asrava*; the waters which accumulate inside the boat and threaten to overturn the boat represent *bandha*. Now the man tries to save the boat from sinking by plugging the hole some way or the other; this is *samvara*. He also tries to rid the boat of the accumulating water by throwing the water out; this is *nirjara*. With great effort, the man crosses the river and reaches the other shore; this is *moksha*.

ANEKANTAVADA

Anekantavada is one of the most important and fundamental doctrines of Jainism. The Sanskrit compound *an-eka-anta-vada* literally means "doctrine

The child should support his parents when he is able to do so. Although the family should work together to aid each other, each one must suffer for his own deeds. One's family is of no use to him at the time of judgement. Then he shall be judged in accordance with his deeds.

of non-exclusivity"; it is sometimes loosely translated into English as "scepticism" or "non-absolutism". It refers to the principles of pluralism and multiplicity of viewpoints, the notion that truth and reality are perceived differently from diverse points of view, and that no single point of view can represent the complete truth. (This is something made familiar to us through the parable of the blind men and the elephant). Mahavira, is thought to have propounded this philosophy and encouraged his followers to study and understand rival traditions in his *Acaranga Sutra*: "Comprehend one philosophical view through the comprehensive study of another one," he urged them. Essentially, this concept encourages us to consider, appreciate and respect the truth represented in another's point of view. Many scholars believe that this doctrine played a pivotal role in the growth as well as the survival of Jainism in ancient India, especially against the onslaughts from other religions at various times.

I forgive all the living beings. All living beings may forgive me. I cherish friendly feelings towards all. I do not hold any illwill towards man, beast or plant.

CLASSIFICATION OF KNOWLEDGE

Jainism classified knowledge in two ways: i) Canonical (*Agamika*), and ii) Philosophical (*Darsanika*). The five kinds of knowledge based on the former are: 1) *Matijnana* (Sensitive knowledge), 2) *Srutajnana* (Scriptural knowledge), 3) *Avadhijnana* (Visual knowledge) 4) *Manahparyayajnana* (Mental knowledge) and 5) *Kevalajnana* (Perfect knowledge). *Pratyaksha* (Direct knowledge) and *Paroksha* (Indirect knowledge) are developments of the latter. *Pratyaksha* is defined as knowledge obtained by the self without the assistance of an external instrument. In Jain terminology, *"aksha"* actually refers to the soul. Thus *Pratyaksha* in Jain *Agamika* tradition does not mean empirical perception, i.e. knowledge obtained through sense organs. *Paroksha* is dependent on others.

THE SACRED SCRIPTURES OF JAINISM

The *Purvas*, translated as ancient or prior knowledge, are fourteen Jain scriptures that were preached by all *Tirthankaras*. However, these have been lost in record.

Apart from the *Purvas*, Jain literature is classified into two major categories:

1. *Agama* Literature consists of original scriptures compiled by the immediate followers of Mahavira, known as the *Gandharas*, and the *Srut-kevalis* i.e. the persons having the knowledge of *purvas*, and accorded the exalted status of "scripturally omniscient persons". They are written in the Prakrit language.

2. Non-*agama* Literature consists of commentary and explanation of *Agama* literature and independent works, complied by elder monks, nuns, and scholars. They are written in many languages such as Prakrit, Sanskrit, Old Marathi, Gujarati, Hindi, Kannada, Tamil, German and English.

It must be emphasised that Lord Mahavir's preaching was methodically compiled by His followers into many texts. These texts are collectively known as *Agamas*, the sacred books of the Jain religion. Hence, the Jain religion does not have one sacred book like the Bible or Qur'an, but it has many books compiled by many followers.

JAIN FESTIVALS

Many Jain festivals are especially connected with the anniversaries of the births and deaths of the *tirthankaras*.

Jain Pilgrims

The main Jain festival of the year is *Mahavir Jayanti*, the birth anniversary of Mahavira, the founder of Jainism. On this day Jain devotees visit sacred sites and worship the *tirthankaras* or the enlightened souls. This usually occurs in the months of March/April.

Deep Diwali is observed during October/November in honour of the final liberation of Lord Mahavira,

Charity without fellow feeling is like sowing a fallow land.

who died on this day at the age of 72, at Pawapuri in Bihar. On this day, Mahavira is worshipped at midnight and early next morning. Sacred scriptures are recited and houses are grandly illuminated. Jains observe Diwali in the month of *Kartik* for three days and all through this period Jains indulge in fasting and recite the *Uttaradhyayan Sutra,* in which the final *pravachans* of Lord Mahavira are recorded. They also reflect upon his teachings. The Jain year commences with *pratipada* subsequent to Diwali. Like their Hindu compatriots, Jain businessmen conventionally launch their accounting year from Diwali.

Paryushana is observed in August/September every year, coinciding with the onset of the South-West monsoon. Jain monks refrain from travelling during this time, in order not to cause any harm or injury to other living organisms. As for the laity, this ten-day period is marked by strict observance of the ten cardinal virtues: forgiveness, charity, simplicity, contentment, truthfulness, self-restraint, fasting, detachment, humility and continence. They also observe a unique custom, by which they ask every individual they may have offended during the year for forgiveness. Old quarrels are forgotten and friendships and relationships are renewed, as they fold their hands and ask for *Micchami Dukadam* or forgiveness.

JAIN MARRIAGES

Marriage and the rearing of families is not enjoined upon all Jains. The institution of marriage is viewed clearly in its social aspect. There is no religious motive whatsoever in the contract of marriage. However, Jains always prefer to marry within their own community so that their children might follow their religion and beliefs. The Jain marriage ceremony is dominated by the customary practices or rituals, which of course vary from community to community. For the Jains, marriage means a community declaration of man and woman's intention of being together for their entire life. The community supports the couple by being a part of it. The elders of the Jain community have condemned the practice of negotiating a dowry before the ritual of marriage. Jains believe that there should be no waste of money or time behind unnecessary extravagances. Nevertheless, marriage is a once-in-lifetime occasion and is often celebrated on a grand scale.

Do not allow yourself to be deluded by evil associates. Make friends with those who are considerate both towards people and towards animals.

UNIQUE FEATURES OF JAINISM

Fight with yourself, why fight with external foes? He who conquers himself through himself, will obtain happiness.

It is safe to say that Jainism was the earliest religion to promote *ahimsa* through the vegetarian diet. Although Hinduism and Buddhism have also espoused this cause with the spirit of assimilation that is typical of India, it is Jains who scrupulously apply the principle of nonviolence even to their everyday activities, including their daily diet. In fact, a strict vegetarian diet is the most significant hallmark of the Jain identity.

Jains consider nonviolence to be the most essential religious duty for everyone. It is an indispensable condition for liberation from the cycle of reincarnation, which is the ultimate goal of all Jain activities. As I said, although Jains share this goal with Hindus and Buddhists, their approach is particularly rigorous, uncompromising and comprehensive.

Jains go out of their way to ensure that no harm is caused even to the smallest of insects while preparing their meals and during the process of eating and drinking. They also believe that harm caused by carelessness is equally blameable as harm caused by deliberate action. Jain scriptures also contain specific instructions on how to avoid unnecessary injury to plants, although they admit that plant foods must be consumed for human survival. The eating of root vegetables and honey is, however, forbidden to Jains.

In modern India, Jains have always been tolerant, liberal and respectful to all other faiths. They have built and maintained several Hindu shrines such as the famous Manjunatha temple at Darmasthala in Karnataka. They have also donated liberally towards building mosques and churches.

Jain trusts and endowments also encourage multi-faith dialogues to promote mutual understanding and religious harmony.

Anekantavada is against the notion of the "battle of ideas", which is equated with *himsa* or violence of the intellect. It encourages its adherents to consider the views and beliefs of their rivals and opposing parties. This has taught Jain thinkers to maintain the validity of their doctrine, while at the same time respecting the views of their opponents. The principle of *anekantavada* also influenced Mahatma Gandhi to adopt principles of religious tolerance, *ahimsa* and *satyagraha*. Jain religious tolerance fits well with the liberal and tolerant view typical of Indian religions.

Modern judicial systems, democracy, freedom of speech, and secularism all implicitly reflect an attitude of *anekantavada*.

According to John Koller, because *anekantavada* is designed to avoid one-sided errors, reconcile contradictory viewpoints, and accept the multiplicity and relativity of truth, Jain philosophy is in a unique position to support dialogue and negotiations amongst various nations and peoples.

Jain cosmology gives paramount importance to mountains, rivers, trees, and other natural resources. Jain scriptures give a vivid description of how plants and other beings can and should be saved by a Jain. These are very important principles laid down by Jainism to avoid harm to water, air, fire, and all forms of life and even to minimise such evils as noise pollution. They also encourage us to practise silence, and to observe carefulness in speaking (*bhasasamiti*), and to protect the forest and plants. These rules apply to all practicing Jains.

Sallekhana, the spiritual decision to choose death, is an exclusively Jain principle which anticipates the modern concept of euthanasia. It is defined as making the physical body and the internal passions emaciated by abandoning their sources gradually at the approach of death with pleasure and not by force. However, in Jain tradition, this is not just done to avoid pain and suffering, but as a conscious decision not to prolong this life.

Rendering service to others is one of the basic disciplines prescribed for all Jain laity. Jainism directs the householder to fix boundaries for business, not to pursue commercial activities causing injury to living beings, exclusively for enlarging one's own wealth. This

The Dilwara Temple

All beings hate pain, therefore one should not hurt or kill them. Ahimsa (non-violence) is the highest religion.

has been at the root of several philanthropic activities of the Jain community in India. Jains also build and maintain *goshalas* and hospitals for animals. They strongly believe that birds and animals are man's younger brothers and sisters in the One Family of Creation.

A man is seated on top of a tree in the midst of a burning forest. He sees all living beings perish. But he doesn't realise that the same fate is soon to overtake him also. That man is a fool.

Judaism is one of the ancient religions of the world. It is also the religious culture of the Jewish people, incorporating a system of Jewish law, custom and practice. The word Judaism is derived from the Hebrew word Yehudah, and its distinct feature is a set of beliefs and practices derived from the Jewish Bible, also known as the Tanakh.

JUDAISM

Judaism is a religion which claims a historical continuity of over 3000 years according to the Old Testament, it is the oldest surviving monotheistic faith in the world. Its texts, traditions as well as some of its practices and beliefs are common to all the Abrahamaic religions such as Christianity, Islam and the Baha'i Faith.

Interestingly, the sacred texts of the faith describe the Jews as a 'nation' rather than a religion. Thus Jews of all denominations are regarded as belonging to one ethnoreligious group, wherever in the world they may happen to live. Originating in the Middle East, Judaism spread to many parts of the world including India, Europe, Russia and the United States, both due to voluntary emigration and forced exile and persecutions. Today, many Jews will subscribe to the idea that what we call 'Jewish identity' arises primarily from belonging to an ancient people and upholding its traditions.

Moses: The Master

Jews consider Judaism to be the expression of the covenantal relationship between the children of Israel (later, called the Jewish nation) and God. According to the biblical tradition, God revealed Himself to Abraham and also propounded to him the doctrine of a monotheistic God, at a time when most religions of central Asia and Europe were actually polytheistic. God also promised special protection to the Jews, who were henceforth known as "the Chosen people".

ORIGINS

The history of the Jewish faith, like Christianity and Islam, may be said to begin with the myth of creation as outlined in the Book of Genesis. However, this ancient history becomes specifically Jewish, with the Life of Abraham, who is regarded as the Founder of the Jewish religion, indeed, the Father of the Jewish people. Son of Terah, and the father of Ishmael and Issac, Abraham was put to the test by God, who demanded that he should sacrifice his son Issac to establish his faith and prove that he was "worthy of becoming the father of a mighty nation, which would be as numerous as the stars in the sky or the grains of

A Jew at prayer

God will judge each man according to his works. All men shall be known by their works. Whatever one undertakes to do, one should do it with all his might. God commands men to work and promises that He will be with them in all good works.

sand on the seashore". Abraham obeyed the command, and was about to kill his son as a sacrificial offering, when an angel intervened to save the boy. Well pleased with Abraham's faith, God promised the prophet that his descendants would 'inherit the land' (i.e. Canaan, which is the ancient name for the territory that includes modern day Israel, Palestine, as well as parts of Lebanon, Syria and Jordan, referred to as "the Promised Land" in the Old Testament) . This is called, The Covenant of Abraham. Most scholars are of the opinion that this event took place around 1800 BC. All the ancient Jews trace their physical lineage of birth to Abraham, and in the Bible, Jews refer to themselves as "the seed of Abraham". All subsequent prophets refer to God as the God of Abraham, and he is thought to be the first of the Prophets of Judaism, Christianity and Islam.

In the days following Abraham, the religion was simple: God was regarded as a benevolent patron; all faith centred on the agreement between Abraham and God. Religious practice consisted of sacrifice and prayer at a sacred altar, stone pillar, or sacred tree. Circumcision was the defining mark of the religious community. Its central doctrine was the promise of land and many descendents to Abraham, the Patriarch.

The Covenant that God made with Abraham was renewed with his son Isaac, and then with Issac's son Jacob.

Trust not in wealth. It is fleeting and may be the cause of much evil and suffering. The poverty of a good man is more to be prized than the wealth of the evil man. If one has wealth, one should use it for good and not for evil.

After Abraham, the chief Prophet of Judaism is Moses. As the Bible tells us, the Jews migrated to Egypt during a famine. Here, they came under persecution and enslavement. God chose Moses to free them from the slavery of the Pharaohs, and lead them out of Egypt into the Promised Land. The story of Moses is one of the most thrilling accounts from ancient scriptures. Born a slave, he was adopted by the daughter of the Pharoah, and brought up as a prince. But his faith asserted itself against his upbringing, and he left the luxurious life of the palace, to become a humble shepherd among his own people, until God revealed Himself to Moses and commanded him to fulfil his destiny as the saviour of his people, the Hebrews.

Moses too, is venerated as a Prophet by all Abrahamaic religions. Like the other great patriarchs of the Faith, he was called upon to take up the leadership of his people, including religious, political, legislative and military roles. God performed many miracles to assist

Moses with a safe passage for the Jews, including the parting of the waters of the Red Sea, which enabled them to escape from the pursuing army of the Pharaoh.

At Mount Sinai, God established the nation of Israel as His own, and gave through Moses, the terms of yet another of his Covenants with them. Here too, He revealed Himself as their true God, and uttered in their hearing, the Ten Commandments which Moses duly recorded on a 'tablet' or book, and 'sealed' the Covenant with a sacrificial ritual. The Covenant required exclusive loyalty to Yehovah, who rescued them from bondage in Egypt. Worship of other gods, veneration of idols (even of Yehovah), and magical practices were strictly prohibited. Rituals and festivals were also established to celebrate God's unceasing benevolence.

In further proof of His promise, the Lord then sustained the Israelites through 40 years of journeying in the wilderness before leading them into Canaan, the land promised to Abraham. Central to all these

Only fools give way to war. The wise seek peace. The peace-loving, the meek, shall inherit the earth. The Lord will judge between nations, and wars are of no avail.

events was Moses, who, however, was not destined to enter the Promised land with his followers.

The Biblical Book of Joshua narrates to us the conquest of Canaan, and the settling of the Israelites in the territory. During this period, they broke the Covenant with God several times, by indulging in idol worship of deities other than Jehovah or Yehovah. The 'Judges' like Eli and Samuel were now the spiritual leaders of the people. Samuel crowned Saul as the first King of the Hebrews. King David, Saul's successor, consolidated the monarchy, and made Jerusalem the spiritual, religious and national capital of Israel.

A Synagogue where the devout pray

David's son Solomon, was one of the greatest monarchs of Israel, and during his forty-year reign, Hebrew glory was at its highest. However, his many intermarriages with women of other faiths, caused Solomon to swerve from the Covenant. After his death, the kingdom was split into two, and both were conquered by the enemies of Israel. This was the starting point of excessive fragmentation among the Israelites. Judea, the split-up half of the kingdom, gradually came under Roman occupation. Jews were persecuted and prevented from following their faith. The nadir of the Roman occupation was the desecration and the destruction of the ancient Temple at Jerusalem, originally built by Solomon at the spot consecrated by Abraham.

Throughout this turbulent period, Jews continued to live in Judea, and to practice their faith. Different sections of the people adopted different responses to the inescapable rigours and oppressions of Roman rule: these ranged from armed revolt (the Zealots), withdrawal from the world (the Essenes), to a renewed focus on preserving tradition in a new situation (the Pharisees), to a new sense of identification and integration with Greek society (the Sadducees) and Greek thought (Jewish Neoplatonists).

The Pharasiac movement gave impetus to the development of what we now call Rabbinical Judaism.

The Lord will help those who are earnest. He is near to the sincere and knows man's inner being. He is not fooled by outward appearances.

Reacting to the destruction of the Second Temple in 70 AD, the rabbis sought to reinterpret Jewish concepts and practices in the absence of the Temple and for their people who were now largely in exile. Apart from some minor movements, Rabbinical Judaism was the dominant form of the Jewish religion for nearly 18 centuries. It was responsible for producing the *Talmud,* the *Midrash,* and the great figures of medieval Jewish philosophy.

The annals of Jewish history after the Roman occupation and the advent of Christ, is a record of a series of persecutions and forced exiles. As we know, orthodox Jews refused to accept Jesus as the promised Messiah, and this led to their persecution by Christians. From the ninth century onwards, the Church forbade to all Christians, any contact or association with the Jews, thus isolating the Jewish community in a predominantly Christian Europe.

Meditation brings understanding. One should contemplate God in all His greatness at all times. This is enjoyable and brings the greatest peace and happiness. To meditate upon the Law of the Lord is the duty of all believers.

This isolation and persecution continued even after the Crusades, leading to 'ghettoisation' i.e. forcing the Jews to live in poor, harsh non-livable environments, separated from other people, under severe anti-semetic rules and regulations. The lowest ebb of this anti-semetism was reached during the Nazi rule in Germany, bringing about the horrors of the holocaust, or the monstrous genocide of the Jews under Hitler. By the end of the Second World War, it had claimed over six million Jewish lives, which was over a third of the world Jewish population.

Out of this horror emerged some good for the Jews – by all accounts, the most tortured, vilified and persecuted people in modern history. On May 14, 1948, the Jewish People's Council met at the Tel Aviv Museum and publicly declared the establishment of the State of Israel. The Jews had campaigned long and hard and had suffered immeasurably, for this day to become a reality. The US and the USSR as well as the United Nations recognised the new state, which was also admitted as a sovereign member of the UN. Millions of Jews worldwide, who had faced harassment and persecution for centuries, migrated in great numbers to their Homeland, after nearly two thousand years of exile and wandering. In this effort, they were aided by several non-Jews, who saw this move as reparation and recompense for the inhuman horrors that the Jews had endured in Hitler's concentration camps.

The God of Abraham and the prophets had promised them that they would be brought back to their Homeland before the coming of their Messiah. In 1998, at the Golden Jublilee of their state, over 36% of the world's Jews were living in Israel, awaiting the arrival of their promised Messiah.

JEWISH BELIEFS AND PRACTICES

At the very outset, it must be emphasised that Judaism does not have an official or systematic creed or set of beliefs. Some Jews adhere to a complex set of beliefs and rituals; but others hold on only to certain ritual practices; all of them are considered to be "Jewish". This term thus refers to a culture and a race, rather than a dogmatic religion.

The Ten Commandments are the core of Jewish belief, although, as we have seen earlier, they are accepted by Christians and Muslims as well. In simple form, the Ten Commandments are:

One should love God with all one's heart. And one should love his neighbour. The stranger has a claim on one's love. God loves the good man, the righteous. He also loves the sinner and seeks to draw him from his sin and to Himself.

1. Worship no other gods
2. Do not worship idols
3. Do not misuse the name of the Lord
4. Keep the Sabbath holy
5. Honour your father and mother
6. Do not murder
7. Do not commit adultery
8. Do not steal
9. Do not give false testimony
10. Do not covet

In the great 12ᵗʰ century Rabbi Maimonides put together "13 Articles of Faith" that he believed every Jew ought to adhere to, and this is often used as a summary of core Jewish beliefs, although it must be emphasised that not all Jews subscribe to them, *in toto*.

1. God exists
2. God is one and unique
3. God is incorporeal
4. God is eternal
5. Prayer is to God only
6. The prophets spoke the truth
7. Moses was the greatest of the prophets
8. The written and oral Torah were given to Moses

The dust will return to dust, and the spirit of man will go to its everlasting home. The Lord will reward the good with eternal life and the spirit of man will dwell forever with God who made it.

The Ten Commandments

9. There will be no other Torah

10. God knows the thoughts and deeds of men

11. God will reward the good and punish the wicked

12. The Messiah will come

13. The dead will be resurrected

TRADITIONAL JEWISH BELIEFS

- Judaism begins with the Covenant between God and Abraham, the Founder-Prophet and originator of the Jewish nation.

- The most important of Jewish doctrines is belief in a single, omniscient, omnipotent, benevolent, transcendent God, who created the universe and continues to govern it.

- According to most branches of Judaism, God established a Covenant with the Israelites and their descendants, and revealed His laws and commandments to Moses on Mount Sinai in the form of both the written and oral Torah.

- Judaism has traditionally valued Torah study and the observance of the commandments recorded in the Torah and expounded in the Talmud.

It is wrong to hate a brother. Hatred begets strife, and strife destroys a people. Only the fool will give way to hatred.

- It is the Jewish belief that the Torah, which contains the fundamental laws and commandments (*mitzvot*) that govern Jewish life, was given directly by God to Moses. To Jews, therefore, it is God's Word. The ancient interpretations of the Torah by rabbis, passed down by word of mouth — the oral tradition – as well as later, written interpretations are now contained in the Talmud.

- Jews believe that the *mitzvot* – which God has given and which relate to all areas of life – food, clothing, prayer, relationships, business dealings, morality and so on – must be obeyed.

Historically, Jews have always placed their faith in divine revelations made to their prophets and leaders. However, there is now no centralised authority to dictate dogma to all believers. Thus it has been said that although Judaism is strictly monotheistic, it has never really been monolithic. Even today, there are different interpretations and formulations of the doctrines found in the Torah.

Judaism is joyous. One who has the Lord on his side should be happy, rejoicing all the time. Happiness results from good works. If people keep the law, they shall be happy.

Moving away from matters of belief, many historians and scholars insist that emphasised practices and observances of Jewish Law are far more important for Jews than religious beliefs. They even associate apostasy with a failure to observe Jewish law, maintaining that the requirements of Judaism as a faith includes circumcision and adherence to traditional customs. These required observances and practices include:

- Praying three times a day — morning, afternoon, and evening — either in the home or synagogue. An additional morning prayer service is added on the Sabbath and Festivals. These prayers can be private or community, but community worship is preferable. (Communal prayer requires a quorum of ten adult Jews, called a *minyan*.)

- Recitation of certain prayers and benedictions throughout the day when performing various acts. Prayers are recited upon waking up in the morning, before eating or drinking different foods, after eating a meal, and so on.

- The *Shema* is an affirmation of Judaism and a declaration of faith in one God. The obligation to recite the *Shema* is separate from the obligation to pray and a Jew is obligated to say *Shema* in the morning and at night. The words of the *Shema* are significant.

- Jewish dietary laws are known as *kashrut*. Food prepared in accordance with them is termed *kosher*, and food that violates them is termed *treifah*. Jews who observe these laws are said to be "keeping *kosher*". (Rabbinic Judaism forbids the consumption of meat and dairy products together.) The idea behind these dietary injunctions seems to be that Jews should avoid eating "negative foods" such as those involving pain, sickness, uncleanliness or cruelty to animals.

- The ceremonies that mark a Jew's passage through life, which include *brit milah* (the covenant of male circumcision), naming, *bar mitzvah* (or *bat mitzvah* for girls), marriage, and funeral rites.

The special building where Jewish people meet together for prayer, to study the Torah and to hear it being read, and to meet fellow members of the community is called a synagogue.

In an Orthodox synagogue, men and women sit separately. The men sit in the main part of the building around a central platform and reading desk known as the *Bimah*. Women and young children will sit apart,

Trust in God, at all times. He will lead you even through the shadows of death and will protect you in the presence of your enemies.

often in an upper gallery. They do not take part in the synagogue services (except on some special occasions).

At the very front of the synagogue is a large cupboard called the Holy Ark in which the scrolls of the Torah are kept. On the Sabbath day, the Torah scroll will be brought to the *Bimah* for the allocated reading for that particular Sabbath. Men wear their prayer shawls for the Sabbath day service and, of course, have their heads covered.

In reform synagogues, men and women sit together, women can take part and might even be rabbis, services might be shorter, and the congregation is more likely to sit facing the front. Whereas most of the service is in Hebrew in an orthodox synagogue, in a reform synagogue much more is in English.

JEWISH SCRIPTURES

Prophet Muhammad called the Jews "People of the Book", and appropriately so. After the destruction of the Second Temple in 70 AD and the subsequent exile, sacrifices became impossible and Jewish religious life turned to Torah study and prayer in the synagogue. Study of Torah and other Jewish texts has been central to religious life ever since.

The Torah, the Talmud, and other Jewish writings are precious sources of Jewish history and divine

What you hate, do to no man. One should love his neighbour as himself.

commandments (the *mitzvot*), both of which continue to play a dominant part in Judaism.

To remember the great things God has done for the Jewish people in history, and what He asks of them in return, selections from the Torah and the Prophets are read in the synagogue several times a week.

To assist in proper interpretation and application of the *mitzvot*, a great body of rabbinical writings has developed and continues to develop to this day.

Study of Torah (preferably in its original language, Hebrew) is an integral part of a Jewish child's education, and even Jewish mysticism is focused on intensive textual study.

The Jewish sacred text is the *Tanakh*, whose name is an acronym of *Torah, Nebi'im* and *Ketuvim* (Law, Prophets and Writings). It consists of the same books as the Christian Old Testament, although in a slightly different order and with other minor differences.

The Old Testament

Although the word "Torah" is sometimes used to refer to the entire Tanakh or even the whole body of Jewish writings, it technically means the first five books of the Tanakh. These books are also known as the Five Books of Moses or the Pentateuch.

Another important Jewish text is the Talmud, a collection of rabbinical writings that interpret, explain and apply the Torah scriptures. The Talmud was written between the second and fifth century CE, but Orthodox Jews believe it was revealed to Moses along with the Torah and preserved orally until it was written down. The Talmud is thus known as the "Oral Torah", with the first five books of the Tanakh designated the "Written Torah".

A third group of Jewish literature is the *Midrash*, which is a large body of rabbinical material derived primarily from sermons (the Hebrew word for "sermon" is d'rash). The primary collections of Midrash were compiled between the fourth and sixth centuries, but the midrashic form continues to the present day.

A further set of Jewish writings is the *responsa*, a vast collection (thousands of volumes) of answers to specific questions on Jewish law. If the Talmud is a law book, the responsa are case law.

The Sefer ha-Zohar (Book of Splendour) is the central text of Kabbalah, the mystical branch of Judaism.

JEWISH FESTIVALS

Sabbath: The most important day of the week for Jewish families is the *sabbath* day (Shabbat). It is a day of rest, reminding people that in six days God created the world and on the seventh day, He rested. It is a reminder that we need rest and a regular break from work, which should be a time of "re-creation". The sabbath day begins at sunset on Friday and ends at nightfall on Saturday.

Passover: This festival, which is celebrated in the Spring, reminds Jewish families of the Exodus of their ancestors from Egypt in the time of Moses. No leavened bread is eaten during this feast, because Moses and the Israelites had to leave Egypt very quickly and had no time to make bread with yeast in it. Before Passover comes, all foods containing yeast are removed from the house. A

Those who have should give to those who have not. The poor should always be helped. One who gives to the poor gives to the Lord. If one does not give when the poor ask, one will not be aided when one is in need.

special Seder meal is prepared for this festival in Jewish homes. This is a great family occasion and provides an opportunity every year for re-telling the story and thus passing on the great event from generation to generation. The story is recited by the father, recreating the events of the first Passover. Symbolic items of food are served, and songs are sung to commemorate the great occasion. The final toast after the meal is always, "Next year, in Jerusalem".

- **Shavuot:** This festival comes 7 weeks after Passover. It is an early harvest festival celebrating the beginning of the harvest season. Appropriately, summer flowers are used in homes and synagogues

The Western Wall in Jerusalem

God is faithful and will preserve the faithful. The man of faith can expect great rewards from God.

to provide bright and joyful decorations. At Shavuot the Jewish community celebrates the giving of the Torah, their guide from God for life.

- **Sukkot:** In this autumn festival, Jews build *sukkot* (tents) in their gardens. A *sukkah* is like a shed but, instead of a roof, it is covered with branches and leaves and inside is decorated with harvest festival fruits. In fact, it is also a celebration of the end of harvest, the final in-gathering of crops. In this country, Jewish families will eat meals in the *sukkot*, but in Israel they might also sleep in them. This reminds Jews of the fact that for forty years, their ancestors lived in tents, as they wandered in search of their Promised Land.

- **Purim:** This festival, coming in February or March, is associated with Queen Esther, who saved the Jews from an attempt to exterminate them during the time of the Persian empire.

- **Chanukah:** This is a winter festival, falling in December. It is a festival of lights and giving of presents. During this festival, Jews remember the persecution meted out to their ancestors under Syrian Greek Rule, when their sacred temple was defiled by the tyrant, Antiochus, and they were forbidden to read from the Torah.

MANY PATHS: ONE GOAL

- **Rosh Hashanah:** This is the celebration of the Jewish New Year, falling on the first day of the Jewish month of Tishri (sometimes in September; sometimes in October). It is a celebration of the creation of the world, as recorded in The Book of Genesis. During the New Year's meal, bread is dipped in honey and eaten. Apples are also dipped in honey and honey-cake is a favourite. This all indicates the expectation of a sweet and happy new year.

- **Yom Kippur:** The tenth day of Tishri is the holiest day of the Jewish year— *Yom Kippur* or The Day of Atonement. This is a day of total fasting. Fasting, afflicting the soul by giving up something really important, is a religious way of showing God that a person is truly sorry for the sins he has committed and the failures of which he has been guilty.

JEWISH MARRIAGES

The Jewish word for marriage is *Kiddushin*, which literally means "made holy". In a Jewish wedding, the bride stands on the right hand side of the groom. The wedding ceremony takes place under a four-poster

The Lord forgives all sins. He is forgiving at all times, if the wicked ones will forsake their ways.

Evil is the cause of suffering. Everyone is evil and must repent. God will reward those who flee from evil and seek the good. God is ever ready to pardon.

canopy called a *Huppah* (or *Chuppah*), situated in the synagogue in front of the *Bimah*. Sometimes, especially in Israel, the ceremony takes place in the open-air. The *Huppah* represents the future home of the couple. Vows are said and then the couple drink from a goblet of wine. The groom places the ring on the right index finger of the bride. The rabbi reads out the *ketubah* — this is a marriage contract which is drawn up before the ceremony. Marriage, in Judaism, is a contract, and the *ketubah* sets out the contractual duties and responsibilities of the husband towards his wife.

A Jewish marriage

Do good at all times, for man will be judged by his works.

The rabbi then pronounces seven blessings, following which the groom stamps on a glass to smash it. This represents the regret over the destruction of the Jewish Temple in Jerusalem by the Romans in 70 AD.

UNIQUE ASPECTS OF JUDAISM

There is a story in wide circulation about a question asked of Rabbi Hillel—a notable rabbi from the 1st century BCE. A non-Jew asked the rabbi to teach him everything about the Torah while standing on one foot. Rabbi Hillel responded: "What is hateful to you, don't do unto your neighbour. The rest is commentary. Now, go and study." Good actions are far more important than doctrines for Jews, who believe that God appointed the Jews to be his chosen people in order to set an example of holiness and ethical behaviour to the world.

The term "God" is used in Jewish writings in English, to respect the Jewish prohibition against spelling the name or title of the deity in full.

There are five main forms of Judaism in the world today. However, the most conservative traditions do not necessarily recognise the most liberal as being part of Judaism. This is a common problem among many of the world's great religions.

Judaism teaches that animals are part of God's creation and should be treated with compassion.

Judaism is not a missionary faith and so doesn't actively try to convert people (in many countries anti-Jewish laws prohibited this for centuries). Despite this, the modern Jewish community increasingly welcomes would-be converts. Not all Jewish conversions are accepted by all Jews. The more Orthodox a community is, the less likely it is to accept a conversion done in a more liberal movement.

A person who converts to Judaism becomes a Jew in every sense of the word, and is just as Jewish as someone born into Judaism. There is a good precedent for this; Ruth, the great-great grandmother of King David, was a convert.

The whole duty of man is to fear God and keep His commandments. This involves love and service to God with one's whole heart .

Nicholas de Lange, a distinguished scholar of Judaism, says that the very idea of religion was artificially imposed on Judaism. "The term 'religion' has been foreign to Judaism until relatively recently," he writes, "when the dialogue with Christianity has compelled Jews to recognise and use it. Indeed the Hebrew language does not really have a word for religion." Judaism is characterised by its extraordinary emphasis on tradition, the deep sense of community, even when there is a complete lack of religious commitment among certain individuals.

Unlike many other religions, Judaism does not focus much on abstract cosmological concepts. Although Jews have certainly considered the nature of God, man, the universe, life and the afterlife at great length, there is no mandated, official, definitive belief on these subjects, outside of the very general concepts discussed above. There is substantial room for personal opinion on all of these matters, because Judaism is more concerned about actions than beliefs.

Judaism focuses on relationships: the relationship between God and mankind, between God and the Jewish people, between the Jewish people and the land of Israel, and between human beings. This is what is emphasised in Jewish scriptures and history.

Many of the world's religions have hope in a future heroic figure who will rescue the righteous, judge the wicked, and restore peace to the world (Kalki in Hinduism, Maitreya in Buddhism and the Second Coming in Christianity). In Judaism, this figure is the Messiah. Christians believe the Messiah has come in the form of Jesus of Nazareth; Jews emphatically do not.

Kabbalah (meaning: receiving) is a discipline and school of thought concerned with the mystical aspect of Judaism. It is a set of esoteric teachings that is meant to explain the relationship between an infinite, eternal and essentially unknowable Creator with the finite and mortal universe of His creation. In solving this paradox, *Kabbalah* seeks to define the nature of the universe and the human being, the nature and purpose of existence, and various other ontological questions. It also presents methods to aid understanding of these concepts and to thereby attain spiritual realisation.

Family love and solidarity is basic to Jewish life. The child must honour and respect his parents and obey them at all times. The parents must teach the child and rear him in the ways of the Lord.

Sikhism is a faith, a way of life, a religious philosophy and a set of practices based on belief in One God, known as Waheguru. *The teachings of the ten great Gurus or teachers of the faith, starting with Guru Nanak Dev up to Guru Gobind Singh; the* Adi Granth *or Primary Volume which is revered as the* Guru Granth Sahib, *which is also thought of as the last and eternal Guru. It is not without significance that the word Guru should occur so often when we talk of Sikhism; the word* sikh *is derived from Punjabi (Sanskrit original* sishya*)and means a 'disciple' or a learner.*

SIKHISM

Guru Nanak: *Prophet of Peace*

Many people believe that this religion is a reformed version or re-purification of the Hindu faith. Some historians regard Sikhism as a symbiotic blend of Hindu, Islamic and Sufi influences, along with the inspiration of the *bhakti* movement of the India of those days. But many Sikhs assert that their religion is a direct revelation from God, and has nothing to do with Hinduism or Islam.

The origins, growth and history of Sikhism are closely associated with the North Western Indian state of Punjab, which is so called because of its five Rivers. Today, the followers of Guru Nanak, known as the Sikhs, are spread all over the world, but by far the largest number of the faith are still to be found in Punjab, and Sikhism is part of Punjabi culture, society and tradition. In this sense, Sikhism may be said to be an ethnic religion.

Even today, in the Punjab, many Hindu families give their first born son to the Gurus, to be baptised as a *Khalsa sikh,* or a soldier of the Guru's army of protectors. It is said that this tradition started from the time of the Tenth Guru, Guru Gobind Singh, who made a clarion call to all the Hindu families to offer their eldest sons to fight for the protection of Dharma, against the forced conversions to Islam prevalent under the Moghul rule. Since then, Sikhism is traditionally regarded as a religion of warriors who were protectors of those who could not defend themselves. Today, there are several diverse orders of Sikhism, such as the *Udasis*, the *Radhasoamis* and the *Nirankaris*. Some scholars regard them as offshoots

Let no man in the world live in delusion. Without a Guru none can cross over to the other shore.

of Sikhism; while others see them as differing Sikh philosophies. The *Khalsa*, ordained by Guru Gobind Singh, is regarded by many Sikhs as being the completion of the development of the Sikh religion.

A well-known contemporary Sikh writer and historian, Khushwant Singh, asserts however, that despite innovations, "this new community, the [Sikh] *Khalsa Panth*, remained an integral part of the Hindu social "and religious system". It is significant that when Guru Tegh Bahadur was summoned to Delhi, he went as a representative of the Hindus. He was executed in the year 1675. His son who succeeded him as Guru later described his father's martyrdom as in the cause of the Hindu faith: "To preserve their caste marks and their sacred thread did he perform the supreme sacrifice". The Guru himself looked upon his community as an integral part of the Hindu social system.

As fragrance abides in the flower
As reflection is within the mirror,
So does your Lord abide within you,
Why search for Him without ?

The Word is the Guru, The Guru is the Word,
For all nectar is enshrined in the Word.
Blessed is the Word which reveals the Lord's
name
But more is the one who knows by the Guru's
grace

The remarkable thing about India's religions is that Hinduism, Sikhism, Buddhism and Jainism have peacefully co-existed for ages. Over and above this, Punjabi Hindus and Sikhs share a close cultural and social identity. In their case, the demarcation is harmonising rather than divisive.

Even when it was founded, Sikhism was a progressive and boldly liberal religion. The famous saying of its founder, Guru Nanak, "There is no Hindu, there is no Muslim," is still one of the basic tenets of the Sikh faith.

ORIGINS

The Sikh religion traces its origins from the life and teachings of Guru Nanak (1469- 1539 AD). During his time, both Hinduism and Islam were widespread in Northern India, as also was the widespread disillusion and discontent among the people with regard to both religions. The *bhakti* movement, dedicated to eradicating several social evils of Hindu society, was also taking shape across India at that time. Devout Vaishnavite Hindus as well as saint-poets like Kabir sought a way of love and devotion to God that was beyond narrow denominations of religious dogma. In fact, Kabir anticipated Guru Nanak with his famous *doha*: "God, whether Thou be Allah or Ram, I live by Thy Name!" It must also be mentioned here that some of Kabir's most beautiful verses were later incorporated into the Guru Granth Sahib.

Nanak Chand was born on April 15, 1469, in the village of Talwandi in Punjab. (Today, after the Partition of India, this village is part of Pakistan and is a sacred pilgrimage centre for all Sikhs, known as Nankhana Sahib). He was the first son of a pious Hindu family, his parents being Bhai Kalu and Tripta Devi, humble and devout folk. Nanak's father was a *patwari* – a farmer and keeper of land records. As a child, he displayed remarkable wisdom and perception. But he was in no way inclined to fulfill his father's worldly ambitions for his future. He was often lost in a divine world of his own, even as his eyes overflowed with intense love for the Almighty.

God is one, but He has innumerable forms.
He is the creator of all and He Himself takes
the human form.

One cannot comprehend Him through reason, even if one reasoned for ages.

The father was a persistent man; he did his best to interest his son in worldly matters. He set the son up to be a cowherd, but Nanak Chand let the cows graze as they pleased while he sat down to meditate! Not one to give up easily, the father put Nanak in charge of a shop, but the son distributed the groceries among the *sadhus* and the poor and the needy.

The father was at a loss to understand his son! In despair, he appealed to Nanak Chand, "My son, it looks as if you are an utter failure in life! Wouldn't you like to be someone in society?" And again, "You must do something or the other to earn wealth. Why don't you take to farming? Be a farmer and plough the fields," he pleaded. "Father, I am ploughing the fields of life," Nanak replied. "I am sowing in my life, the seeds of the Name Divine!"

At the age of 19, Nanak Chand was married to Sulakhni, for the parents felt that marriage and family life would change him. Nanak and his wife had two sons, Sri Chand and Lakhmi Chand. One day, when he was about thirty years old, people saw Nanak Chand going for a dip in the river. Casting his garments on the shore he plunged into the river Ravi. Forthwith, he disappeared. He was taken to be drowned! At the end of the third day Nanak re-appeared. On his face shone a strange light. He had a vision and a revelation. In the vision he heard a voice tell him: "Nanak, I am with Thee. Repeat My Name and ask others to repeat My Name; mingle with men and show them the way!"

Now his life's mission became clear to Nanak. He prepared to go forth among the people, to sing to them the Name of God, and to share with them the Truth revealed to him – that the word of the Lord was the Guru. He undertook several long journeys, mostly by foot, to propagate the message of unity, harmony and love, based purely on his personal experience and revelation, without reference to any scriptures. He travelled far and wide; he travelled all over India, visiting Benaras and Kashmir, Peshawar and Delhi, Chennai and Kurukshetra; he also went to Mecca, Baghdad, Afghanistan, Ceylon and Tibet; he was imbued with the zeal of the missionary and the illumination of a true Guru. Wherever he went, he awakened the souls of the people. He revealed to the

The Lord can never be established nor created; the formless one is limitlessly complete in Himself.

*He who shows the real home in this body is
the Guru.
He makes the five sounded word reverberate
in man.*

prince and the peasant, the Hindu and Muslim, the
educated and illiterate, the way to reach God.

Accompanied by his childhood friend and close
companion, the minstrel Mardana, Guru Nanak
moved from village to village, town to town. He was a
great reformer, a great singer of songs. He would enter
a village or town, and Mardana's *kirtan* would draw
crowds; to them the Guru would proclaim, "There is
no Hindu and no Mussalman!" People were at first
bewildered by this cryptic message; but he took the
trouble to explain to them that there was but One
great God, and that He was loving and kind, and above
all narrow denominations and distinctions of caste
and creed.

Towards the closing period of his life he settled down
at Kartarpur. Everyday *satsangs* were held which were
attended by many devotees. In the year 1539, Guru
Nanak departed from his earthly pilgrimage. But
before then, he appointed his own successor, Guru
Angad. A succession of gurus followed Guru Angad,
one of whom was Guru Arjan Dev, who compiled
the Granth Sahib during his leadership. The following
is a list of the Sikh Gurus who followed Guru Nanak:

1. **Guru Nanak** Himself.

2. **Guru Angad** (1504-52), who is said to have
   invented the *Gurumukhi* script, and widely
   propagated the hymns of the Guru and also
   preached the life of the Guru.

3. **Guru Amardas** (1552-74), who is thought to have
   initiated the tradition of *Langar*, the fellowship
   meal cooked in a community kitchen, meant to
   remove caste distinctions and establish social
   harmony among his followers. *Baisakhi* and Diwali
   were chosen as days for the get-together of all
   Sikhs under the Guru.

4. **Guru Ramdas** (1574-81), who was Guru
   Amardas's son-in-law and was responsible for
   founding the holy city of Ramdaspur, which is now
   known as Amritsar. The construction of the sacred
   shrine of Guru Harmandir Sahib (the Golden
   temple) also began here during his time. He also
   introduced the *Gurbani* among his followers.

*Even kings and emperors with heaps of
wealth and vast dominion cannot compare
with an ant filled with the love of God.*

5. **Guru Arjan Dev** (1581-1606), was the youngest son of Guru Ramdas. He compiled the Adi Granth which is the most important segment of the Guru Granth Sahib. Under his leadership, Sikhism began to spread rapidly among the people, thus attracting the negative attention of the Moghul rulers. The Fifth Guru became the first Martyr of the Sikh faith, rousing the wrath of Hindus and Sikhs against the Moghuls.

Guru Arjan Dev: The Great Martyr

Those who act in ego do not go beyond karma. It is only by Guru's Grace that one is rid of ego.

By the karma of good actions, some come to serve the Perfect Guru.

6. **Guru Har Gobind** (1606-1644) was the son of Guru Arjan Dev. He tried to mobilise the Sikhs and the Hindus against the Moghuls; he was imprisoned by Emperor Jehangir, but released due to the intervention of his wife, Nur Jehan on *Bandi chor diwas*. He was the founder of the *Akhal Takht* or the Eternal Throne, the symbol of the temporal and religious power of the Gurus.

7. **Guru Har Rai** (1644-1661) travelled and preached extensively to spread the Faith. He supported Dara Shukoh, the elder brother of Aurangazeb in his conflict with the latter, and lost his elder son in the cause. He himself died, by being poisoned at the age of 31, at the behest of Aurangazeb.

8. **Guru Har Krishan** (1661-1664) was the second son of Guru Har Rai, who succeeded his father at the age of five, due to the demise of his elder brother. He had been instructed by his father to stop the Sikh faith from becoming a political tool of the Moghul empire. He did his best to keep away from the Delhi *durbar*, and concentrated instead on social work.

9. **Guru Tegh Bahadur** (1644-1675): Though he was able to spread Sikhism to a greater degree, Sikhism also suffered from schism during his time. He too, was executed by Aurangazeb, as he dared

to fight for freedom of religion and faith, especially for the protection of persecuted Kashmiri pandits. He was thus a great Sikh Martyr for the cause of the Hindus.

10. **Guru Gobind Singh** (1675-1708) was the tenth and last Guru and also the most famous after Guru Nanak. He was born at Patna. Because of the execution of his father, he became the Guru at the age of nine. He organised the Sikhs into the *Khalsa* – a disciplined army of devoted and courageous soldiers, baptised by the sword to defend their faith to the death, against the

The Initiation of the Khalsa Panth

He, who sings (with love) the praise of the Lord for an instant, mounts to all the heavens, and is delivered and released.

Seek not the abode of heaven, nor fear the depths of hell. For, that which has to happen must happen, so build no hopes in the mind. Utter thou the Lord's praise. For, from Him one gathers the Treasures of Eternal Bliss.

oppression of the Mughals. He began the tradition of adding the suffix 'Singh' to the names of the Sikhs. He did not nominate a successor, but abolished the succession of the Gurus and made the Guru Granth Sahib the symbol of the Guru himself. He spent most of his time opposing the Mughals to whom he lost his two sons and finally he himself was assassinated by a Pathan at Nanded.

After the death of the tenth Guru in 1708, the loyalty of the Sikhs was transferred from the personal authority of the Guru to the sacred book, the Guru Granth Sahib, and so it remains today.

From the idealism, the missionary zeal and the deep and devout mysticism of its Founder, Guru Nanak, Sikhism had evolved into a militant faith of trained warriors by the time of the Tenth Guru. This was undoubtedly due to the constraint of political, historical conditions, under which Sikhs were severely persecuted and killed, with many of their own Gurus becoming martyrs to the cause. However, the basic religious beliefs and convictions of Sikhism, were always adhered to uncompromisingly.

FUNDAMENTAL TRUTHS OF SIKHISM

Any attempt to outline Sikh beliefs must begin with the opening invocation of the prayer at the Gurdwara:

Ek Onkar… Satnaam…

All true Sikhs believe in the one and only one God, who has infinite qualities and names. He is the same for all religions, and is the Universal Creator, Sustainer and Destroyer. He is manifest everywhere, in every aspect of Creation. He is fearless and without enmity. His form is indestructible. He doesn't need to take up any living form. He is without birth or death. He is enlightened with his own light. He has and will exist forever. In the words of the Adi Granth, He is *nirankaar, akal* and *alakh* – formless, shapeless, timeless and beyond sight. He is omnipotent and omnipresent and is signified by the opening term of the scripture : *ek onkar*. In the beginning, He alone existed; and the Creation of the Cosmos was at His will or *Hukam*.

God is knowable only to the spiritually awakened. In the task of knowing God and attaining salvation, the role of the Guru is indispensable. The Guru is the

---

One in whose heart there is love, he attains salvation.

As you sow, so you shall reap; This body is the result of your actions.

---

voice and light of God, and the source of all wisdom and salvation. The Sikhs believe that the spirit of Nanak was passed from one guru to the next, "just as the light of one lamp, which lights another and does not diminish." Outward practices, rites and rituals are irrelevant to this pursuit: inward remembrance of the Name and the *shabad* (Divine Word) are essential.

The following lines from the Guru Granth Sahib emphasise this basic principle:

There is only the one Supreme Lord God; there is no other.
Soul and body are all Yours. Whatever pleases You shall happen.
Through the Perfect Guru, one becomes perfect. O Nanak, meditate on the True One.

Simran and *jap* – remembrance and recital of the Name Divine – are fundamental to the Sikh way of life. Only by keeping the Name of God in mind, can the soul progress towards salvation. Therefore, the Sikh Gurus ask the devotees to meditate with single mindedness, dispel doubt, remain focused and subdue their ego. Thus glory will be obtained.

Sikhism also insists on the brotherhood of all humanity, the equality of all people. "We are all sons and daughters of *Waheguru*, the Almighty," proclaimed Guru Nanak. Thus discrimination on the basis of birth, caste, social class or gender, is strictly forbidden to the Sikhs.

Sikhism emphasises *sangat* and *pangat* – that is congregations of the faithful, and fellowship meals shared by all devotees irrespective of caste, creed, colour or social status.

Sikhism does not deny the validity and truth of other faiths. However, Sikhism does teach that unlike other faiths, it is a more direct and a simpler path to salvation.

Every true Sikh is enjoined to defeat and destroy the five thieves who dwell within the self: lust (*kaama*), anger (*krodha*), greed (*lobha*), attachment (*moha*) and pride (*ahankar*). It is the duty of each Sikh to subdue and control these emotions. The best way to conquer the thieves is with five weapons: contentment (*santokh*), charity (*daan*), kindness/giving (*daya*), positive energy (*chardi kala*) and humility (*nimrata*). The four fruits of life that we may obtain through this are: Truth, contentment, contemplation and *Naam* (the Name of God).

All your actions without remembering Him, are as futile as decorations on a corpse.

O foolish mind! Why do you grumble, When you are rewarded according to your own actions?

Naam japo, kirat karo, wand chhako – i. e. meditate on the Name, undertake honest, good work, share your earnings with others – are the injunctions laid on all Sikhs. The recitation of *Japji Sahib* in the morning, *sadar* at sunset, and *sohila* at night are regular features of all Sikh congregations.

Like the other religions of India, Sikhs also believe in *karma* and reincarnation. Guru Nanak taught that *karma* can be modified by divine grace.

The essence of Sikh teaching is summed up by Guru Nanak in the following words: "Realisation of Truth is higher than all else. Higher still is truthful living."

PRACTICES ENJOINED UPON SIKHS

Simple, precise and practical guidelines are laid out by the Gurus for the practice of the "Sikh way of life". The Gurus emphasise that a Sikh should lead a disciplined life engaged in *Naam Simran*, meditation on God's name, *Kirat Karni*, living a honest life of a house-holder, and *Wand chako*, sharing what one has with the community. This translates into hard work,

*I belong to no sect: I adore but one God!
And I see Him in the Earth below. And the
Heavens above and in all directions!*

honest living, love of fellow humans and through them service of God, the Universal power. This way of life is stripped of all complications, esoteric rituals and exploitation of others in the name of religion. No benefits are gained by birth or station of life or social status; everyone has to undertake the rigours of *Simran* (meditation) and *Seva* (selfless service) to progress spiritually. The Sri Guru Adi Granth asks the Sikh to "practise truth, contentment and kindness; this is the most excellent way of life. One who is so blessed by the Formless Lord God renounces selfishness, and becomes the dust of all."

Personal regulations include the 5Ks as they are called:

WEARING THE 5KS AS ARTICLES OF FAITH

1. *Kesh* – long and uncut hair and a turban to protect the hair on the head.

2. *Kanga* – small comb to be used twice daily to keep the hair in clean and healthy condition.

3. *Kaccha* – underwear in the form of shorts to exercise self-control.

4. *Kara* – a steel slave bangle on the dominant arm to remind the Sikh to always remember the Guru before undertaking any action.

5. *Kirpan* – a short, often dagger-sized sword to remind the Sikh that he has to defend the weak against all forms of repression.

PROHIBITIONS

All true Sikhs are prohibited from the following:

1. Cutting Hair

2. Intoxication

3. Adultery

4. Blind spirituality, superstitions and rituals

5. Material obsession and accumulation of material wealth

6. Sacrifice of creatures, or any ritual animal sacrifice

7. Non-family-oriented living: (A Sikh is encouraged not to live as a recluse, beggar, yogi, monastic (monk/nun) or celibate).

8. Worthless talk including bragging, gossip, lying, slander, "back-stabbing", etc.

9. No priestly class: Sikhism does not have priests, who were abolished by Guru Gobind Singh. The only position he left was a *Granthi* to look after the Guru Granth Sahib; and any Sikh is free to

become *Granthi* or read from the Guru Granth Sahib

10. Eating meat killed in a ritualistic manner (*Kutha* meat)

11. Having premarital or extramarital sexual relations

THE SACRED SIKH SCRIPTURES

The holiest of the Sikh scriptures is the Guru Granth Sahib. It was called *Adi Granth* (first scripture) until Guru Gobind Singh conferred on it the title of the Guru in 1708, after which it was called Guru Granth Sahib.

Sikhs are proud to claim that the *Adi Granth* is the only world scripture which was compiled during the lifetime of its sacred composer, unlike other world scriptures which were compiled many years after the death of the prophet. (e.g. the gospels, written about 60 years after the death of Christ; Quran, written about 80 years after the death of Mohammed, and the *Three Baskets* and *Angas* written about 40 years after the death of Buddha and Mahavir respectively).

The later version of *Adi Granth*, the Guru Granth Sahib was compiled by Guru Arjan Dev, the fifth Guru of the Sikhs. The work of compilation was started in 1601 and finished in 1604. The Granth, called by Guru Arjan as Pothi Sahib, was installed at Golden Temple (then called 'Harimandir' - the house

How great is God! The greatest of the great is He, and great is His Word! Men are specks: yet alas! they depart this life in pride!

of God) with great celebrations. This scripture, as it stands now, includes along with the *Adi Granth*, the sacred *bani* of many *pirs*, saints and *bhagats* from different faiths and different parts of India, from Kabir to Namdev, from Sadna, the butcher to Jaidev, and Farid, Pippa, Surdas and Raidas.

The *Adi Granth* also contains the *Japji Sahib*. Consisting of about forty *shlokas*, it is the prayer of initiation of the Guru. It is believed to have been composed by Guru Nanak himself, and he exhorted

The Golden Temple, Amritsar

his disciples to recite it at the sacred *amrit vela* or early morning.

For every devout Sikh, the recitation of the Guru Granth Sahib precedes all important activities. This scripture replaces the *agni* of the Hindu tradition in Sikh marriages and the couples go around this scripture during the consecration of their marriage.

SIKH FESTIVALS

Sikhs celebrate many Hindu festivals like *Raksha Bandhan, Holi, Karva Chauth* and *Diwali*. But their chief festivals are the *Gurpurabs*, which are anniversaries associated with the lives of the Sikh

A Sikh Procession

Gurus. Sikhs celebrate ten *Gurpurabs* in a year, each one honouring the ten gurus of the *Khalsa Panth*. Of these the important ones are the birthdays of Guru Nanak and Guru Gobind Singh and the martyrdom days of Guru Arjan Dev and Guru Tegh Bahadur.

Guru Nanak's Jayanti is usually celebrated in the month of Kartik (October / November). As the Sikhs believe that Guru Nanak brought spiritual illumination and enlightenment to humanity, this festival is also called *Prakash Utsav*, the festival of light.

The Tenth Guru, **Gobind Singh's birthday** is observed on December 2. The martyrdom day of the fifth Guru, Arjan Dev falls in the months of May/ June and that of the ninth Guru, Tegh Bahadur, in November.

All Sikh sacred days follow a beautiful spiritual routine. The *Prabhat Pheris*, early morning religious processions that go around localities singing *shabads* (hymns), start as early as three weeks before each important festival. Devotees offer refreshments to the faithful when the procession passes their homes.

O Lord! If I had hundreds of thousands of tons of paper, and if my ink were inexhaustible; and if my pen moved swift as the rushing wind, I should still be unable to anticipate all Thou art!

None is mine enemy, and none to me a stranger is! Saith Nanak, servant of all: "All, all are my brethren in the One Beloved!"

Gurpurabs mark the culmination of *Prabhat Pheris*. There is *akhand path* or continuous recitation from beginning to end of the Guru Granth Sahib, without a break for three days. It is also concluded on the day of the festival. The Granth Sahib is carried in procession on a flower decorated float. Five armed guards, who represent the *Panj Pyares*, head the procession carrying *Nishan Sahibs* (the Sikh flag). Local bands play religious music and marching school children form a special part of the procession.

In the Gurdwaras, special programmes are held, including *katha* (discourse), religious lectures and recitation of poems in praise of the Guru. *Kirtan-darbars* and *Amrit Sanchar* ceremonies are also held in the Gurdwara hall. After *Ardas* and distribution of *Karah Parshad* (sweet pudding), *Langar* (fellowship meals) are served to one and all and there is *kirtan* till late in the night.

Sweets and community lunches are offered to everyone irrespective of religious faith. They are given with a spirit of *seva* (service) and *bhakti* (devotion). Sikhs visit Gurdwaras, where special programmes are arranged and *kirtans* are held. Houses and Gurdwaras

are lit up for the festivities. On the anniversary of the martyrdom of Guru Arjan Dev, sweetened milk is offered to commemorate the death of the Guru.

Gurpurabs remind the Sikhs that many of their Gurus and ancestors had to sacrifice their lives in the defense of the Faith. Whether it is *Diwali* (*Bandi Chhor Diwas*), *Baisakhi* (*Khalsa Sajna Diwas*) or Martyrdom day of Guru Arjan Dev Sahib (*Shahidi Diwas*), Sikhs never fail to gather and remember their Gurus and pay homage to the great Martyrs. All the *Gurpurabs* are celebrated with great fervour and enthusiasm by the Sikhs throughout the world.

SIKH MARRIAGES

Sikhism does not encourage ascetic practices, and marriage is enjoined upon all the faithful. Sikhs are required to marry when they are of a sufficient age (child marriage is strictly forbidden).

The preliminary social ceremonies consist of a *baraat*, in which the bridegroom mounts upon a decorated horse to go to the bride's house. This is followed by the *milni* ceremony in which elders from both sides meet and exchange greetings. *Shabad* (the Word) is sung and *ardaas* (invocation to the Gurus) is recited.

The religious ceremonies take place in the Gurdwara. Sikh couples are united in holy wedlock through the

> *Make compassion thy mosque, and sincerity*
> *thy prayer-carpet, and justice thy Quran:*
> *So mayst thou be a true Mussalman!*

anand karaj ceremony, which includes hymns specially composed for the purpose by Guru Ramdas. They sit together to hear the recitation of the sacred scripture. The marriage ceremony is performed in the company of the Guru Granth Sahib, around which the couple circles four times, as hymns from the scriptures are sung. During the fourth and final hymn, flowers are showered on the couple as they circle the holy book. A final hymn is sung, expounding their responsibilities to each other and to their elders. After the ceremony is complete, the husband and wife are considered "a single soul in two bodies." A wedding feast is offered to all visitors as *langar prasad*.

According to Sikh religious rites, neither husband nor wife is permitted to divorce. Today, some Sikh couples take to divorce through civil courts – but such a divorce has no religious sanction.

UNIQUE FEATURES OF SIKHISM

The liberal and progressive view of its founder has led to Sikhism being one of the most broad-minded and tolerant of modern religions. Sikhs believe that no faith or preceptor or prophet has the monopoly over the truth; rather, truth can be discovered by different people of diverse faiths, following their chosen paths. Each and everyone of these paths is a valid route to God and salvation. Thus the Guru Granth Sahib tells us: "Some read the Vedas, and some the Qur'an. Some wear blue robes, and some wear white. Some call themselves Muslim, and some call themselves Hindu. Some yearn for paradise, and others long for heaven. Says Nanak, one who realises the *Hukam* of God's will, knows the secrets of his Lord and Master." And again: "By His power the Vedas and the Puranas exist, and the Holy Scriptures of the Jewish, Christian and Islamic religions. By His power all deliberations exist."

The Guru Granth Sahib

Universal humanism is at the heart of the Sikh faith. Social inequalities, sectarianism and distinctions of caste and creed are swept aside to emphasise community living, social consciousness and brotherhood of all men. This gives dignity and respect to each individual, and asserts the individual's right to faith and liberation through good work. Devotees sing, "O Lord! I am neither high, low nor of the middle; I am God's devotee and seek His protection." The principles of universal equality and brotherhood are essential beliefs of Sikhism.

Sikhism insists that service to one's fellow men is one of the greatest good actions that human beings can perform. It insists equally, that *seva* should be offered to everyone, over and above any distinction of caste and creed. *Seva* is regarded as one of the best methods of inner cleansing and purification, along with *simran*, remembrance of the Name. In the Gurdwara, service may take any form: sweeping the floor, fetching water, cooking food in the community kitchen, washing the dishes, and collecting the footwear of devotees. Each of these tasks is done with love and devotion, as an offering to God and Guru. Sikhs are exhorted to infuse this spirit of love and devotion in all their actions.

All true Sikhs are enjoined to:

1. Wake up early in the morning

2. Bathe and cleanse themselves thoroughly

3. Cleanse the mind by spending some time in meditation and prayer

4. Engage in family life and assume all responsibilities within the family

5. Attend to work or study routine and earn a living by honest means

6. Undertake to help the needy with monetary and/ or physical help

7. Exercise their responsibilities to the community and take an active part in the safeguard of the community

Simple living is stressed upon for all Sikhs. A Sikh is expected to rise early, meditate and pray, consume simple food and perform an honest day's work, carry out duties to his family, lead a good and wholesome life and always be positive, charitable and supportive to the poor and weak. Salvation is obtained by one's actions – Good deeds, remembrance of God – *Naam Simran*, *Kirtan*, etc. All Sikhs are encouraged to share and give at least a tithe (10%) of their earnings in charity. They are urged to perceive joy and sorrow, happiness and misery as one – for it is the will of God that causes them. Such a life brings as its rewards the Four Fruits: Truth, contentment, contemplation and *Naam*.

Five be thy prayers, - The first is truth, The second is righteousness, The third is charity, The fourth is pure aspiration, And the fifth is the praise and glory of God! And let deeds of service Be Thy creed, O brother! So mayst thou be a true Mussalman!

Sufism can best be described as Islamic mysticism or the inner, esoteric, purely spiritual dimension of Islam. It is essentially an Islamic tradition, derived from the Qur'an and Prophet Muhammad's teachings and has been seen as "the movement from within, as an aspect of Islam". Some western scholars regard Sufism largely as the product of diverse philosophical and spiritual influences, derived from Islam, but including Christian, Neoplatonic and others.

The Whirling Dervishes

SUFISM

Sufism, referred to as *tasawwuf*, in Arabic, is understood by many scholars and Sufis to be the inner, mystical or psycho-spiritual dimension of Islam. There are some Muslims and non-Muslims who believe that Sufism is outside the sphere of Islam. Nevertheless, Seyyed Hossein Nasr, one of the foremost scholars of Islam, in his article, 'The Interior Life in Islam' contends that Sufism is simply the name for the inner or esoteric dimension of Islam. It is founded on the pursuit of spiritual truth as a definite goal to attain. This very logical principle is based on a typically succinct saying of Prophet Muhammad: "Whoever knows oneself, knows one's Lord." Most scholars agree that it is impossible to relate Sufism to any religion outside of Islam.

Victor Danner says in his book *The Islamic Tradition* (1988), "Sufism is the Spiritual Path (*tariqah*) of Islam and has been identified with it for well over a thousand years...It has been called 'Islamic mysticism' by Western scholars because of its resemblance to Christian and other forms of mysticism elsewhere. Unlike Christian mysticism, however, Sufism is a continuous historical and even institutionalised phenomenon in the Muslim world that has had millions of adherents down to the present day. Indeed, if we look over the Muslim world, there is hardly a region that does not have Sufi orders still functioning there."

Although some people refer to this tradition as Sufism, others refer to it as the *Sufi Way.* They draw this distinction because they feel that the term, "Sufism" refers to a philosophy or a school of thought like capitalism or socialism, and they feel that the *Sufi Way* describes a practical path to follow.

ORIGINS

Sufism is thought to have originated in the time of Prophet Muhammad. The first Sufis were actually contemporaries of the Prophet. Etymologically, the origin of the word *sufi* is thought to be from *ahl-al-suffa*, which literally means, "Companions of the porch" or "Companions of the bench". The early Sufis were actually a group of devout but impoverished Muslims, who spent their days and nights on benches outside the mosque where the Prophet worshipped. They kept away from the world and worldly activities. They were men of non-possession. They ate what was given to them, and wore simple, coarse garments.

According to some scholars, the word *sufi* is derived from the Arabic *suf,* which means wool. Thus the Sufis were ascetics who wore coarse garments of wool – this being a symbol of voluntary poverty and renunciation of the world. The two were combined

One day Hasan of Basra and Malik, son of Dinar and Shakik of Balkabh, came to see Rabia (al-adawiya) when she was ill. Hasan said, "None is sincere in his claim (to love God) unless he patiently endure the blows of His Lord." Rabia said, "This smells of egoism." Shakik said, "None is sincere in his claim unless he gives thanks for the blows of his Lord." Rabia said, "This still needs to be improved." They said, "Do Thou speak." She said, "None is sincere in his claim unless he forgets the blows in beholding his Lord."

by Al-Rudhabari who said, "The Sufi is the one who wears wool on top of purity."

These Sufis were devoted to prayer and spent their time on the porch of the Prophet's mosque, eager to memorise each new increment of the Qur'an as it was revealed. Yet another etymology, advanced by the 10th century Persian historian al-Buruni, is that the word *sufi* is linked with Greek word *sophia*, which means "wisdom". Thus the true sufi is actually a seeker of wisdom.

There are some who associate the word *sufi* with the word *safa*, meaning pure. The great Sufi poet-saint, Jalal ud-Din Rumi, when asked, "What makes the Sufi?" answered: "Purity of the heart, not the patched mantle!" The true sufi is a man of purity, inner purity of the heart. He rejoices in a life of poverty and prayer, of simplicity, sympathy and sacrifice. He accepts suffering and pain as gifts from God and grows in inner purity. He believes that there can be no inner illumination without purification; and without inner illumination, there can be no unification, which is the goal of the sufi's quest.

As the worshippers of Allah, Sufis belong to different *Tariqas*, or orders, established in the first few centuries after the Prophet's death. These orders have a master or *murshid* who imparts sacred knowledge to others in the group.

Thus, the foundations of Sufism were essentially Islamic and were connected directly with the Prophet and His teachings. The early Sufis who had close links with the Prophet, were the founders of Sufism. Among the most famous of these individuals were: Salman Farsi, Ammar Yasser, Balla'al, Abdullah Masoud and Oveyse Gharani. Their disciples adopted their techniques of self-understanding and discipline, and carried sufi thought and practices to lands as far apart as Persia, India, Indonesia, Syria, Egypt, Mesopotamia and North Africa.

FUNDAMENTALS OF SUFI THOUGHT

The faith of the Sufi rises above all creeds and all denominations and religions. It is a way of life – the life of faith and freedom and love. It seeks to set men

The true saint goes in and out amongst the people and eats and sleeps with them and buys and sells in the market and marries and takes part in social intercourse, and never forgets God for a single moment.

free from the bondage of creeds and dogmas, of rites and ceremonies, calling them away from all things extern to the interior life of the Spirit. The Sufi emphasis is on the inner experience and ecstasy, rather than on deductive reasoning or positive tradition. It is the way of the Heart – the Heart which turns, at all times and in all conditions, to the One and Only Beloved.

The goal of life, according to the Sufi mystics, is union with God. And the very first step on the path is repentance *(tauba)*, or conversion. True conversion is a change of mind and heart. It is a gift of grace. When God or a God-man looks upon someone in grace, the soul within him is awakened. And he realises that the years spent in accumulating the wealth or honours of the earth were wasted in vain. Life is too short and no further time must be wasted in pursuing the vanities of the world. The awakened soul turns his back on worldly pleasures and longs for union with the One Beloved. He lives a life of self-control and self-denial, without which no progress may be made on the path.

Awakening comes in a variety of ways. But it is always a gift of grace. With awakening comes the realisation that the body is a Temple of God. It must not be soiled; it must be kept clean and pure, so that it might become a channel of God's forces in this world of darkness and death. In this thought lies the seed of true repentance or conversion – the very first step on the Path. And the second step is the fear of God. The

Abandon life and the world, that you may behold the Life of the World.

penitent soul lives in fear, lest he may do something which offends the Lord.

Fear of God leads to detachment mundane the third stage on the Sufi Path. For the love of God, the soul renounces everything that is non-God. The root of all sin and suffering lies in the attachment to mundane things. True detachment is inner – it is detachment from desires which stain the purity of the soul.

As the pilgrim treads the Path, he learns to be detached even from his detachment: he is absorbed in the love of God. The world and its pleasures and power no longer attract him. He has attained to freedom.

Then comes the fourth stage, a very important step on the Path. It is poverty, the inner poverty of the Spirit. It does not consist merely of non-possession of worldly wealth or goods, though it includes it. "I have not found the true knowledge of God," said Bayazid, "except in a hungry stomach and a naked body." True poverty, however, is more an emptiness of the heart than of the hand or the stomach. A man may possess all the world and yet be poor. Another may possess nothing and yet not be poor. For, true poverty is the humility of the heart. It is the knowledge of one's own nothingness.

The fifth stage is that of patience. Patience is the alchemist who turns every blow into a blessing, every burden into a benediction. As the pilgrim moves on the Path, he is tried and tested, as gold is tested by being thrown into the crucible. Significant are the words of Hudayafa al-Yaman, "When God loves a servant, He proves him by suffering." If he is patient, he will not avoid suffering, but will greet it with a smile, knowing that all that comes from God is good.

The man of patience thrives on suffering: the more he suffers, the more his soul shines. The great Sufi teacher and mystic, Jalal ud-Din Rumi, unfolds a very beautiful picture in his *Masnavi*. He writes, "There is

The Mystic Rumi's Tomb

an animal called the porcupine. It is made stout and big by blows of the stick. The more you cudgel it, the more it thrives. The soul of a true believer is, verily, a porcupine. The more it is chastised, the more it thrives. So it is that God's chosen ones have to bear a greater share of suffering than other worldly men. Suffering gives strength to their souls."

The sixth stage is that of *tawakkul* or self-surrender. It is entrusting oneself to God, completely, entirely, utterly. It is passing out of oneself so that nothing of oneself remains – alone, the Beloved exists!

Once Bayazid was asked by an *imam* to assist him at the Friday congregational prayer. At the close of the prayer, the *imam* asked Bayazid, "You do not work for wages and you do not beg for alms: how do you live?" To this Bayazid answered, "Let me offer the prayer again! A prayer recited behind an *imam*, who does not know who gives us our daily bread, cannot be valid."

I desire not to desire, for my will is without value, since I am ignorant in any case. Therefore choose Thou for me what Thou knowest to be best and do not put my perdition in what my autonomy and free choice prefer.

It was Hatim who said, "It is our business to worship God as He bade us. It is His business to provide us with daily sustenance, as He promised us."

The seventh and the last stage is gratitude. The pilgrim on the Path has now arrived at a stage where he is grateful to God for whatever comes his way. Does he fall sick? He praises the Lord. He feels sure that the Beloved can never mean harm, the Creator's pen can never slip! He is always happy and contended. In his prayers, he will never ask God for a thing to happen or another to be averted. He knows that not a leaf moves, not a straw turns, not a lip stirs, except if it be the will of God. And whatever God wills is the very best that can ever happen. God's will becomes his own will. Significant are the words of Jami who said, "The Sufi has no individual will. His will is obliterated in the will of God, nay, indeed, his will is the very will of God." And when this happens, man wants nothing: he lacks nothing. He lives in a state of at-one-ment with God. And as those around him look at him, they exclaim, "We have seen God!"

So lived the Sufi mystics, the Friends of God: concerning whom Gurudev Sadhu Vaswani – who himself was a "Friend of God" – had so much to tell us. To them God was the One Only Reality of Life. And they found God in the heart within. The way by which they walked was the Way of Love. And love, as a great Sufi mystic said, lies in this, that you account yourself as very little and God very great. Love means giving all that you have to Him whom you love so that nothing remains to you of your own. As you tread the Path of Love, you find that the "you" in you has vanished – alone the Lord remains. It was Hafiz, who sang, "My heart is so full of the thought of the Beloved that the thought of self has disappeared from my consciousness." In another place, he says, "Betwixt the lover and the Beloved there must be no veil. Thou myself, O Hafiz, art the veil. Get out of the way!"

Getting out of the way, the Sufi mystics sought to realise their unity with God. They loved God for His own sake, not for any reward. They sought the Giver, not His gifts. They sought God, not 'experiences', nor 'miracles', nor 'powers'. Thus it was that Rabia once said, "It is the Lord of the house whom I need. What have I to do with the house?"

Rabia: The Mira of Islam

Having found God, they did not forsake humanity. They came and lived in the midst of men, to share with them the treasures of the Spirit, which have been given them. Their ideal was to be *in* the world but not *of* the world. One thing only they insisted upon, "Never forget God!"

They lived ever united to the Beloved. In that union, they beheld the Light, nothing but the Light. And wherever they turned, they found God, nothing but God. They became the "Friends of God". They met Him, face to face, and saw Him "unveiled within the abode of Peace".

SUFI TEACHINGS

Sufism has been defined as a type of knowledge by the great Sufi masters. Shaykh Ahmad Zarruq, a 15th century Sufi who wrote *The Principles of Sufism*, defined Sufism as, "a science whose objective is the reparation of the heart and turning it away from all else but God." Ibn 'Ajiba, one of the best known Sufi masters, defined Sufism as, "a science through which one can know how to travel into the presence of the Divine, purify one's inward from filth, and beautify it with a variety of praiseworthy traits."

The concept of *Wahdat* or "Unity with God" is central to Sufism. Two distinct versions of this concept are prevalent: *Wahdat-ul-Wujood* (Unity of Being)

essentially states that the only truth within the universe is God, and that all things exist within God only. *Wahdat-ul-Shuhud* (Unity of Witness), on the other hand, holds that any experience of unity between God and the created world is only in the mind of the believer and that God and His creation are entirely separate.

In Sufi psychology, three concepts are emphasised: *Nafs* (the ego), *Qalb* (the heart) and *Ruh* (the soul). The origin and basis of these terms is from the Holy Qur'an and they have been expounded upon by several Sufi mystics.

The association between the three is illustrated in a beautiful myth by Amr al-Makkî:

God created the hearts seven thousand years before the bodies and kept them in the station of proximity to Himself and He created the spirits seven thousand years before the hearts and kept them in the garden of intimate fellowship with Himself, and the consciences — the innermost part — He created seven thousand years before the spirits and kept them in the degree of union with Himself. Then he imprisoned the conscience in the spirit and the spirit in the heart and the heart in the body. Then He tested them and sent prophets, and then each began to seek its own

O reason, to gain eternal life tread everlastingly the way of death.

station. The body occupied itself with prayer, the heart attained to love, the spirit arrived at proximity to its Lord, and the innermost part found rest in union with Him.

The self, ego or *nafs* has the potential of functioning from the grossest to the highest level. At its lowest level this refers to our negative traits controlled by emotions and sensual desires and their gratification. Seven levels of the *nafs* are identified in Sufi psychology, based on the Qur'an. The process of spiritual evolution depends on our progress through these levels. These are: tyrannical self, regretful self, inspired self, serene self, pleased self, pleasing self and the pure self.

Qalb in Sufism is not the physical organ, but the spiritual heart. According to Sufi psychology emotions are from the self or *nafs*, not from the heart. *Qalb* is the home of man's deepest intelligence and wisdom. It also holds what is called the divine spark. The goal of the sufi is to develop a heart that is sincere, loving and compassionate, and also to develop the heart's intelligence, which is deeper, and more grounded than the rational, abstract intelligence of the mind. Just as the physical heart supplies blood to the body, so too, the spiritual heart nourishes the soul with wisdom and spiritual light, and it also purifies man's grosser personality traits.

The soul or *ruh* is in direct contact with the Divine, even if one is unconscious of that connection. In Sufi psychology the soul has seven levels or facets: mineral, vegetable, animal, personal, human, secret and secret of secret souls. Each level represents the stages of evolution. The soul is holistic, and extends to all aspects of the person, i.e. the body, the mind and the spirit. Each level of the soul has valuable gifts and strengths, as well as weaknesses. The goal is to develop the strengths and to achieve a balance between these levels, not forgoing the lower ones to focus only on the higher ones.

Sufis believe that the soul never dies. Death is only the separation of the *Ruh* from the physical body, which was mixed by God to provide life. We can make our souls strong by following the disciplines taught by our spiritual teachers or *pirs*. If the soul is made strong according to the teachings of Islam, then it is possible for us to get on the way which leads to Allah.

Fanaa is the Sufi term for extinction. It means annihilation of the self, while remaining physically alive. Persons having entered this state are said to have no existence outside of – and be in complete unity with – Allah. *Fanaa* is equivalent to the concept of *nirvana* in Buddhism or *moksha* in Hinduism which also aim for annihilation of the self.

The nature of *fanaa* consists of the elimination of evil deeds and lowly attributes of the flesh. In other words, *fanaa* is abstention from sin and the expulsion from the heart of all love other than the Divine Love; that is, the expulsion of greed, lust, desire, vanity, etc. In the state of *fanaa,* the reality of the true and only relationship asserts itself in the mind. One realises that the only real relationship is with Allah.

Baqaa, which literally means permanency, is another important sufi concept. It describes a particular state of life with God. Inayat Khan writes in his book *A Sufi Message of Spiritual Liberty* :

The ideal perfection, called *Baqaa* by Sufis, is termed *Najat* in Islam, *Nirvana* in Buddhism, *Salvation* in Christianity and *Mukti* in Hinduism. This is the highest condition attainable, and all ancient prophets and sages experienced it, and taught it to the world.

Baqaa is "abiding in God" or "affirmation of universal consciousness". At this state every being must arrive some day, consciously or unconsciously, before or after death. The beginning and the end of all beings is the same, the difference only exists in their journey.

Perfection is reached by the regular practice of concentration, passing through three grades of development: *Faná-fi-Shaikh*, annihilation in the astral plane, *Faná-fi-Rasul*, annihilation in the spiritual plane, and *Faná-fi-Allah*, annihilation in the abstract. After passing through these three grades, the highest state is attained of *Bá qi-bi-Allah*, annihilation in the eternal consciousness, which is the destination of all who travel by this path.

Can the water of the (polluted) stream clear out the dung? Can man's knowledge sweep away the ignorance of his sensual self?

How shall the sword fashion its own hilt? Go, and trust this wound to a surgeon.

Flies gather on every wound, so that no one sees the foulness of his wound.

Those flies are your thoughts and your possessions; your womb is the darkness of your states;

And if the Pir (spiritual master) lays a plaster on your wound , at once the pain and lamentation are stilled,

So that you fancy it is healed, (whereas in reality) the ray of the plaster has shone upon the spot.

Beware! Do not turn your head away from the plaster, O you who are wounded in the back, but recognise that (healing of the wound) proceeds from the ray: do not regard it as (proceeding) from your own constitution.

Haqiqa or *Haqiqat* is the Sufi term for the Supreme Truth or Absolute Reality.

Marifa is a term used by Sufis to describe mystical intuitive knowledge, knowledge of spiritual truth as reached through ecstatic experiences rather than revealed or rationally acquired.

Ihsan is an Arabic term meaning "perfection" or "excellence". *Ihsan* is the goal or aim of Sufi practices.

The fundamental principles of Sufism are beautifully captured in this anonymous Persian poem, translated by A. A. Godlas:

What is *Tasawwuf*?

What is *Tasawwuf*? Good character and awareness of God.
That's all *Tasawwuf* is. And nothing more.
What is *Tasawwuf*? Love and affection.
It is the cure for hatred and vengeance. And nothing more.
What is *Tasawwuf*? The heart attaining tranquility.
Which is the root of religion. And nothing more.
What is *Tasawwuf*? Concentrating your mind. Which is the religion of Ahmad (PBUH). And nothing more.
What is *Tasawwuf*? Contemplation that travels to the Divine throne. It is a far-seeing gaze. And nothing more.
Tasawwuf is keeping one's distance from imagination and supposition.
Tasawwuf is found in certainty. And nothing more.

Surrendering one's soul to the care of the inviolability of religion;
This is *Tasawwuf*. And nothing more.
Tasawwuf is the path of faith and affirmation of unity;
This is the incorruptible religion. And nothing more.
Tasawwuf is the smooth and illuminated path.
It is the way to the most exalted paradise. And nothing more.
I have heard that the ecstasy of the wearers of wool
Comes from finding the taste of religion. And nothing more.
Tasawwuf is nothing but *shari'at*.
It is just this clear road. And nothing more.

SUFI ORDERS

The traditional Sufi orders emphasise the role of Sufism within Islam. Therefore, the *Sharia* (traditional Islamic law) and the *Sunnah* (customs of the Prophet) are seen as crucial for any Sufi aspirant. Among the oldest and most well known of the Sufi orders are the *Qadiri, Chisti, Oveyssi, Shadhili, Jerrahi, Ashrafi, Bektashi, Nimatullahi* and *Mevlevi*. One proof traditional orders assert is that almost all the famous Sufi masters of the past Caliphates were also experts in *Sharia* and were renowned as people with great *Iman* (faith) and excellent practice. Many were also *Qadis* (*Sharia* law judges) in courts. They held that Sufism was never distinct from Islam and to fully comprehend and practice Sufism one must be a practicing Muslim obeying the *Sharia*.

O God! make me busy with Thee, that they may not make me busy with them.

However, in recent times there has been a growth of non-traditional Sufi Movements in the West. Some examples are the Universal Sufism Movement, the Golden Sufi Center, the Sufi Foundation of America, the Universalist Sufis and Sufism Reoriented.

SUFI SACRED TEXTS

Some of the most famous and beautiful literature of the Islamic world has been written by Sufis. Sufism has produced a large body of poetry in Arabic, Persian, Punjabi, Sindhi, Turkish, Pashto and Urdu which notably includes the works of Jalal ud-Din Muhammad Rumi, al-Hallaj, Ibn al-Farid, Hafez, Jami, Ibn Arabi,Farid Ud-Din Attar, Abdul Qader Bedil, Bulleh Shah, Amir Khusro, Yunus Emre, Shah Abdul Latif Bhittai, Mujaddid Alf Sani, Sachal Sarmast, Muhammad Iqbal as well as numerous traditions of devotional dance, such as Sufi whirling, and music, such as Qawwali. The Sufi poetry of Shah Karim Buleri and Shah Abdul Latif is truly enchanting. The soulful songs of Sami and Sachal are emotionally purifying. In them you will find the vision of the One.

Sufi texts include the works of great *pirs* and poet-saints such as:

1. Abdul-Qadir Gilani
2. Mohiuddin Ibn-Arabi
3. Shams Tabrizi
4. Jalal ud-Din Muhammad Rumi
5. Mansur Al-Hallaj
6. Al-Ghazali
7. Data Ganj Baksh (also known as Hujwiri)
8. Amir Khusro
9. Farid ad-Din Attar
10. Bulleh Shah
11. Hafez-e Shirazi
12. Saadi
13. Ibn 'Ata Allah
14. Ahmed Zarruq
15. Sultan Bahu
16. Khwaja Farid
17. Mawlana Faizani
18. Muhammad al-Jazuli
19. Riaz Ahmed Gohar Shahi
20. Muhammad Tahir ul-Qadri

Sufis are emphatic that Islamic knowledge should be learned from teachers and not exclusively from books. Modelling themselves on their teachers, students hope that they too will glean something of the Prophetic character.

Through the centuries Sufis contributed hugely to Islamic literature for example Rumi, Omar Khayyám and Al-Ghazali's influence extended beyond Muslim lands to be quoted by philosophers, writers and theologians in the East and West.

UNIQUE FEATURES OF SUFISM

Although outside movements have had some influence on Sufi terminology, Sufism is definitely rooted in Islam itself. Its development was instrumental in checking the worldliness and loose morals in ruling *Umayyad* circles in the early days of Islam. Pirs such as Hasan of Basra urged the Muslim community to heed the Qur'enic call to fear God, and its warnings for The Judgment Day, and its reminders of the transitoriness of life in this world. A new emphasis on the love of God brought the transition from asceticism to mysticism. The woman

A Sufi Festival

There is no hell but selfhood, no paradise but selflessness.

saint Rabia of Basra called for love of God "for His own sake," not out of fear of hell or hope for heaven.

The Sufi emphasis on intuitive knowledge and the love of God increased the appeal of Islam to the masses and made possible its extension beyond the Middle East into Africa and East Asia. Sufi brotherhoods multiplied rapidly across the continents and their success was due primarily to the humanitarian attitude of their founders and leaders, who not only ministered to the spiritual needs of their followers but also helped the poor of all faiths.

In fact, a number of Sufi scholars in the West, assert that Sufism is a projection of "the perennial philosophy" of man's true nature to the Divine and as such forms a subterranean current in many religions and mystical traditions and practices.

At first, Sufism was criticised by those who feared that the Sufis' concern for personal experiential

For thirty years I went in search of God, and when I opened my eyes at the end of this time, I discovered that it was really He who sought for me.

knowledge of God could lead to neglect of established religious observances and that the Sufis' ideal of unity with God was a denial of the Islamic principle of the "otherness" of God. By combining a traditional theological position with a moderate form of Sufism, al - Ghazali made mysticism widely acceptable in the Muslim world.

Sufism exercised a tremendous influence, partly through mystical poetry, for example, that of Jalal ud-Din Rumi, and partly through the formation of religious brotherhoods. The latter grew out of the practice of disciples' studying under a mystical guide (*pir* or saint) to achieve direct communion with God.

Sufi psychology has influenced many areas of thinking both within and outside of Islam, drawing primarily upon the three concepts: a lower self called the *nafs*, a faculty of spiritual intuition called the *qalb* or spiritual heart, and a spirit or soul called *ruh*. These interact in various ways, producing the spiritual types of the tyrant (dominated by *nafs*), the person of faith and moderation (dominated by the spiritual heart), and the person lost in love for God (dominated by the *ruh*).

Sufi mysticism has always exercised a fascination upon the Western world, and its orientalist scholars. Figures like Rumi have become household names in the

Rumi: The Great Singer

United States, where Sufism is perceived favourably as quietist and apolitical.

The Islamic Institute in Mannheim, Germany, which works towards the integration of Europe and Muslims, regards Sufism as particularly suited for inter-religious dialogue and intercultural harmonisation in democratic and pluralist societies. It has described Sufism as a symbol of tolerance and humanism – undogmatic, flexible and non-violent.

The Sufi tradition of *Qawwali* music is an ecstatic singing and listening experience that transports participants to a state of *wajad*, where they feel one with the Divine, attaining to a spiritual ecstasy. Originally performed mainly at Sufi shrines or *dargahs* throughout South Asia, it has also gained mainstream popularity throughout the world.

Speaking tongues are the destruction of silent hearts.

Zoroastrianism is one of the oldest monotheistic religions of the world, which first began as a widely accepted religion of the ancient Iranian people. Zoroastrians believe in the one universal and transcendental God, Ahura Mazda, the one uncreated Creator to whom all worship is ultimately directed. In some European languages, it is therefore referred to as Mazdaism.

ZOROASTRIANISM

The religious beliefs and philosophy of this ancient faith are based on the life and teachings of the Prophet Zarathustra, or Zoroaster, as the Greeks referred to him. The religion may be described as the worship of Ahura Mazda, exalted by Zoroaster (Zarathustra) as the supreme divine authority. Though most adherents of this faith refer to themselves as Zoroastrians, some also call themselves Behdin, meaning, "follower of Daena" or the "Good Religion". It is one of the most widely respected religions of the world today, but its faithful adherents are very few in number, compared to the other major religions of the world. Most of the world's Zoroastrians today think of India as their home, although there are a few still living in Iran.

Zarathustra: An Illumined Soul

Zoroastrianism is first described recognisably in the *Histories* of Herodatus, as the culture and faith of the Persians, as Iranians were called at the time. Both the famous Persian emperors, Cyrus II and Darius are thought to have been worshippers of Ahura Mazda, and their faith encouraged them to be liberal rulers who practised tolerance towards all faiths. However, the Zoroastrians, who once enjoyed great prestige and political power in Iran, came under severe economic and political pressure to convert when Iran was brought under Arab Muslim rule.

Although Zoroastrianism had begun in Iran almost three millennia ago, and was for some time the state religion in that part of the world, it was marginalised by the influx of later faiths, until the faithful who refused to convert, were forced to migrate to other lands under more benign and tolerant rulers. Thus it was that a considerable section of them from North Eastern Iran migrated to Gujarat, on the western coast of India, where the locals began to call them *Parsis* – i.e. people from Persia. Others remained in Iran, shifting to the provinces of Yazd and Kerman, which remain centres of Zoroastrian culture even today. By the tenth century AD, their fond hopes of establishing a Zoroastrian state vanished almost completely. However, many Zoroastrian practices continue to be an ineradicable part of Iranian life and culture.

ORIGINS

Many scholars believe that Mazdaism pre-dated Zoroaster, and was part of the society and culture of Persia for thousands of years. But modern history regards Zoroaster or Zarathustra as the Founder of the faith, and the Prophet of Ahura Mazda.

Though records of his life are scant, there is no doubt regarding his name, his birth or his family. He was born the son of Pourushaspa, a name which literally means 'full of horses'. We therefore presume that his father was a horse breeder/trader. His mother was called Dughdova, which is translated as 'milkmaid'. It is difficult to date his life in exact terms, although many scholars believe that he must have lived around 1500 BC. He belonged to the Spitama clan.

Very little is known to us about his early life, though a few legends have come down to us through the generations. It is said that when his mother was carrying him in her womb, she saw a terrible vision in which the world was destroyed; however, an angel assured her that her son would protect the world

Doing good to others is not a duty, it is a joy, for it increases our own health and happiness.

against such a destruction. It is said that when the baby was born, he did not cry like other infants; instead, he had a radiant smile on his face, and he seemed to emanate a divine glow. It was perhaps due to this that his parents decided to call him Zarathustra, which according to one translation, means 'golden light' or 'golden star'.

He was a brilliant and bright child, and at the age of seven, he went to study under one of ancient Iran's most wise teachers, a man famous for his wisdom and knowledge. For eight years, Zarathustra sat at his feet to receive the knowledge of the sun, the moon and the stars, of planets in their courses and of the cycle of seasons, of light and wind and rain, of men and birds and animals and of their Creator. It is said that at the age of nine, his friends arranged for a colloquy with the head priest of the local temple, so that some of the profound questions that troubled the young lad could be answered; but Zarathustra could not get satisfactory replies to any of his pressing questions.

He would spend much of his leisure out in the open pastures, perhaps hoping for enlightenment from communion with Mother Nature. It is thought that he was married to a girl named Havovi, but not much is known of his married life. What we do know is that he retired from the world to spend years in meditation and contemplation, seeking to find answers to his questions.

His biographers tell us that when he was thirty years old, one early morning, he went to fetch some water from the river. It was around dawn. The sky had just turned colour and the sun was about to rise. As he had gone into the waters of the river, *Vohu Manah* (the angel of the Good Mind) appeared to him, and opened the portal to the Divine Light of Ahura Mazda. This was the first moment of Illumination and the first Revelation of Zarathustra.

In his vision, he perceived Ahura Mazda as the Wise Lord of Creation, and the six emanations of Ahura Mazda, the *Amesha Spentas*, as the guardians and artisans of this physical world. He perceived the laws upon which the universe operated, and understood the inter-relationship between Ahura Mazda, the *Amesha Spentas*, and the Creation.

After initial reluctance, Zarathustra first spoke to his family of his vision; and some of his close relatives became his first followers. But the antagonism of the ruler and the priestly classes made the progress of the faith very slow in those initial years; so much so, it is said that the prophet had just twenty-two followers

Taking the first footstep with a good thought, the second with a good word and the third with a good deed I entered Paradise.

in the first twelve years after his vision. This was largely due to the vested interests of the ruling classes and the priests, as well as the ignorance of the common people and their unwillingness to accept any change.

Soon, he decided to move out of the land of his birth along with his chosen disciples, but wherever he went, he faced opposition. It was King Vishtaspa, a wise and just man, who gave the prophet an opportunity to expound his views in a court-debate. He was so convinced by Zarathustra's powerful arguments, that he willingly embraced the faith. But here again, jealous rivals plotted his overthrow, and he was imprisoned on false accusations of practising black magic. Divine Powers came to his rescue. All of a sudden, the king's favourite horse took ill, and no one could cure the animal. Zarathustra offered to treat the animal, and successfully rescued the creature from death. The king had a change of heart and punished Zarathustra's detractors, restoring the prophet to a position of eminence in the kingdom. Zoroastrianism was now made the state religion.

I who have set my heart on watching over the soul, in union with Good Thought, and as knowing the rewards of Mazda Ahura for our works, will, while I have power and strength, teach men to seek after Right. I have become an alien in a foreign land.

This was a major turning point in Zarathustra's life and a remarkable breakthrough in the spread of his faith. He was now free to preach extensively, and successfully propagated his faith in the neighbouring countries as well. It was at the court of King Vishtaspa that he is thought to have composed the *Gathas* – seventeen beautiful and profound hymns which are still venerated as the most sacred scriptures of Zoroastrians.

None of the stories of his life portray Zarathustra as a divine being, not even the most extravagant legends that have been built up later. He remained a man like all others, though divinely gifted with inspiration and closeness to Ahura Mazda. Unlike the Qur'an, the *Gathas* of Zarathustra are not 'channeled' – that is, the *Gathas* are regarded as the inspired composition of a poet-prophet rather than a text dictated by a heavenly being. His life is an inspiration for all Zoroastrians, precisely for this reason: in his innovations, in his loving relationship with God, and spiritual courage, he is a model for all his followers. In fact, many Zoroastrians regard their prophet as the first priest of their millennia-old faith.

The prophet probably spent almost three decades at the king's court, before his death at age 77. Again, we do not know how Zarathustra died. Many legends and Zoroastrian traditions say that he was killed, while praying in the sanctuary, by a foreign enemy of the king. Others believe that Zarathustra died peacefully.

The influence of his teachings spread to Greece and Rome. It is said that Socrates had a Zoroastrian instructor named Gobyras. Plato is also said to have wished to visit Persia to study with Zoroastrian teachers but his wish remained unfulfilled due to the outbreak of a war.

ZARATHUSTRA'S TEACHINGS

Zarathustra preached that there were only two gods, the "wise lord" Ahura Mazda and his eternal rival Ahriman. It was the duty of all believers to be on the side of Ahura Mazda.

Zoroastrianism believes in one God, Ahura Mazda who is:

- Omniscient
- Omnipotent
- Omnipresent
- Impossible for a normal human being to conceptualise
- Unchanging
- The Creator of everything
- The Source of all the goodness and happiness in the world

This Supreme God is to be worshipped and his prophet is Zoroaster. Zoroaster is not worshipped but is followed, as the path of truth and righteousness that he directed, namely *asha* will lead men and women to God.

Amesha Spentas are God's divine attributes. By knowing them, man can know God. These aspects are like the rays emanating from the single eternal source of light. The first three aspects represent the Father-aspect of God while the remaining three represent the Mother-aspect. They are:

Vohu Manah - Good mind and good purpose

Asha Vahishta - Truth and righteousness

Spenta Ameraiti - Holy devotion, serenity and loving kindness

Khashathra Vairya - Power and just rule

Hauravatat- Wholeness and health

Ameretat - Long life and immortality

Mainyu - The spirit of Ahura Mazda

Sacrificial rituals called *Yasnas*, rituals and prayers are used to invoke these divinities on different occasions to sanctify the world and help the faithful in their lives.

Combating the goodness is God's adversary, *Angra Mainyu* who resides in hell. This dualism is two fold cosmic and moral. There is the cosmic dualism between God and the Angra Mainyu who is the destructive spirit that introduces the evils of death, sickness, etc. into God's pure and beautiful world. There is also a moral duality that points towards the inherent good and evil sides of a human being.

Zoroastrians believe in the duality of existence – i.e. the presence of good and evil in the world. They also believe in the divinity of all creation, which God created out of His own astral body.

Human beings are born pure and have a choice either to follow the teachings of God and remain righteous or follow the ways of the evil one and be damned. Depending upon their choices and their actions, God decides their fate in the spiritual realm. God offers knowledge of righteous conduct and provides instructions for the expiation of sin.

Zoroastrianism believes in the final judgment day, on which God would resurrect all the dead and subject to a second scrutiny. All the good souls would be given a permanent place in heaven and the rest will be condemned into a purgatory till eternity.

They also believe that the birth of Zoroaster heralded the beginning of the current cycle of creation, which would last for 3,000 years. During this period a

One's friends should be holy people. A holy man will radiate holiness to all his friends.

prophet would appear on earth at the end of each millennium to preserve the teachings and guide humanity. The third prophet, will be a future son of Zoroaster, whose name would be Shoshyant, who would herald the Judgment Day and the eventual destruction of evil powers in the material world.

Zarathustra gave three important commandments to his followers to enable them to lead perfect lives and work for their own spiritual progress. These are *humata* (good thought), *hukhta* (good word) and *havarshta* (good deeds). Good thoughts are very important in the spiritual journey of man, because all else comes out of thoughts. Without good thoughts one cannot subject oneself to the Divine Will. Thinking good alone is not sufficient, for one must have the courage to speak Truth all the time. One must be truthful to oneself and to others, for there is no place for hypocrisy or duplicity in the life of a true Zoroastrian. Performance of good deeds is equally important. The Supreme Power of God, in the aspect of *Khashathra Vairya* comes to him who engages himself in good actions. Good actions also include *Sraosha* or service, obedience and devotion to God. When we cultivate this virtue we will be able to see the path of salvation clearly in front of us.

THE BASIC TENETS OF ZOROASTRIANS

1. All the scriptures are sacred, including the *Gathas, Yashts* and the *Vendidad*. The devout recite them in the Fire temples in the presence of the sacred fire.

2. All the fire-temples and rituals of the *Yasna* are sacred and are necessary for the religion. The performance of these sacred rituals, increase the power of good in this world and decrease the power of evil.

3. *Dakhma-nashini* is the only method of corpse-destruction for a Zoroastrian, as enjoined in the *Vendidad*. This is the destruction of the dead body in the stone-enclosed *Dakhma*, by the flesh-eating birds or the rays of the Sun, this being the most spiritually powerful method as commanded by Ahura Mazda to Zarathustra.

4. For the devout Zoroastrian, ethnic identity and religion are synonymous, as declared in the *Vendidad* by Ahura Mazda himself. Therefore, all Zoroastrian men and women are enjoined to marry within their community.

A Zoroastrian Temple, Yazd

5. Zoroastrians do not believe in conversion. They believe that the righteous of every religion go to heaven, that all religions are equal, and it is folly to convert. Conversion also goes against the Master Law of *Ereta* (righteousness) itself, because God has given us birth in our respective religions, to adore Him in them, and not to mistrust His Judgement and rebel and go over to another faith. For, each faith leads ultimately to God.

6. Faith and Hope in the coming of the *Saoshyant* (Saviour) sustains the Zoroastrian religion through

---

Courage begets strength by struggle with hardships. Courage grows from fighting danger and overcoming obstacles. Develop the courage to act according to your convictions, to speak what is true, and to do what is right.

---

the centuries. They firmly hope and pray, that Ahura Mazda sends the *Saoshyant* to the earth to defeat evil and further righteousness (*Ashoi*). Their religion also proclaims that Ahura Mazda will send the *Saoshyant*, born of a virgin (a belief adopted by other later religions).

7. They firmly believe that when the *Saoshyant* comes, the final spiritual battle between the forces of good and evil will commence, resulting in the utter destruction of evil. *Ristakhiz*, the ressurection of the dead will take place – the dead will rise, by the Will of Ahura Mazda. The world will be purged by molten metal, in which the righteous will wade as if through warm milk, and the evil will be scalded. The Final Judgement of all souls will commence, at the hands of Ahura Mazda the Judge (*Davar*), and all sinners punished, then forgiven, and humanity made immortal and free from hunger, thirst, poverty, old age, disease and death. The world will be made perfect once again, as it was before the onslaught of the evil one.

When a man makes an honest effort to cleanse himself day by day of his evil thoughts, evil words, and evil deeds, then will follow in their wake, as the day the night, good thoughts, good words and good deeds.

Observing the Fire Festival

Zoroastrians are thought to be fire-worshippers. Fire is to them a sacred symbol of God's light and purity, and no other symbol is permitted by Ahura Mazda.

THE SACRED SCRIPTURES OF ZOROASTRIANISM

The central scripture is the *Avesta*. The most sacred sections of the *Avesta* are the *Gathas* or Hymns of Zarathushtra; they are also the most enigmatic. Later sacred literature includes the Pahlavi Texts, which contain extensive quotations and paraphrases from lost *Avesta* texts. The *Gathas* are the most sacred scriptures of the faith, but they are very complex and profound, and can only be understood with the help of later commentaries.

The *Avesta* consists of three sections. The first is the *Vendidad*, which is actually an enumeration of various manifestations of evil spirits, and ways to confound them. It also sets down religious laws and ancient mythical tales. The second is *Visparad*, which is a collection of invocations or litanies which are recited before other prayers. The third is *Yasna,* a liturgical collection which contains prayers addressed to the Supreme Lord and other deities who form the spiritual hierarchy. The *Avesta* contains direct conversations between Zoroaster and Ahura Mazda, the Supreme Lord.

The date of their composition is uncertain. Some of these sacred scriptures are said to have been lost or destroyed during Alexander's conquest of Persia. Only texts in the Avestan language are considered part of the *Avesta.*

Scholars have found remarkable linguistic and cultural similarities between the texts of the *Avesta* and those of the *Rigveda*; this suggests that the ancient cultures of India and Iran shared some common beliefs.

The use of the expression *Zend-Avesta* to refer to the Avesta in general is a misunderstanding of the phrase Zand-i-Avesta (which literally means "interpretation of the Avesta").

The *Yashts* (from *yesti,* "worship by praise") are a collection of 21 hymns, each dedicated to a particular divinity or divine concept.

The *Siroza* ("thirty days") is an enumeration and invocation of the 30 divinities presiding over the days of the month, according to the Zoroastrian calendar.

Only texts preserved in the Avestan language count as scripture and are part of the *Avesta.* Several other secondary works, in the Pahlavi dialect, are thought to have been composed later; but they are nonetheless crucial to Zoroastrian theology and scholarship.

ZOROASTRIAN FESTIVALS

Zoroastrians celebrate several festivals and holy days, all of which are bound to the Zoroastrian calendar.

The seasonal festivals, called *gahambars* (meaning "proper season") occur six times a year. They commemorate the creations of Ahura Mazda. The six festivals are:

- *Maidyozarem Gahambar* ('mid-spring' feast)
- *Maidyoshahem Gahambar* ('mid-summer' feast)
- *Paitishahem Gahambar* (feast of 'bringing in the harvest')

- *Ayathrem Gahambar* ('bringing home the herds')

- *Maidyarem Gahambar* ('mid-year'/winter feast)

- *Hamaspathmaidyem Gahambar* (feast of 'all souls', literally 'coming of the whole group')

Each of these festivals is celebrated over five days.

Eleven divinities of the Zoroastrian pantheon have both a day-of-the-month and a month-of-the-year dedicated to them. A special *Yasna* or *Jashan* (meaning "worship", "oblation") service is then held in their honour on those days and months. These are known as *Name Day Feasts.*

Naoroze or New Year's day.

Pateti which was originally a day of introspection and penitence.

Sadeh, a mid-winter festival, traditionally celebrated with a bonfire.

Zartosht No-Diso, the death anniversary of Zarathustra. In the seasonal calendar, Zoroaster's death anniversary falls on December 26.

Khordad Sal, which celebrates the birth anniversary of Zoroaster. In the seasonal calendar, Zoroaster's birth anniversary falls on March 26.

ZOROASTRIAN MARRIAGES

Marriage from a Zoroastrian point of view is a sacrament and not just a civil contract. This sacrament can only be given by a qualified Zoroastrian priest when both parties to the marriage are Parsi Zoroastrians.

A number of religious texts, in particular, the *Avestan Vendidad* and the *Pahlavi Dinkard* have proscribed mixed marriages. These texts have considered "mixing of the seed" (intermarriage) as sinful.

This apart, the Zoroastrian religion takes a very positive view of marriage. Marriage is considered as an institution that finds favour with the mighty God. Ahura Mazda says:

"O Spitama Zarathushtra: Indeed, I thus recommend here unto thee, a man with a wife above a *magard* (i.e. an unmarried man), a man with a family above one without any family, a man with children above one who is without children."

Do not do unto others all that which is not well for yourself.

Marriages are meant to be celebrated, with due pomp and ceremony, in the presence of an assembly (*Anjoman*), which can bear witness to the event.

In Parsi weddings in India, the bride and groom wear traditional garments. Two plates of rice are placed on either side of the couple. There is a pot of clarified butter placed before the bride, as well as a bowl of molasses.

When the bride and bridegroom seat themselves opposite each other, separated by a curtain, the two officiating priests pass round the chairs of both a piece of cloth, so as to enclose them in a circle. This circle symbolises unity. The ends of the cloth are tied together with the recital of the sacred formula of *Ahunwar* or *Yatha Ahu Vairyo*. This signifies the tying of the marriage knot.

Now, the officiating senior priest places the right hand of one in the right hand of the other and fastens or unites them with the recital of the sacred *Ahunwar* formula. He fastens them with raw twist, which he puts round the hand seven times. This is the hand fastening ceremony.

The raw twist is then passed around the marriage knot seven times. The raw twist itself can be easily broken, but when several threads are twisted into one, they cannot easily be broken. So, this ceremony indicates a wish that the tie of union, in which the couple is now united, may not easily be broken.

The bride and bridegroom are given a few grains of rice in their left hands when their right hands are fastened together. They throw the rice over one another, to indicate their love and respect for each other. The assembly claps its hands to express approval and goodwill for the union of the couple.

This is followed by the strictly religious part of the ceremony, which is performed by two priests. This consists of:

1. Preliminary blessings
2. Questions to the witnesses and to the marrying couple
3. Joint address by the two priests

   The ceremony ends with the recital of the *Tandorosti* prayer, which is a form of benediction.

UNIQUE FEATURES OF ZOROASTRIANISM

It is widely accepted that Zoroastrianism has had a considerable influence on major Western religions such as Judaism, Christianity and Islam. Many of its

Those who believe, their minds awaken to higher consciousness and to the inner knowledge of all spheres.

concepts such as one God, day of judgment, heaven and hell, are reflected in the later religions.

But Zoroastrianism has never been an aggressively monotheistic religion. Rather it represents an original attempt at unifying under the worship of one supreme God, a polytheistic religion comparable to those of the ancient Greeks, Latins, Indians, and other early peoples.

Zoroaster taught that man must enlist in the cosmic struggle between good and evil because of his capacity of free choice. Thus Zoroastrianism is a highly ethical religion in which the choice of good over evil has almost cosmic importance. He also taught that humans are free to choose between right and wrong, truth and lies, and light and dark, and that their choices would affect their destiny for eternity.

The Zoroastrian after-life is determined by the balance of the good and evil deeds, words and thoughts of the whole life. For those whose good deeds outweigh the bad, heaven awaits. Those who did more evil than good go to hell (which has several levels corresponding to degrees of wickedness). There is an intermediate stage for those whose deeds weigh out equally.

Zoroastrians do not proselytise and living Zoroastrianism has no missionaries. Zoroastrian communities are generally not supportive of conversion.

As one of the world's oldest revealed religions, it is also, arguably, the world's first proponent of ecology, through caring for the elements and the earth. The faith endorses the caring of Seven Creations (sky, water, earth, plant, animal, human and fire), as part of a symbiotic relationship. Zoroastrians believe that at the end of time, humanity must give to Ahura Mazda a world of purity, a world in its original perfect state. As an example of their concern, it is a tradition that Zoroastrians never enter a river, to wash in it or pollute it in any way. Purity of nature in their tradition is seen as the greatest good.

The Tower of Silence

Zoroastrians in India remember their traditional story of The *Crisis*: how, once upon a time, Mother Earth was in trouble. She asked God (Ahura Mazda) if He could send her a prince, with warriors, to stop the people from hurting her, using force. But Ahura Mazda said he could not. Instead he would send Her a holy man, to stop the people from hurting her, using words and inspirational ideas. And thus was born the prophet, Zoroaster.

India is considered to be home to the largest Zoroastrian population in the world. Like the Sindhis, the Parsis also constitute a minority community that has contributed richly to Indian education, industry, economics, philanthropy and culture. They are today, one of the most prosperous and peace-loving communities in the country, having achieved social integration and wide acceptance, even while maintaining their unique cultural and religious identity.

A beautiful story is told to us of the arrival of the first Zoroastrians in India. Fleeing from Arab occupation, persecution and forced conversion in Persia, they had fled Eastward, arriving at the port of Navsari in Gujarat in the 9th century. An emissary was sent to the local ruler to request him for patronage and shelter to the refugees. The local ruler, Jadi Rana, sent to them an unusual welcome gift: a bowl brimming over with milk. It was a gesture meant to indicate to the intelligent community, that his kingdom was full, and could not really accommodate the new arrivals. The Parsi High-Priest sent for some sugar, mixed the sugar thoroughly with the milk and sent it back to the Rana, who was absolutely delighted: for the return-gift indicated to him symbolically that the newcomers would not only blend smoothly and harmoniously with the local population, but also add sweetness by way of their loyalty and respect for the land of their adoption. To this day, the Parsi community in India has remained true to this 'sweet' promise that their ancestors made.

Obedience, peace, charity, humility, truth, and righteousness should prevail in every home and the children should respect the parents at all times.

THE PATHS ARE MANY...

BRIEF INTRODUCTION TO OTHER WORLD RELIGIONS

CONFUCIANISM

Confucianism is known as "the school of the scholars". It is an ethical and philosophical system based on the teachings of the Chinese sage Confucius. Although there have been attempts to make Confucianism a religion, and deify Confucius himself as a saviour, it is essentially a way of life taught by Confucius in the 6th–5th century BC. Regarded by some as a philosophy, and by others as a religion, Confucianism is perhaps best described as an all-encompassing humanism, although it is not very much concerned with spiritual matters. It originated in China but has spread to Korea, Taiwan and Vietnam. Most people who adhere to the teachings of Confucius follow Chinese traditional religion, which is a blending of Confucianism, Buddhism, Taoism and age old local practices and beliefs.

K'ung Fu Tzu (551-479 BC) was a contemporary of Gautama the Buddha. (Confucius, the name we know him by, is a Latin rendering of original Chinese name). It is thought that he was born in Province of Lu in ancient China. He was an extremely studious child, and by fifteen, he had set his mind on becoming a scholar. Though he was forced to take up a tedious government job to earn his living and look after his mother, his heart lay in the study of the ancient classics, which offered him both delight and peace.

We do not know who his teachers were, but it is widely believed that Confucius was well versed in all the arts valued by ancient China – namely, ritual, music, archery, charioteering, calligraphy and arithmetic – and he was self-taught in the classics which he had always loved. Very soon, he quit his job to become a teacher of the people, and was elevated to the position of a respected and admired man, "a travelling university" as he was often called. Followed by his devoted students, he moved about in an ox-cart, drawing wisdom from the incidents of everyday life that he and his students witnessed, as they travelled across north-eastern and central China. Like Socrates, he moved among the common people, listening to their problems and worries, and counselling them to live a life based on virtues and ethical principles.

Surprisingly for modern scholars, Confucianism lays a lot of emphasis on rites and rituals: but this has a special significance. Internalisation is the main process in rituals. The formal and disciplined behaviour associated with rituals and ceremonies, becomes progressively internalised; negative desires are channeled into constructive avenues and personal cultivation becomes the mark of social correctness. Observing rituals with sincerity makes ritual the most powerful way to cultivate oneself. Thus, as Confucius says, "Respectfulness, without the rites, becomes laborious bustle; carefulness without the rites, becomes timidity; boldness without the rites, becomes insubordination; straightforwardness without the rites, becomes rudeness". (*Analects* VIII, 2).

Sadly, his teachings were not accepted by the rulers and their circles of influence; in fact, many records speak of Confucius' frustration at not finding acceptance in the larger political arena; but he had an ever growing number of personal followers, gaining a great reputation as, "a man of vision and mission".

Confucius often claimed that he never invented anything but was only transmitting ancient knowledge; however, he did produce a number of new ideas. Many western admirers say that the revolutionary idea of replacing the nobility of blood with one of virtue, was first proposed by Confucius. *Juniz* was a term which had meant "nobleman" before Confucius; slowly it assumed a new connotation in the course of his writings, more or less as "gentleman" did in English.

Another of his new ideas was that of meritocracy, which led to the introduction of the Imperial examination system in China. This system allowed anyone who passed an examination to become a government officer, a position which would bring wealth and honour to the whole family. We can say that this system was promoted largely due to the Confucian emphasis on education.

In the two millennia after his death, Confucius' principles gained wide acceptance in China, perhaps because of their basis in everyday ethics, humanitarian values, emphasis on personal relationships, and respect for morality and common Chinese tradition and belief. He advocated familial loyalty, reverence for ancestors, and respect for all elders among the younger generation. Troubled by the moral laxity and social disharmony of the times, he urged the people to value humanism, justice, truth and morality. Rather than setting out a code of ethics or a formal set of dogmas, rules, he encouraged his disciples to think for themselves, learn their values from the ancient classics, and foster virtue and goodness by personal example rather than by doctrinal precepts.

Few followers of Confucius today have a clear belief in any Divine existence, or in after-life. Yet they believe in the world of spirits and souls, and some even practise ancestor worship. As such, there is no concept of God in Confucianism.

Some of the chief concepts of Confucianism are: *ren* (humaneness or benevolence); *li* (ritual norms), *zhong* (loyalty to one's true nature), *shu* (reciprocity) and *xiao* (filial piety). Together these constitute *de* (virtue). The essence of all his teachings may be summed up under this one word 'Jen'. The nearest equivalent to this difficult word is "social virtue". All those virtues which help to maintain social harmony and peace like benevolence, charity, magnanimity, sincerity, respectfulness, altruism, diligence, loving kindness, goodness are included in Jen.

His "Golden Rule" is: "What you do not want done to yourself, do not do unto others." "The injuries done to you by an enemy should be returned with a combination of love and justice."

SACRED TEXTS:

The *Lun-yü* (*Analects*) are regarded as the most revered sacred scripture in the Confucian tradition. These were not written by the Sage, but compiled after his death by a later generation of his disciples, in the manner of the Socratic Dialogues compiled by Plato. It is based primarily on the Master's sayings, preserved in both oral and written transmissions, and captures the Confucian spirit in such an impressive manner, that it was translated into Latin and widely popularised in Europe by Jesuit scholars.

The Confucian Canon includes the Five Classics and the Four Books.

The Five Classics are:

1. *Shu Ching* (Classic of History)

2. *Shih Ching* (Classic of Odes)

3. *I Ching* (Classic of Changes)

4. *Ch'un Ching* (Spring and Autumn Annals)

5. *Li Ching* (Classic of Rites)

The Four Books are:

1. *Lun Yu* (Analects) of Confucius

2. *Chung Yung* (Doctrine of the Mean)

3. *Ta Hsueh* (Great Learning)

4. *Meng Tzu* (Mencius)

Confucianism has been followed by the Chinese for more than two millennia. It has deeply influenced the spiritual and political life in China; its influence has also extended to Korea, Japan, and Vietnam. East Asians may profess themselves to be Shintoists, Taoists, Buddhists, Muslims, or Christians – but seldom do they cease to be Confucians. In fact, the followers of Taoism, Shintoism and Buddhism equally believe in Confucianism as a philosophy compatible with their own. Hence they coexist in a diffused form, which is something remarkable in the case of the religions of the world.

TAOISM

The founder of Taoism is thought to be Lao-Tse (604-531 BC), whose life overlapped that of Confucius

(551-479 BCE). However, many historians feel that he is actually a mythical figure, or a popular synthesis of a number of historical figures. Such scholars point out that the Chinese term *Laozi* literally means "Old Master" and is generally used as an honorific reference or title. Lao-Tse is revered as a wise man in philosophical forms of Taoism, but regarded as a god in more religious and 'practising' forms of Taoism, much like The Buddha in some schools of Buddhism.

There are not many details of his life available to us. But several popular legends have grown around his life and personality. Some people say that he was conceived when his mother gazed upon a falling star; that he stayed in the womb for sixty-two years, and was born when his mother leaned against a plum tree. He accordingly emerged a grown man with a full grey beard and long earlobes, which are a symbol of wisdom and long life. In other versions he was reborn in thirteen different incarnations since the days of Fuxi; in his last incarnation he was Lao-Tse, and he lived to be nine hundred and ninety years old, and even travelled to India to reveal the Tao.

One interesting legend tells us that Lao-Tse was so disillusioned with the corruption and moral decay of urban life that he headed west to live as a hermit in the unsettled frontier at the age of 160. At the western gate of the kingdom, he was recognised by a guard. The sentry asked the old master to produce a record of his wisdom. This is the legendary origin of the *Tao Te Ching*. Thus the *Tao Te Ching* came into being, put down in black and white by the Master himself.

Some traditions actually state that the 'Old Master' was the teacher of The Buddha, or even that he was himself, the original Buddha.

The *Tao Te Ching* or *Dao De Jing* is a Chinese classic text. Its name comes from the opening words of its two sections: *dào* or "way," and dé or "virtue," and *jing* or "classic." According to tradition, it was written around the 6th century BC by Lao-Tse, although many people say that it was compiled by his disciples later. Many artists, from China and other countries, as well as poets, painters, calligraphers and even gardeners have used the *Tao Te Ching* as a source of inspiration. Its influence has also spread widely outside East Asia, aided by hundreds of translations into Western languages.

Tao (pronounced "Dow") can be roughly translated into English as path, or the way. As Chinese scholars say, it is basically indefinable. It has to be experienced. According to the followers of the faith, it "refers to a power which envelops, surrounds and flows through all things, living and non-living. The Tao regulates natural processes and nourishes balance in the Universe. It embodies the harmony of opposites (i.e. there would be no love without hate, no light without dark, no male without female)."

One of the key concepts of Taoism is *Wu wei*, literally "non-action" or "not acting". The concept of *wu wei* is complex and reflected in the word's multiple interpretations: it can mean "not doing anything", "not forcing", "not acting" in the theatrical sense, "creating nothingness", "acting spontaneously", and "flowing with the moment." Lao-Tse is thought to have used the term in conjunction with simplicity and humility as key virtues, often in contrast to selfish action. On a political level, it means avoiding violent events such as war, harsh laws and unjust taxes. Some Taoists see a connection between *wu wei* and esoteric meditation techniques, such as "sitting in oblivion" (i.e. emptying the mind of bodily awareness and thought).

The concept of a personified deity or God is foreign to Taoism, as is the concept of the creation of the universe. Each believer's goal is to become one with the Tao, the force which flows through all life and is the first cause of everything.

Taoism started as a combination of psychology and philosophy but evolved into a religious faith in 440 AD when it was adopted as a state religion. At that time Lao-Tse became popularly venerated as a deity. Taoism, along with Buddhism and Confucianism, became one of the three great religions of China. But, by the end of the Ch'ing Dynasty in 1911, state support for Taoism ended. Much of the Taoist heritage was destroyed during the next period of warlordism. After the Communist victory in 1949, religious freedom was severely restricted. During the 'cultural revolution' in China from 1966 to 1976, much of the remaining Taoist heritage was destroyed. Some religious tolerance has been restored in China under Deng Xiao-Ping from 1982 to the present time.

Taoism currently has about 20 million followers, most of whom live in Taiwan. Over thirty thousand Taoists live in North America and Canada as well. Taoism has had a significant impact on North American culture, especially in areas such as "acupuncture, herbalism, holistic medicine, meditation and martial arts...".

TAOIST CONCEPTS, BELIEFS AND PRACTICES :

Tao is the first-cause of the universe. It is a force that flows through all life. "The Tao surrounds everyone and therefore everyone must listen to find enlightenment."

Each believer's goal is to harmonise themselves with the Tao.

Taoism has provided an alternative to the Confucian tradition in China. The two traditions have coexisted in the country, region, and generally within the same individual.

The concept of a personified deity is foreign to Tao, as is the concept of the creation of the universe. Thus, they do not pray as Christians do; there is no God to hear the prayers or to act upon them. They seek answers to life's problems through inner meditation and outer observation.

- Time is cyclical, not linear as in Western thinking.

- Taoists strongly promote health and vitality.

- Five main organs and orifices of the body correspond to the five parts of the sky: water, fire, wood, metal and earth.

- Each person must nurture the Ch'i (air, breath) that has been given to them.

- Development of virtue is one's chief task. The Three Jewels to be sought are compassion, moderation and humility.

- Taoists follow the art of "wu wei," which is to let nature take its course. For example, one should allow a river to flow towards the sea unimpeded; not erect a dam which would interfere with its natural flow.

- One should plan in advance and consider carefully each action before doing it.

- A Taoist is kind to other individuals, in part because such an action tends to be reciprocated.

- Taoists believe that "people are compassionate by nature...left to their own devices [they] will show this compassion without expecting a reward."

Taoist Sacred Texts:

Tao-te-Ching is believed to have been written by Lao-Tse himself. It describes the nature of life, the way to peace and how a ruler should lead his life.

Chuang-tzu (named after its author) contains additional teachings.

The Yin Yang symbol:

This is a well known Taoist symbol. According to Tao scholars, "It represents the balance of opposites in the universe. When they are equally present, all is calm. When one is outweighed by the other, there is confusion and disarray." Yet another source states: "The most traditional view is that 'yin' represents aspects of the feminine: being soft, cool, calm, introspective and 'yang' the masculine: being hard, hot, energetic, moving, and sometimes aggressive. Another view has the 'yin' representing night and 'yang' day." Ultimately, the 'yin' and 'yang' can symbolise any two polarized forces in nature. Taoists believe that humans often intervene in nature and upset the balance of Yin and Yang.

Tai chi techniques

Tai chi exercises are another popular form of therapy associated with Taoism today. The concept of the *Taiji* "supreme ultimate" is derived from both Taoist and Confucian philosophy. It is thought to represent the fusion of Yin and Yang into a single ultimate, represented by the *Taijitu* symbol. *Tai chi chuan* is generally classified as a form of traditional Chinese martial arts of the *Neijia* (soft or internal) branch. It is considered a soft style martial art – an art applied with internal power – to distinguish it from other hard martial art styles. Since the first widespread promotion of *Tai chi's* health benefits in the early twentieth century, it has developed a worldwide following among people with little or no interest in martial training, for its benefits to health and health maintenance. Medical studies of *tai chi* support its effectiveness as an alternative exercise and a form of martial arts therapy. Focusing the mind solely on the movements of the form purportedly helps to bring about a state of mental calm and clarity. Traditional Chinese medicine teaches that illness is caused by blockages or lack of balance in the body's "*chi*" (intrinsic energy). *Tai Chi* is believed to balance this energy flow.

ZEN BUDDHISM

The Japanese word *Zen* and the corresponding Chinese term, *Ch'an* are derived from the Sanskrit word *dhyana*, meaning "meditation". Zen is a school of Mahayana Buddhism, which focuses on attaining enlightenment (*bodhi*) through meditation, even as Gautama The Buddha did. According to Zen belief, all human beings have The Buddha-nature, or the potential to attain enlightenment within them; but The Buddha-nature has been clouded by ignorance in most people. Zen Masters say that the way to overcome this ignorance is not the study of scriptures, or the performance of religious rites, devotional practices, and good works, but sustained meditation; this, they say, will eventually lead to insight and awareness of the ultimate reality. Training in the Zen path is usually undertaken by a disciple under the guidance of a master.

An interesting story is narrated in the early Buddhist scriptures of the origin of Zen. One day, a number of disciples had gathered around The Buddha, eager to hear his sermon. But on that particular occasion, the Buddha chose to remain utterly silent, only holding out a lotus flower for his disciples to see. Most of them were utterly puzzled by this silence. Only one of them, Mahakashyapa, gazed intently at the flower, and realised the inexpressible meaning of The Buddha's gesture. He had obtained inspiration directly from The Buddha's gaze, and the flower that the Master had held. He smiled at The Buddha in gratitude, and The Buddha smiled back in recognition of his disciple's subtle sense of insight. Thus was born a new school of Buddhism, in which experiential wisdom took precedence over sermons and scriptures; and in which revealed transmission bypassed the need for words and rituals. Zen draws its inspiration from these words attributed to The Buddha: "*Bodhisattvas* never engage in conversations whose resolutions depend on words and logic."

To this day, Zen Masters do not use words to transmit their wisdom, relying instead on intuitive thought processes and the grasp of unspoken truths. It is believed that *Bodhidharma*, the South Indian Pallava prince-turned-monk, was the one who first brought Zen to China; he himself is thought to have been in the direct lineage of the disciples of Mahakashyapa. The essence of Zen philosophy is expressed in the *Bloodstream Sermon* attributed to him:

Buddhas don't save Buddhas. If you use your mind to look for a Buddha, you won't see the Buddha. As long as you look for a Buddha somewhere else, you will never see that your own mind is the Buddha. Don't use a Buddha to worship a Buddha. And don't use the mind to invoke a Buddha. Buddhas don't recite sutras. Buddhas don't keep precepts. And Buddhas don't break precepts. Buddhas don't keep or break anything. Buddhas don't do good or evil.

To find a Buddha, you have to see your nature.

Although Zen rejects words as a channel of teaching wisdom, the early Zen Masters were well versed in the various *sutras* of Buddhism; it was just that they felt that actual practice of the Buddha's ways was more worthwhile than reading or reciting from the scriptures. By the Seventh Century, Zen Buddhism as taught by *Bodhidharma* was well established in China as a separate and distinct school.

Kubota Jiun, the Zen Scholar and writer tells us: "Although it would be inaccurate to say that writings in the Zen sect are not traditional scriptures, Zen is distinguished by lacking a *single scripture* upon which everything depends. And although we could stretch a point, perhaps, and say the *Hannyashingyo* (*Heart Sutra*) is such a traditional scripture, as long as study of this *sutra* ends in intellectual discussion, it has no relation to Zen whatsoever."

However, Dwight Goddard's best selling book, *A Buddhist Bible*, mentions the *Lankavatara Sutra*, *The Diamond Sutra*, *The Prajna Paramita Sutra* and *The Heart Sutra* as "Favourite Zen scriptures."

At the heart of Zen practice is seated meditation, widely known by its Japanese name *zazen;* it recalls both the posture in which the Buddha sat under the *Bodhi* tree, and the elements of mindfulness and concentration which are part of the Eightfold Path as taught by the Buddha.

Zen training emphasises daily practice, along with intensive periods of meditation. Practising with others is also considered important. Zen historian D.T. Suzuki writes that aspects of Zen are: "…a life of humility; a life of labour; a life of service; a life of prayer and gratitude; and a life of meditation." The

Chinese Chán Master Baizhang (720–814 CE) left behind a famous saying which had been the guiding principle of his life, "A day without work is a day without food."

It is often said in Zen history, that "a five-petalled flower blossomed" in China. This Zen expression means that Zen opened up like a flower with five petals and spread throughout the whole country. These schools were *Igyo, Hongen, Soto, Unmon, and Rinzai*. Thousands of temples were constructed across the Chinese countryside, in forests and mountains, where tens of thousands of people devoted themselves to the study and practise of the Zen Dharma. Zen philosophy and practise permeated and elevated Chinese culture, making its art and thought sublime, until it was systematically rooted out in the Communist movement of the Twentieth Century.

Although Zen Buddhism arrived in Japan as early as the 7th century, it did not develop significantly in that country until the 12th century. The *Rinzai* sect of Zen was introduced to Japan by the Chinese priest Ensai in 1191. Rinzai Buddhism emphasises the use of *koans*, paradoxical puzzles or questions that help the practitioner to overcome the normal boundaries of logic. *Soto* Buddhism was another Zen sect that was transmitted from China to Japan. It emphasises the practice of *zazen* and tells the aspirant simply to clear the mind of all thoughts and concepts, without making any effort towards enlightenment, until enlightenment occurs naturally.

Zen has exercised a profound influence on the daily lives of the Japanese people. This influence can be seen and appreciated in many aspects of Japanese life, including eating, clothing, painting, calligraphy, architecture, theatre, music, gardening, decoration, etc.

Zen is perhaps the most well-known school of Buddhism in the West today. Its concepts have been influential on western society since the latter half of the 20th century. There are about 9.6 million Zen Buddhists in Japan today, and numerous Zen groups have developed in North America and Europe in the last one hundred years.

SHINTOISM

The word Shinto is derived from two Chinese words *shin tao*, meaning The Way of the Gods. Shintoism is unique in the sense that it has no real founder, no written scriptures, no body of religious law, and only a very loosely-organised priesthood. Some scholars describe the faith as "an amorphous mix of nature worship, fertility cults, divination techniques, hero worship, and shamanism."

Shinto or *kami-no-michi* as it is called, incorporates spiritual practices derived from many local and regional traditions of Japan and the Japanese people of the Yamato and Izumo cultures. Even early Japanese writings do not refer to a unified "Shinto religion", leading scholars to believe that Shintoism was not institutionalised for a long time.

Shinto is a religion in which practice (actions) and ritual, are more important than words or doctrines. It is pantheistic in its leanings, characterised by the worship of nature, veneration of ancestors, polytheism, and animism. There is also a strong focus on ritual purity, involving honouring and celebrating the existence of *Kami* ("spirit", "essence" or "deities") , that are associated with more abstract "natural" forces in the world (mountains, rivers, lightning, wind, waves, trees, rocks). Shinto teaches that everything contains a *kami*. Perhaps *kami* may best be described as "sacred" elements and energies. In Shinto belief, *kami* and people are not separate; they exist within the same world and share its interrelated complexity.

The Shinto myth of creation states that the Japanese islands were directly created by the Gods for the Japanese people, and were ordained by the higher spirits to be a paradise on earth. Shinto is the way of God – the fundamental connection between the power and beauty of nature (the land) and the Japanese people. It is the path to understanding the divine power of Nature. Aesthetics is thus a vital aspect of Shintoism.

Also allied to this belief is the doctrine of Japanese superiority over the rest of the world: because of their divine descent, the Japanese people are gifted with courage and intelligence. They "are honest and upright of heart, and are not given to useless theorising and falsehoods like other nations." Thus Shinto is associated with nationalism and racial purity and pride. This being the case, there is no concept of a saviour, as the race itself is of celestial origin.

There are "Four Affirmations" in Shinto:

1. Tradition and the family: The family is seen as the main mechanism by which traditions are preserved. Their main celebrations relate to birth and marriage.

2. Love of nature: Nature is sacred; to be in contact with nature is to be close to the Gods. Natural objects are worshipped as sacred spirits.

3. Physical cleanliness: Followers of Shinto take baths, wash their hands, and rinse out their mouth often.

4. *Matsuri*: The worship and honour given to the *kami* and ancestral spirits.

Purity is one of the fundamental virtues of Shinto ethics. There are two significations of purity. One is outer purity or bodily purity and the other inner purity or purity of heart.

Shinto has been called "the religion of Japan", and its influence on Japanese life and culture is significant. For example, the Shinto ideal of harmony with nature underlies such famous Japanese arts as flower-arranging (*ikebana*), traditional Japanese architecture, and garden design. Also linked with Shinto is the world famous art of Sumo wrestling, where, even today, many Shinto-inspired ceremonies are performed before a bout, such as purifying the arena by sprinkling it with salt. The elaborate Japanese greetings and respectful bowing also represent a continuation of the ancient Shinto belief in *kotodama* (words with a magical effect on the world).

There are different types of Shinto expression:

Imperial Shinto is associated with the family of the Japanese Emperor in their own imperial shrines.

Shrine Shinto is the most popular among the Japanese people, and includes ritual worship offered in over 80,000 shrines all over Japan.

Folk Shinto includes the numerous and assorted folk beliefs in deities and spirits. Its practices include divination, spirit possession, and shamanic healing, derived from ancient local traditions.

Ko Shinto is a tradition that values the systematic methods of exercise and training. It is also one of the oldest Shinto sects.

To these we may also add *Sect Shinto*, which are numerous cults that have grown around the Shinto faith over a period of time.

The principal worship of *kami* is done at public shrines or at small home shrines called *kamidana*. The public shrine is a building or place that functions as a conduit for *kami*. A few shrines are also natural places called *mori*. These may be sacred groves of trees, or mountains, or waterfalls. The shrines are elaborate structures in the typical Japanese architectural style, separated from the public space and designated as sacred space. They are 'protected' from the outside world by special gates, protective statues, ropes, fences and barriers. Periodic rituals as well as yearly celebrations are held at these shrines, all of them conducted by special priests who are also administrators.

Since Shinto has a large number of deities, a systematic worship of all such deities is impossible. Only a few deities are regularly worshipped, the chief being the sun-goddess, Amaterasu. The fact that the highest deity is a female makes Shinto unique among world religions.

Although Shinto does not consider any one volume as the wholly inspired revelation on which its religion is based, two books are considered sacred and have done much to influence the beliefs of the Japanese people. The works are *Ko-ji-ki*, the "records of ancient matters", and *Nihon-gi*, the "chronicles of Japan".

Shinto has co-existed with Buddhism in Japan for well over a millennium. Though Buddhism and Shinto have very different perspectives on the world, most Japanese do not see any challenge in reconciling these two very different religions, and practise both.

Swami Sivananda, an Indian mystic and spiritual leader, asserts that Shinto is closer to Hinduism than any other faith. He sums up the ethics of Shinto as follows:

Ten Precepts Of Shinto

i)   Do not transgress the will of the gods

ii) Do not forget your obligations to ancestors

iii) Do not offend by violating the decrees of the State

iv) Do not forget the profound goodness of the, gods, through which calamity and misfortunes are averted and sickness is healed

v)   Do not forget that the world is one great family

vi) Do not forget the limitations of your own person

vii) Do not become angry even though others become angry

viii) Do not be sluggish in your work

ix) Do not bring blame to the teaching

x)   Do not be carried away by foreign teachings

ATHEISM

If religion is primarily associated with a doctrine, a deity, a belief system centred around certain worship-practices, then the question may well be asked: can we consider atheism as a 'religion'?

The term "theism" derives from the Greek *theos,* meaning God. Atheism in its broadest sense is the rejection of *theism*, or belief in a deity. It can also be interpreted as non-theism, the negation, rejection, or absence of theism. In modern terms, we may say that atheism regards the existence of God as unproved and therefore unbelievable hypothesis or proposition. As one writer phrases it: it can be *no belief in God*, or *belief in no God.* (The difference, he says is crucial.)

The Greek word *atheos*, meaning "without gods", was a derogatory term applied to anyone who did not believe in the accepted gods of those days, or believed in false gods, or no gods. However, with the spread of free enquiry, scepticism, criticism of religion and the general loss of faith associated with modern civilisation, atheism began to be 'professed' by more and more people. It is thought that about 2.3% of the world's population is atheist today, while a further 11.9% is described as non-theist.

While atheism denies God, *agnosticism* expresses uncertainty about the existence of God. The dictionary defines an agnostic as "a person who holds the view that any ultimate reality (as God) is unknown and probably unknowable; broadly speaking, one who is not committed to believing in either the existence or the non-existence of God or a god." Some famous agnostics of recent times are: Charles Darwin, Thomas Huxley, Robert Ingersoll, and Bertrand Russel. Prominent atheists include Auguste Comte, Sigmund Freud, Karl Sagan, Jean-Paul Sartre and Issac Assimov. (Atheists and Agnostics are often included in each others' lists, which makes the classification rather fluid.)

There is no one ideology or set of beliefs to which all atheists adhere. Some atheists tend toward secular philosophies such as humanism, rationalism, and naturalism, while many base their attitude on scepticism, which dismisses religious beliefs as irrational, illogical and superstitious. In the Western world, atheists are assumed to be irreligious or unspiritual. However, many Westerners regard spiritual belief systems such as Buddhism, Shinto and Tao as atheistic religions.

Atheism is not a complete religion in the sense that Christianity, Islam and Judaism are. For one thing, it does not offer a guideline for living as many religions do. However, atheists derive their own ethics, philosophy of life and worldview using their atheism as a starting point. Thus we have a recent phenomenon called 'positive atheism' which promotes the moral uprightness, understanding and tolerance towards others' religious beliefs, avoiding all attempts to denigrate religion or preach atheistic philosophy.

Theoretical atheism is derived from a particular rationale or philosophical argument, such as Marxism or Nihilism. Practical or pragmatic atheism has no arguments to offer; it is simply indifference to and ignorance of the idea of gods.

The Universal Encyclopedia of Philosophy tells us that practical atheism can take many forms:

- Absence of religious motivation – belief in gods does not motivate moral action, religious action, or any other form of action;

- Active exclusion of the problem of Gods and religion from intellectual pursuit and practical action;

- Indifference – the absence of any interest in the problems of Gods and religion; or

- Unawareness of the concept of a deity.

Theoretical atheism dates as far back as the early Vedic age in India, where the *Charvaka* School, the *Samkhya* and *Purva Mimamsa* philosophies were materialistic or non-theistic. In a sense, Buddhism and Jainism also reject the concept of a God or saviour, though they pay homage to enlightened masters. In Western philosophy, the Greek philosopher Diagoras is cited as the "first atheist" by Cicero. Critias (thought to be Plato's uncle) viewed religion as a human invention used to frighten people into moral living. As we know,

Socrates himself was accused of impiety, because he questioned the state gods. Epicureanism, a materialistic philosophy, did not rule out the existence of gods, but asserted that if they did exist, they were unconcerned with the human condition. The early Christians were labeled as atheists in the Roman empire, because they did not believe in pagan gods. While Christians were persecuted by the Romans in those early days, the Christian Church, when it was established, executed or burnt non-believers as heretics.

Criticism of Christianity became frequent in the 17th and 18th centuries, especially in France and England. Protestant thinkers like Thomas Hobbes espoused a materialist philosophy and scepticism toward supernatural occurrences, while the Jewish-Dutch philosopher Spinoza rejected divine providence in favour of a pantheistic naturalism. In the latter half of the 19th century, atheism rose to prominence under the influence of rationalistic and freethinking philosophers like Ludwig Feuerbach, Arthur Schopenhauer, Karl Marx, and Friedrich Nietzsche. In the twentieth Century, atheism was promoted by new schools of thought such as existentialism, objectivism, secular humanism, nihilism, logical positivism, Marxism, feminism and the general scientific and rationalist movement. Religion and all forms of worship were severely repressed under the Russian revolution and the Chinese Communist movement.

In 1966, Time magazine famously asked on its cover page, "Is God Dead?" This was in response to the *Death of God* theological movement, and also because statistics cited that nearly half of all people in the world lived under an anti-religious power, and millions more in Africa, Asia, and South America seemed to lack knowledge of the specifically Christian God of the West. In the following year Albania was declared as the world's first officially atheist state.

Atheists claim that they are the most misunderstood and maligned 'religious' minority, severely discriminated against, in the United States.

AFRICAN TRADITIONAL RELIGIONS

The traditional, indigenous religions of Africa occupy a very distinct and special place among the world faiths. This is despite the fact that the majority of people in the African continent today are followers of either Christianity or Islam. The zeal of the missionary religions has more or less wiped out the tribal religions practiced by the Africans for centuries; but native practices and cults have prevailed despite the dominance of the institutionalised faiths. Thus we find a fascinating situation where large numbers of Africans profess the faith of the Abrahamaic religions, while traditional/ethnic/tribal/folk practices and rituals are still adhered to in one form or another. This syncretism has taken such roots in African society, that even established churches and religious authorities have not been able to dislodge what they regard to be 'idolatrous' or 'pagan' practices.

Here is what one scholar has to say about Africa: "The indigenous religions remain very much the living faith of many rural dwellers in Africa. Both in urban and rural areas, religions continue to adapt to the changing circumstances of life of the people... Traditional priests, diviners, mediums and shrine attendants dress in modern outfits for traditional religious cult of deities in present-day African societies. In another development, the beliefs and rituals of several traditional African deities like the Yoruba Orisha continue to be maintained by many adherents and practitioners of the Voodoo, Santeria and Cumina cults...which... combine indigenous African religious stuff with elements from Christianity."

The African Traditional religions (ATR) do not fall within the category of universal or missionary religions. They are classified among traditional or folk religions of the world. They thrive in stable and homogenous ethnic societies. They have no founders, reformers, or prophets, and are handed down through the family system from one generation to the next. In the words of the writer Mbiti, African traditional religions "have no missionaries to propagate them. As folk religions, they are said to be community-based. People simply assimilate whatever religious ideas and practices are held or observed by their families and communities".

The African scholar Godfrey Onah points out that one problem that we encounter in analysing ATR is the absence of scriptures. The oldest religious traditions of the continent have been handed down in orally preserved form and are reflected in the cultural and religious artefacts of African peoples. This reduces the possibility of their survival in a globalised society. Even for faithful adherents, it is impossible to understand and follow a religion properly, if one does not know its history, its antecedents and its values and beliefs well.

Another difficulty lies in the fact that ATR is not a proselytizing religion. There is a popular proverb in Ghana, which says: "No one teaches a child, God." When the basic religious issues are taken for granted, there is bound to be a lot of flexibility and variation, even about the meanings of some important concepts, especially the concept of God and of spirits.

The problem of understanding ATR is further compounded by the fact that the major religions are constantly engaged in trying to reinterpret ancient beliefs and practices in the light of their own value systems.

According to Onah, there are three principal dimensions of ATR.

1. Belief: The main objects of traditional religious belief are: God, the divinities, spirits and the ancestors. Belief in God, conceived as one Supreme Personal Being seems to be shared by the majority

of African cultures. It must be stressed that experts disagree on whether these faiths are polytheistic or monotheistic; but it is safe to say that these religions clearly distinguish between one supreme power and lesser deities.

2. Worship: Religion is an integral part of life for the Africans, and worship touches every aspect of their lives. Strictly speaking, only God and the divinities are worshipped and this is done through sacrifices, offerings, prayers, invocation, praises, music and dance. ATR is not pantheistic, although some special trees, rivers, forests and mountains are considered manifestations of the sacred, and often serve as places of worship.

3. Community Loyalty: Africans believe that all human beings are born/placed in a given community to protect and nurture their lives, and thus it is within this community that their destiny should be worked out. Living harmoniously within a community is therefore a moral obligation ordained by God for the good of mankind. As the scholar John Mbiti puts it so beautifully, "*I* am because *we* are; and since we are, therefore I am."

Conscience is the oracle of the heart, the inner voice of God in every man. When he obeys this inner voice, a man can be at peace with himself and his neighbours. A man who disobeys this voice, lives in constant fear of divine retribution. Thus we have the Igbo proverb:

"It is only one who has committed perjury that is afraid of the thunder."

Religion in Africa is not a discreet or separate human activity, kept apart from other aspects of living. In African traditional religion, as in many other ancient belief systems in other parts of the world, the spiritual permeates every aspect of life. The landscape is a source of spiritual contemplation and worship. Ancestral spirits are easily accessible and well placed to give advice and warnings. There is a holistic approach to health, involving both physical and spiritual dimensions.

Ancestor worship is something fundamental to all traditional religion, even though the monotheistic religions reject the idea. But these very religions have been more or less constrained to accept rituals that are still sacred to Africans. Thus even Christianity and Islam, which are the dominant religions of Africa, have become part of the African cultural heritage and acquired a distinct African identity. In sociological terms, this is known as *inculturation.*

It is also necessary to mention that ATR has given rise to African Diasporic Religions which have arisen, typically in the Western hemisphere, among Africans who have retained much of their traditional culture and beliefs but adapted them to new environments. These include Santeria, Candomble, Vodoun, Shango, etc. These are prevalent in countries as far apart as Brazil, Cuba, Haiti, Jamaica and the U.S. In many areas the African elements exist side by side with modern European influences. Adherents of African diasporic religions typically have no real tribal affiliation, and are not necessarily African or black in their race and ethnicity. They are classified as Afro-Caribbean and/or Afro-Brazilian syncretistic religions, and have given a new life to ATR.

Paganism, Heathenism, Animism, Fetishism, Ancestor-worship, Idolatry and Totemism, are some of the labels that outsiders have used to describe ATR. These labels are misguided and misunderstood attempts to come to terms with a complex faith and culture. Daniele Mezzana argues that for centuries, African traditional religions have been subjected to the same kind of misrepresentation, underestimation and basic stigmatisation by Western society.

African writer and Nobel laureate, Wole Soyinka believes that Christianity and Islam would be conservative forces that would impede Africa's ability to cope with the modern world, whereas the indigenous traditions would be far more open, liberal and flexible, enabling Africans to adapt to a changing world.

JUCHE

Scholars of comparative religion describe Juche as the world's newest religion. As a concept, Juche was first proclaimed in North Korea by President Kim Il-Sung, in 1955. Juche is a Communist government sponsored mixture of ideology, philosophy and religion for an estimated 22,000,000 people of the Democratic People's Republic of Korea (North Korea). Initially, Juche was just an ideology of political expediency to promote the Korean Workers' Party, and to establish Kim Il-Sung as a supreme leader of the party. Later, Confucian ideas were added with reference to family values, self-sacrifice and material possessions, to make it more holistic.

Should we regard such a politically motivated system of beliefs as a religion? Many scholars classify Juche as a North Korean form of Marxist Communism. From its origins, it was the official philosophy promulgated by the North Korean government and educational system. Its promoters describe Juche as simply a secular, ethical philosophy and not a religion. But, from a sociological viewpoint Juche is clearly a religion, and in many ways more overtly religious than Soviet Communism or Chinese Maoism. It does not have any independent spiritual or theocratic elements – it is essentially secular, using religion only for political purposes, if it does not reject religious faith outright.

In the terminology of sociology, a political religion is an ideology with cultural and political power equivalent to those of a religion, and often having many sociological and ideological similarities with religion. Such political religions vie with existing religions, and try, if possible, to replace or eradicate them. Christian scholars of comparative religion have linked the concept to modernity, mass society and the rise of the bureaucratic state, and see in political religions "the climax of the rebellion against the religion of God" (meaning their own religion); these political religions have also been described as 'pseudo-religions', 'substitute religions', 'surrogate religions', 'religions manipulated by man' and 'anti-religions'.

One of the first demands of Juche is loyalty to the state or dominant political party and acceptance of the government/party ideology. Dissenters and opponents are ruthlessly eliminated or forced into exile or subjected to social ostracism. Loyalty oaths are required for employment, government services, or simply as routine. Criticism of the government is regarded as a serious crime. Enforcements range from imprisonment to execution.

The power base of the ideology is reinforced by instilling fear of some kind in the population. For example, North Korea holds frequent air raid drills to emphasise the possibility of imminent invasion.

Another tactic of Juche is to pin blame for the nation's problems on a particular entity or group. North Korea blames its economic problems on the Western world.

A political religion like Juche often elevates its leaders to near-godlike status. Display of leaders in the form of posters or statues is mandatory in public areas and even private homes. Children are required to learn the state's version of the leaders' biographies in school.

Political gatherings may supplement or replace religious ceremonies to help reinforce loyalty. The state usually controls the mass media for similar reasons, filling it with propaganda.

The North Korean government has promulgated Juche as a political alternative to traditional religion. The doctrine is fundamentally opposed to Christianity and Buddhism, the two largest religions on the Korean peninsula. Juche theoreticians have, however, incorporated religious ideas into the state ideology. The public practice of all other religions is overseen and subject to heavy surveillance by the state.

Juche teaches that "man is the master of everything and decides everything," and that the Korean people are the masters of Korea's revolution. Translated to mean "self-reliance" Juche gradually emerged as a systematic ideological doctrine under Kim Il-Sung, who outlined the three fundamental principles of Juche in 1965:

1. Independence in politics (*chaju*)
2. Self-sustenance in the economy (*charip*)

3. Self-defense in national defense (chawi)

The Juche outlook requires absolute loyalty to the revolutionary party and leader. In North Korea today, these are the Workers' Party of Korea and Kim Jong-Il, respectively.

In his book, *A Christian Study of North Korea's State Religion,* Thomas J. Belke tells us that Juche has "more adherents than Judaism, Sikhism, Jainism or Zoroastrianism." Certainly there are more "followers" of Juche, by nature of their nationality, than there are Jews or Jains. Belke also reports a few centres in India, and Juche websites indicate some centres in Australia, Europe and Japan. But despite the presence of these outreach centres set up by the North Korean government, there do not appear to be any established communities of adherents outside of North Korea. Thus Juche is restricted by nationality to a single country, although the adherents in that country are numerous, making it one of "the significant religions of the world." Moreover, although it was founded as a subset of Communism, today's Juche has developed into a distinct, unique system and has officially repudiated its Marxist-Leninist roots.

NEO–PAGANISM

The term "Neo-Paganism" is thought to have been coined by Tim Zell, editor of *The Green Egg,* a publication of the Church of All Worlds Faith. It refers to a group of religions which share certain common characteristics.

A Neo-Pagan religion, as its name indicates, is a revival of ancient faiths reconstructed from beliefs, deities, symbols, practices and other elements of an ancient religion. Thus we have the *Druidic* religion, which is based on the faith and practices of the ancient Celts; followers of *Asatru* adhere to the ancient, pre-Christian Norse religion; *Wiccans* also trace their roots back to the pre-Celtic era in Europe. Other Neo-Pagans follow *Hellenismos* (ancient Greek religion), *Religio Romana* (ancient Roman religion), *Kemetism* (ancient Egyptian religion) and other traditions.

To some fundamentalists, all religions other than Judaism and Christianity are actually varieties of Satanism (i.e. Devil Worship). To them, even Islam, Buddhism, Hinduism, Sikhism, Taoism and the various Neo-Pagan religions are all forms of Satanism, or at least are led by Satan or his demons. But to almost everyone else, Neo-Pagan religions are simply individual faith groups with little or no connection to Satanism.

We use the term Neo-Paganism as an umbrella term for several modern revivals of ancient ethnic and magical traditions. Many of them are polytheistic, but some regard their faith as pantheistic. In fact, there are diverse concepts of deity among Neo-Pagans.

Subdivisions within Neo-Paganism include Wicca, Magick, Druidism, Asatru, Neo-Native American religion and others.

It is only in recent times that Neo-Paganism has become a sizable and indeed visible movement. Many practitioners in America allege that they kept their Neo-Pagan faith secret, for fear of prejudice and vilification in society. However, they have begun to profess their faith openly now, and public gatherings and seasonal celebrations are frequently held. Reliable statistics on Neo-Paganism are still not available, but it is obviously "a rapidly growing religion/religious category" according to experts. Estimates regarding its worldwide followers range from under one hundred thousand to over four million. Independent surveys and government-based figures do not tally with estimates provided by Neo-Pagan and Wiccan organisations themselves.

Thus two points can be stressed about Neo-Paganism: 1) Neo-Paganism is not a single religion, but an umbrella term for many disparate religions. 2) It could also be said that Neo-Paganism could be classified as a subset of primal-indigenous religion. But both these statements need to be qualified; for each of these faiths has developed its own cultural and social identity; and though their roots are in primal ethnic religions, Neo-Paganism has its distinct modern ideology influenced by the emerging philosophies of the Twentieth Century, such as Environmental Protection, Peace, Brotherhood and Religious Freedom. And,

remarkably, many of these religions have more in common, in terms of shared beliefs and common values, than the two major religions of the world. In other words, they are remarkably cohesive in their beliefs and practices, often getting together to celebrate events like *Proud to be Pagan*, which has become an annual socio-cultural or socio-religious festival in the US.

Why are these ancient religions being revived today? Charlotte Hardman says in her book, *Paganism Today*, "The interest in Paganism today in the UK and USA may be interpreted as a response to an increased dissatisfaction with the way the world is going ecologically, spiritually and materially. People are disillusioned by mainstream religion and the realisation that materialism leaves an internal emptiness."

According to Neo-Pagan websites, the main branches of Paganism in the U.K. and United States are *Shamanism, Goddess Spirituality, Sacred Ecology* and other various Magical Groups, the two most predominant of these being *Wicca* and *Druidry*.

The Pagan Federation statement reflects the basic principles of Paganism:

1. Love for and kinship with Nature: Rather than the more customary attitude of aggression and domination over Nature; reverence for the life force and its ever-renewing cycles of life and death.

2. The Pagan Ethic: "Do what thou wilt, but harm none". This is a positive morality, not a list of thou-shalt-nots. Each individual is responsible for discovering his or her own true nature and developing it fully, in harmony with the outer world.

3. The Concept of Goddess and God as expressions of the Divine reality: female and male, rather than the suppression of either the female or the male principles.

An anonymous Pagan oath is found on several Pagan websites. It describes a personal Pagan spiritual path, including the use of spiritual energy to help others, of tolerance, avoidance of harm to others, Karma, the Three-fold Law, the Goddess and God within, etc. It is attributed to the Pagan writer, Selena Fox:

A PLEDGE

I am a Pagan and I dedicate myself to channelling the Spiritual energy of my inner self to help and to heal others and myself.

I know that I am part of the Whole of Nature. May I grow in understanding of the Unity of all Nature. May I always walk in balance.

May I always be mindful of the diversity of Nature as well as its Unity. May I always be tolerant of those whose race, appearance, culture and ways differ from my own.

May I use my psychic powers wisely and never use it for aggression or for malevolent purposes.

May I never use it to curtail the free will of others.

May I always remember that I create my own reality and that I have the power within me to create positivity in my life.

May I always take responsibility for my actions; be they conscious or unconscious.

May I always act in honourable ways, being honest with myself and others, keeping my word whenever I have given it, fulfilling all responsibilities and committments I have undertaken to the best of my abilities.

May I always remember that whatever is sent out returns magnified to the sender. The forces of *karma* will move swiftly to remind me of my spiritual commitments when I have begun to falter from them.

May I use this *karmic* feedback to remain strong and committed to my Spiritual ideals in the face of adversity or negativity. May the force of my inner Spirit eliminate all malevolence directed my way and transform it into positive light. May my inner light shine so strongly that malevolence cannot even enter my realm of existence.

May I continually grow in wisdom and understanding. May I see every problem that I face, as an opportunity to learn and grow and to develop spiritually.

May I act out of love for other beings on this planet— to other humans, plants, animals, minerals, elementals, spirits or other entities.

May I ever be mindful that the Goddess and God in all their forms dwell within me and that this divinity is reflected through my own Inner Self, my Pagan Spirit.

May I always channel love and light through my being. May my inner Spirit, rather than my ego self, guide all my thoughts, feelings and actions.

TENRIKYO

Tenrikyo is classified in Japan as *Shinshukyo* i.e. a Japanese term used to describe new religious movements. It is essentially a monotheist religion founded in the nineteenth century by a woman named Miki Nakayama. In her lifetime, she became known to her followers as *Oyasama* ('honoured parent'), and was described as 'a shrine of God'. The aim of the religion she founded was to teach people the art of 'the joyous life' as she described it.

Miki Nakayama was chosen as the Shrine of God in 1838, after her son and husband suffered from ailments. The family had called a Buddhist monk to exorcise the spirit causing the ailments. During this time, Miki was possessed by the One God (*Tenri-O-no-Mikoto*), who revealed that she would thenceforth become a shrine of God. Miki then left her home and her family to live a life of poverty and seclusion, giving away everything she had to the poor and the needy. She also worked numerous healing miracles, enabling the blind to see, the insane to regain their sanity, and making painless childbirths possible. Sufferers were saved by *Oyasama* from any illness, and people began to call her a living goddess.

She chose Jiba, a green and beautiful village as the sacred place of Tenrikyo, and identified it as the origin, the home of all mankind, where creation began. Today, Jiba is the headquarters of the Tenrikyo faith, and is known as 'the home of the Parent'.

Her followers refer to God as The Parent, as *Tenri-O-no-Mikoto*. God the Parent is God of Origin, God in Truth. He is the originator of mankind and the giver of life for the whole of creation. God creates us, provides for us, as well as sustains and nurtures all of us. God is also the Truth of Heaven. He is the foundation of the way things are. There is nothing in the entire universe that does not embody the Truth of Heaven. God the Parent taught his people the Truth of Heaven and the path to the Joyous Life by becoming openly revealed through *Oyasama*, taking Her as the Shrine of God.

Followers of Tenrikyo believe that the joyous life is characterised by charity and the rejection of avarice, greed, selfishness, hatred, anger and arrogance. Negative tendencies are not regarded as sins in Tenrikyo, but rather as "dust" that can be swept away from the mind through *hinokishin* (voluntary efforts) and ritual.

Though she is no longer in her physical body, her followers believe that *Oyasama* remains at the Jiba shrine and continues to lavish her boundless parental love on all people in the world as the Mother of all humanity.

While Tenrikyo is considered as an independent religion by its followers, many people regard it as a teaching about the universe which does not interfere with their other religious beliefs.

Although there have been various new religions and cults that have arisen in Japan, many scholars agree that none have had the success of Tenrikyo. It is estimated that the faith has over two million followers and fifteen thousand "churches." They are found in Japanese American communities across the U.S. and several congregations in Hawaii, Brazil, Korea, China, the Philippines and other countries.

OTHER WORLD RELIGIONS

No documentation of world faiths can ever be regarded as satisfactory or even adequate. Apart from some of the beliefs and faiths we have discussed, there are several non-theistic belief systems such as: Agnosticism, Apatheism, Deism, Falun Dafa and Falun Gong, Humanism, New Age, Self-spirituality, New Spirituality, Objectivism, Osho, Thelema, Unitarian-Universalism and many more.

Side by side with these, native religions and faiths are still practiced in many parts of the world, like Shamanisms, Animism and other ethnic and tribal faiths.

Indeed, the paths are many…

CONVERSION

I must open this controversial topic which has become an issue of heated debates both in India, and elsewhere in the world, from the point of view of a culture, a society and way of life which has never believed in proselytisation or conversion. To me, the religion one is born into is like one's mother: can one change his or her mother?

One of my friends informed me last year, that a court in the US had actually permitted a child to change his parents – i.e. revert from the family he was born into, and seek adoption from his foster parents on grounds of cruelty or ill-treatment.

I am sure you will agree with me, that this is an aberration, and not exactly the kind of example which we would wish to hold up for others to follow.

It is said that a Professor of Philosophy from Poland named Krezenski, once came to meet Mahatma Gandhi. By then, Gandhiji was already very well known in Europe and America, as a saintly soul who was bringing about a bloodless, peaceful, social and political revolution in British India. Prof. Krezenski too, like others, admired and revered the Mahatma. In all earnestness, the Professor said to him, that Catholicism is the only true religion and if only Gandhiji converted to the faith, he would be as great as St. Francis. Gandhiji had a simple question for him: why can't a poor Hindu be St. Francis?

Of course, I agree that all of us should follow our religion with faith and loyalty. Of course we must assert the value of our own culture and its form of religious worship. We must all aim to be good human beings – as well as good Hindus, good Christians, good Muslims or good Jews. But asserting our faith must never degenerate into the very unholy act of heaping abuse and denigrating the culture and spiritual identity of other faiths.

How can intelligent, educated people ever believe that their God or His prophet is the only true Divinity, and claim that they have a monopoly on salvation and liberation for the whole of mankind?

Psychologists are at a loss to account for the mindset and attitude that makes people convert to other faiths.

Very few nations, India, being one of them, actually give people the fundamental freedom to practise their faith, and to 'choose their belief' or 'change their belief' at will. In India, many foreign missionary organisations view this as 'the right to preach', 'the right to proselytise' and 'the right to convert people to their own faith'. Once again, Gandhiji's words come to my mind: "I disbelieve in the conversion of one person by another. My effort should never be to undermine another's faith but to make him a better follower of his own faith. This implies the belief in the truth of all religions and respect for them."

The fellowship of all religions: is this not the one great, piteous, urgent need of India and the nations today?

A young man said to me, "The sun of religion is setting." I said to him, "The sun never sets. When the sun appears to set here, it rises elsewhere. The sun of religion, too, is rising, ever rising!"

If you will come to Sadhu Vaswani Mission Campus, you will find a large hoarding on which are given the words of our revered founder Sadhu Vaswani: "Religion! Let us *talk* of it less, *practise* more!" It is on the practice side that we have failed. Religion has not failed us, it is we who have failed religion. Jesus said: "Be not hearers of the Word, be doers of the Word!" He also said: "Everyone who heareth these words of mine but doeth them not, shall be likened unto a foolish man who built his house upon the sand!" On yet another memorable occasion, he said, "Why call ye Me Lord, Lord, and do not the things which I say?"

Religions are not rivals but comrades in the One Service of the Spirit. They are all inspired, in the minds of their prophets by the motive of purifying, enriching and uplifting the life of Humanity.

As I have studied the different religions of the world and the teachings of their great founders, – the prophets and *avataras* of humanity – it has seemed to me that there is a beautiful similarity in their teachings. And I have exclaimed: "What a beautiful harmony! What a wonderful synthesis!" I sometimes wonder why there are people who say that some religions are true and some others are not true!

To study different religions in the right Spirit, the spirit of sympathy and understanding is to know that each one of them emphasises the same fundamental truths."

"Go within!" said the *rishis* of ancient India to the pupils, in the long ago. And Jesus said, "The Kingdom of God is within you!" And the great Buddhist teacher said to his disciples, "O, *bhikkhus!* Ordinary people look outwards, while followers of the Way look into their own minds." And so, you will find the truth of the "within" proclaimed and re-proclaimed by the leaders and interpreters of the different religions of the world. The Beyond is within you! God, the Beyond, is within you! The Transcendent Being is within you! The Kingdom of God is within you!

The question arises, how may we reach the Kingdom of God that is within us? To this question, the great prophets of humanity have given us an answer which is one, simple, emphatic. If we would enter the Kingdom of Heaven, we must do two things. One of them is meditation. If we would enter the Kingdom that is within us, we must learn to meditate, we must practise silence, we must learn to enter the depths within us through silence. The Rishi of the *Katho-upanishad* says, "None beholds Him with the eyes for He is without visible form, yet in the heart is He revealed, through self-control and meditation." And in the Psalms, we have the oft-quoted words, "Be still and know that I am God!" And in the Buddhist scripture, the *Dhammapada*, we have the words, "The disciples of the Buddha are always awake and their minds, day and night, delight in meditation!" and in the Taoist Scriptures we read, "Touch ultimate emptiness. Hold steady and still."

To touch the Kingdom within, two things are needed. The first is meditation. The second is *seva*, loving service. In the Bhagavad Gita, the great Indian scripture which enshrines the teaching of the Lord Sri Krishna, we have the words: "Selfless service opens the way to the Highest!" And Jesus said: "This that you do unto the least of the little ones, you verily do unto Me!"

All sensitive and liberal intellectual people in India and the rest of the world agree that freedom of faith and religion is not really freedom to convert others. In fact, Western psychologists and sociologists perceive conversion as an insidious attack made on the most vulnerable groups in society. This is true of the 'evangelical' work in tribal belts, fishing villages and remote and interior areas of India where the underprivileged live. In the West too, it is observed that the target audiences for conversion are in the same category of vulnerable people, such as new immigrants; mind you, we must state that in the US, conversion is often from one denomination of Christianity to another; from Roman Catholicism to Unitarianism or from Protestantism to Antibaptism and so on. Single mothers, divorced women and economically underprivileged youngsters are 'persuaded' to embrace the faith of the proselytising groups who openly canvas for this end.

Can we 'use' God to denigrate and convert followers of another belief system? Can we go back to evil colonial practices and claim that Europeans/Whites/Christians are the chosen of the Lord, and that the Lord Himself is someone who regards the rest of the world as 'lesser' children?

And the means of conversion – can we use propaganda, fear psychosis, inducements and brainwashing against vulnerable people whose very existence is precarious?

Gandhiji's words come to mind again: "No propaganda can be allowed which reviles other

To set up cults and sects is to cut up the Great God into fragments.

religions…The best way is to publicly condemn it…"And further, "If I had the power and could legislate, I should stop all proselytising…it is the deadliest poison that ever sapped the fountain of truth."

Sri Aurobindo, one of India's great seers was also disturbed by this inherent bigotry and posed this question about a certain religion: "You can live with a religion whose principle is toleration. But how is it possible to live with a religion whose principle is, 'I will not tolerate you'? How are you going to have unity with these people?"

Many people belonging to the missionary faiths believe, that their founder and their scriptures oblige them to convert others to their faiths. I seriously doubt whether any scripture will ever advocate prejudice and intolerance towards other human beings! Ecologists are voicing vociferous protests against damage to the planet's environment. How much more must we protest against conversions which often do great harm to the harmonious, heterogeneous societies and cultures, often leading to the destruction of the very fabric of such a culture of tolerance and reverence for all religions that almost every Indian has imbibed from this land? As we all know, Hinduism has never claimed that it has the monopoly over truths and revelations.

As Dr. Radhakrishnan put it so beautifully: "The Hindu Faith is wholly free from the strange obsession of some faiths that the acceptance of a particular religious metaphysics is necessary for salvation, and non-acceptance thereof is a heinous sin meriting eternal punishment in Hell."

The main note of The Hindu Faith is one of respect and goodwill for other creeds. The Hindu Faith does not believe in proselytisation or conversion. The Hindus never went out to conquer or convert. They have always been worshippers of truth and believe that ultimate victory belongs to the truth – *satyameva jayate!* Truth alone triumphs!

A legal expert teaches us how a category of improper proselytising can be discerned:

- It would not be proper to use coercion, threats, the weight of authority of the educational system, access to health care or similar facilities in order to induce people to change their religion.

- It would be improper to try to impose one's beliefs on a 'captive audience', where the listeners have no choice but to be present. This would presumably require restraint in the exercise of their right to free speech, by teachers in the classroom, army officers to their inferiors, prison officers in prison, medical staff in hospitals, so as to avoid impinging on the rights of others.

- It would not be proper to offer money, work, housing or other material inducements as a means of persuading people to adopt another religion.

Moving outside India, we may see that since the collapse of the former Soviet Union and the rise of democracy in the Eastern Bloc, the Russian Orthodox Church has enjoyed a revival. However, it takes exception to what it considers illegitimate proselytising by the Roman Catholic Church, the Salvation Army, Jehovah's Witnesses and other religious movements in what it refers to as its canonical territory. In fact, the Orthodox Church of the East as well as Anglicans believe that the 'gentleman's agreement' between the Roman Catholic Church and its sister-sects (i.e. the unwritten agreement not to interfere with each other's followers) has been violated by such activities.

There are some who believe that they have the one full and final revelation of the truth; so that those who stand outside the circle of their own faith must necessarily be in error. Again, there are some who approach religious issues without the spirit of sympathy. They fix their attention on what they regard as the aberrations and extravagancies of a particular religion and say, "This religion is a monstrosity!" Saddest of all, we have people who hurt and kill in the name of religion. They are ignorant of the fact that they are killing their own brothers and sisters!

Faith is a matter of the heart; faith relates to the spirit; faith is conviction; faith is at the very core of our being. To attack, to cast doubts and aspersions on someone's faith is to hit him where it hurts most. It is violence of the worst kind.

In the wonderful environment of trust and tolerance that prevailed in ancient and medieval India, many faiths were welcomed and accepted on the Indian soil. Hinduism, like Zoroastrianism and conservative Judaism, is a non-converting faith. All three religions therefore, do not interfere in the practice of other faiths. If our detractors were to say that the current environment in India is not one of peace and harmony, I would still say to them that the modern Hindu attitude is to live and let live; to follow one's own faith and respect others' faiths.

One of India's spiritual leaders, Swami Dayananda Saraswati, describes Hinduism as a non-aggressive faith, for it makes no effort to convert others. In this aspect, those religions who wish to impose their beliefs on others, those who believe that their faith is superior to others, those who push the agenda of conversion, are necessarily aggressive faiths, are they not?

There is one other fact that cannot be lost on the intelligent observer; the aggressive faiths never attempt to interfere with each others' flocks; other aggressive faiths are left alone, perhaps for fear of

---

All world-religions are mirrors of the One Face. In them all shines the One Light.

---

reprisal, perhaps for fear of open conflict. This is where a secular democracy like India with its teeming millions offers attractive possibilities for these faiths to pursue their agenda of conversion.

Conversion and interchange of faith within the Indic religions has always been a common phenomenon in India; the example of Emperor Ashoka is well known. We also know that the Chola and Pandya and Pallava kings of the South, switched over from Hinduism to Jainism and back, due to the powerful inspiration they derived from visiting Jain scholars and monks. One of the greatest intellectuals of the first century AD, the saint-poet Thiruvalluvar, is thought to have been influenced by Jainism, and perhaps even converted to the faith.

In none of these cases can we suspect coercion, aggression or other devious means. No one would question a genuine and voluntary change of heart which is not forced on a man. Let me also stress, these kings were powerful and benevolent; they all exercised firm authority over their people; and yet, in no case were the people of these kingdoms ever induced to convert to the new faith embraced by the monarch. In fact, history tells us that their Queens often remained firmly rooted in the faith they were born into!

It is said too, that Adi Shankara brought many atheists and fearsome *kaabalikas* back into the Hindu fold. In those days, we also had the tradition of great saints and scholars indulging in *tarka* or philosophical debates which often lasted for days on end. The losers in these debates not only conceded defeat, but often embraced the faith of the winner, due to their own conviction. It is also said, that they entered into such debates on the mutual agreement that if they lost their intellectual ability to convince the other, that would be grounds to accept the other's faith.

As we can see, the scenario today is very different. Abuse and denigration is heaped on the Hindu faith, and vulnerable sections of society are offered inducements, or coerced through false promises or fear psychosis to convert. I am sure my readers will agree that this is not the same as voluntary change of heart.

One of the reasons given by such aggressive missionaries is that Hinduism is riddled with internal contradictions like the caste system, and that is why some sections convert willingly. I can easily point to you aspects of other faiths that are problematic and controversial: polygamy, women's status, exploitation of ignorance through so-called miracles and fear psychosis, inducement of a sense of guilt and shame, as well as threatening hell fire and damnation. Hindus know that such things exist in other faiths, and yet they have never capitalised on these weaknesses. It is no use telling a Hindu, "If you can, go out and convert others to your faith. It is a level and open playing field!" This is a useless and futile offer which every thinking Hindu will reject, for we are just not a converting faith!

Hinduism just does not permit such intrusion, such violation of another's life and faith and dignity!

There is another irony of conversions by the so-called low caste people from Hinduism. Their converters claim that they have liberated these people from oppression and abuse and segregation in Hindu society. But the fact of the matter is their own churches and local religious bodies continue to discriminate against them even after conversion! This should make them realise that casteism and untouchability (which, incidentally has been banned under the Indian constitution) are *social* evils, social aberrations and not *religious* abominations. Else, how is it that these evils do not disappear instantaneously when people enter the new religious community into which they have converted?

Why, the Nazis under Hitler and the White Racist regimes of South Africa often used the Bible to justify their superiority and intolerance and the horrors they perpetrated on the Jews and Blacks respectively. Can we therefore describe Nazism and Apartheid as "Christian" evils?

The culture of any society is a delicate and rare and beautiful fabric into which faith, religion and customs and traditions are woven integrally. To pull out the strands of belief and faith from the fabric of culture is to destroy and damage that culture beyond repair. We have allowed this to happen to the Mayan culture of South America; the ancient cultures of Egypt and Mesopotamia have disappeared without a trace; Greece, the cradle of modern thought is but a pale shadow of its past glory. The loss is not theirs alone, but the world's as a whole.

I repeat, freedom of religion does not include freedom to convert; it only assures that all of us may practise our faiths without interference and aggression from others.

A few years ago, when I was in the US, a lady came to meet me in Key West, Florida. She had attended several of my lectures over the years, and on her own, she had read the *Srimad Bhagavad* and the *Gita*. She was so inspired by these scriptures that she wanted to become a Hindu. She came to me for advice on how she should go about it.

I said to her, "You must give up this idea. You say you are inspired by Lord Sri Krishna. You can never draw closer to Krishna simply by labelling yourself as a Hindu. What the *Srimad Bhagavad* and the *Gita* offer, is as valuable and as true as what the Bible offers. You must make an attempt to find it out and practise being a good Christian. A Christian can be equally dear to Sri Krishna as a Hindu. For in the Kingdom of God, there are no labels, no sects and no denominations!"

May I humbly submit to you, true conversion is not just a change of label. When Jesus spoke of conversion, he did not mean a change of creed or dogma; he meant a change of heart, a change of mind and attitude. It is not entrance to a new church or mode of worship; it is inner transformation. How can we believe that God wants numbers from us? And how can we imagine that He wants us, imperfect creatures, to bring about the changes, perform actions that He Himself cannot achieve? Why should an Omnipotent, Omniscient, Omnipresent Supreme Being require pathetic 'warriors' like us to fight and shoot and torture and kill others – that too, on His behalf? Is this not heresy of the worst order? Is this not an apostasy of true faith? And can we really bring ourselves to believe that we are walking on the primrose path to heaven and salvation by treading on the beliefs and sanctity of other people's convictions? Is this not a gross and serious transgression?

In the Kingdom of God, we will not be judged – in fact, we cannot even gain entry through our labels, but by the lives we have led!

My religion is like my mother! All other religions are her sisters! If Krishna is my father, Jesus Christ is my uncle!

As we do not choose the family into which we are born, even so we do not choose the religion into which we are born. For the choice made by God is surely for our highest good. We cannot give up our mother and adopt another's!

I once met an American Christian brother in New York, who said to me, "Why do our missionaries take the trouble of visiting distant lands and converting people to Christianity? Why can't they convert the *Christians* in America to Christianity?"

All great religions are equally true. They are like branches of a tree – the tree of religion.

This, therefore, is the essence of my plea: that instead of conversion, we should try to be better human beings – Hindu, Christian or Muslim.

FELLOWSHIP SONG

The whole earth is our Country,
    And the sky is its dome;
The nations are as mansions
    In th' Heavenly Father's Home!

We of China and Japan,
    Of 'merica and Ind,
We all are brothers, sisters,
    Of Soviet and Sind!

Hindus, Muslims, Christians, all,
    Buddhists and Bahai's,
We share each other's friendship,
    And th' love that never dies!

One is the faith we live by:
    One is the song we sing!
With little deeds of service
    We worship Him our King!

We feed those that are hungry:
    We work for no reward:
We help the poor and needy
    'For love of Him, our Lord!

We're friends of all the friendless,
    Servers of those in pain!
We're brothers of the voiceless,
    The cow, the dog, the hen!

We trust in God, His mercy,
    And in ourselves believe:
All what today we hope for
    We shall one day achieve!

Hand in hand we march on still:
    A better world to build,
A world of love and laughter,
    With peace and plenty filled!

J. P. Vaswani

GLOSSARY

A

Aarti	A Hindu ceremony in which lights are offered to one or more deities daily. Also the name for the devotional song that is sung during this ritual
Abhidharma	Analytical texts which contain an entire system on mind training
Acaranga Sutra	Part of the *agamas* (Jain scriptures)
Adharma	Unrighteousness
Adhyant Beda-darsana	The doctrine of absolute differences
Adi Granth or Guru Granth Sahib	Primary Volume of Sikh scripture compiled by Guru Arjan Dev, which is revered as the last and Eternal Guru
Adi Guru	The first spiritual master of a disciple succession
Adinath	First Lord
Advaita Philosophy	Non-dualism philosophy derived from the Upanishadas and elaborated by Shankaracharya
Advent	Adventus, coming, marks the beginning of the church year and the approach of Christmas

Agamas	1. "Operating instructions" for Hindu worship in the three main sects of Hinduism — the Vaishnava, Shaiva and Shakti sects
	2. The sacred scriptures of Jainism comprising Lord Mahavira's teachings and His sermons
Agamika	Canonical
Agni	Fire
Ahal-al-sufa	Companions of the bench
Ahankar	Pride
Ahimsa	Non-violence
Ahunwar or Yatha Ahu Vairyo	Tying of the marriage knot
Ahura Mazda	The Lord of Creation
Ajiva	Non-living things
Akal Takht	The Eternal Throne, the symbol of the temporal and religious power of the Gurus
Akhand path	Continuous unbroken recitation of the entire Guru Granth Sahib
Akhriah	Faith in a resurrection after death
Akká	Acre

Aksha	Soul
Alakh	The One that is not seen
Al-Amin	Trustworthy
Al-Buruni	Wisdom
Al-furqan	Discernment (name of Qur'an)
Al-hikmah	The wisdom (name of Qur'an)
Al-huda	The guide (name of Qur'an)
Al-jihad fi Sabil Allah	Striving in the way of Allah
Al-kitab	The book (name of Qur'an)
Al-Qadr	Acceptance of pre-destination
Al-Rudhabari	One who wears wool on top of purity
Ameretat	Long life and immortality
Amesha Spentas	Divine attributes of God as per Zoroastrianism. By knowing them, man can know God
Amrit Sanchar	Ceremony of accepting of the nectar
Amrit vela	Early morning
Anand karaj	Holy wedlock ceremony
Anatta	Liberation from suffering
Anekantavad	Jain doctrine of non-exclusivity
Angra Mainju	One who resides in hell
Anjoman	An assembly
Aparigraha	Non-possession
Apaursheya	Not of human endeavour
Arahat	Realised souls worthy of respect
Ardas	Invocation to the Gurus
Arhatship	A Buddhist, monk, an enlightened one, from Sanskrit: worthy of respect
Artha	Possessions, Wealth, Prosperity, Glory
Asatru	Adhere to the ancient, pre-Christian Norse religion
Ash Wednesday	It is the first day of Lent, a period of fasting that leads up to Easter. Its central ritual is placing of ashes on the forehead
Asha	Hope
Asha Vahishta	Truth and righteousness
Ashad	The month of July/August
Ashoi	Pure of heart
Ashrama	A house where a true Guru is living and teaching
Asrava	The influx of karma
Aswayuja	The month of September/October
Atharvaveda	It is one of the four Vedas. A major portion of this Veda is concerned with diseases and its cure and some magical formulas

Atheos	Without gods
Atman or Atma	The soul
Atma-shakti	Soul power
Atma-vidya	The science knowledge of the soul, spirit
Avadhijnana	Visual knowledge
Avatara	Divine incarnation
Avesta	Containing direct conversations between Zoroaster and Ahura Mazda, the Supreme Lord
Ayathrem Gahambar	Bringing home the herds
Ayyam-i-Ha	Essence of God Festival

B

Bá qi-bi-Allah	Annihilation in the eternal consciousness
Báb	Gate, from a Shia Muslim concept
Bábís	One who hosts a gathering of the most eminent followers of the Báb
Bahá'	Glory or 'splendour'
Baisakhi	A Sikh festival
Bandha	The bonds of *karma*

Bandi chor diwas	Day of release of the captives
Bani	An abbreviation of Gurbani of the Guru Granth Sahib
Baqaa	Permanency
Bar mitzvah	A Bar Mitzvah is a boy, and a Bat Mitzvah a girl, who has gone through a Jewish coming-of-age ceremony. The terms also commonly refer to the ceremony itself, which normally takes place when the child turns 13
Baraat	Marriage party — with bridegroom mounted upon a horse to fetch the bride
Basant Panchami	Spring festival falling on the 5th day of the month *Magh* (January/ Febuary). It heralds the coming of spring season – a time when spiritual aspirants commence their spiritual practices
Bayán	A book by The Báb
Behdin	Follower of Daena or the Good Religion
Bhadra or Bhadrapad	The month of August/ September
Bhagats	Holy person/Devotee

Bhagavad Gita	A scripture containing Lord Sri Krishna's teachings. A dialogue between Sri Krishna and Arjuna
Bhajans	Devotional songs
Bhakti	Devotion
Bhakti Marga	Way of devotion
Bharatavarsha	India
Bhasasamiti	To observe carefulness in speaking
Bhikkhus	Buddhist monks
Bhodisattva	One who has attained enlightenment, one who is willingly reborn out of compassion for other suffering men
Biblia	Books
Bimah	Reading desk
Binokishin	Voluntary efforts
Bismillah	In Thy name, O Allah
Bodhi	Enlightenment
Bodhicaryavatara	Influential text in Mahayana and Vajrayana traditions
Brahma Purana	One of the major eighteen *Puranas* (Hindu religious text). Divided into two parts, namely the Purva Bhag and the Uttar Bhag
Brahmacharya	The first of the four stages in the life of a Hindu. It is the stage of celibacy of the student/disciple
Brahman	All pervading self existing power. The supreme entity of the Universe, from which all things emanate and to which all return. It is the unchanging, infinite, immanent and transcendent reality which is the Divine Ground of all matter, energy, time, space, being and everything beyond in this Universe. For want of a better word we call it God
Brit milah	Covenant of male circumcision
Buddha Purnima/ Buddha Jayanti	The thrice-blessed day; of Lord Buddha's life — his birth, his enlightenment and his death or *nirvana*
Buddhaghosa	Theravada teachings with quotes from the Pali Canons

C

Caliph	Shadow of God on Earth
Ch'un Ching	Spring and Autumn Annals
Chaitra	The month of March/April
Chaju	Independence in politics

Chakravarti	Ruler of men
Chandogya Upanishad	An ancient source of principal fundamentals of Vedanta philosophy
Chardi kala	Positive energy/Waxing energy
Charip	Self-sustenance in the economy
Charvaka philosophy	System of philosophy that assumes various forms of philosophical scepticism and religious indifference
Charvaka School, the Samkhya and Purva Mimamsa	Philosophies
Chawi	Self-defense for national defense
Chi	Air, breath
Ching	Classic of Changes
Christes maesse or Christ's mass	Marks the celebration of the birth of Jesus
Chung Yung (Doctrine of the Mean)	A sacred text Ch'an Derived from the Sanskrit word *dhyana*, meaning "meditation"

D

Daan	Charity
Dakhma-nashini	The corpse-destruction for a Zoroastrian, in stone enclosed Dakhma

Dar al-Harb	House of War, the rest of the world, inhabited by non-believers
Dar al-Salam	House of Islamic Peace, in which Muslim governments rule and Muslim law prevails
Dargahs	Sufi shrines
Darsanika	Philosophical
Darshanas	Six basic philosophical expositions relating to Hinduism
Dashavatar	Ten incarnations of Lord Vishnu
Davar	Judge
Day of Arafat	During one day of the Hajj, pilgrims gather at the Plain of Arafat to seek God's mercy, and Muslims elsewhere fast for the day
Daya	Kindness/Compassion
De	Virtue
Death of God	Theological movement
Deep Diwali	Festival observed during October/November in honour of enlightenment of Lord Mahavira
Deepavali	A row of lights. It falls on the last day of the month *Kartik* (October/November) to celebrate the return of Sri Rama to

Ayodhya after defeating Ravana. A three day festival:

- *Dhanteras*. The 13th day of the dark half of the month *Kartik* and the first day of Deepavali Festival
- *Narak Chaudas*. The *Chaturdashi*. The second day of Deepavali Festival
- *Laxmi Puja*: The third day of Deepavali Festival

Devi	Generic designation for any female diety
Dhamma	Teachings of the Buddha
Dhammapada	Buddhist scripture
Dharma	One's righteous duty or religion
Dhikrallah	The remembrance of God (Name of Qur'an)
Dhyana	Meditation
Digambara Jains	Order of naked ascetics, the followers of Lord Mahavira
Digha Nikaya	Respect given to one's spouse
Doha	Stanzas of two rhyming lines
Druidic religion	Faith and practices of the ancient Celts
Dukkha	Suffering
Durga Puja or	This festival is observed twice a
Navrathri	year, once in *Chaitra* and *Aswayuja*. It lasts for 9 days in honour of the nine manifestations of Goddess Durga
Dussehra	Hindu festival which celebrates the victory of Lord Sri Rama over Ravana, the demon king
Dwesha	Hate

E

Easter Sunday	Marks the solemn and joyous occasion of Christ's resurrection
Eid al-Adha	Festival of Sacrifice
Eid al-Fitr	Festival of Fast-Breaking
Eid al-Nabi	Birthday of Prophet Muhammad
Ek onkar	Omnipotent and omnipresent
Ekam	One Eternal Light
Epiphany	Manifestation
Epistle to the Son of Wolf	Important text written by Bahá'u'lláh, in the Bahá'í Faith
Ereta	Righteousness
Essene	Withdrawal from the world

F

Fanaa	Extinction
Faná-fi-Allah	Annihilation in the abstract

Faná-fi-Rasul	Annihilation in the spiritual plane
Faná-fi-Shaikh	Annihilation in the astral plane
Fasad	Illegitimate violence
Folk Shinto	Includes the numerous and assorted folk beliefs in deities and spirits
Four Ashramas	Four stages of human life: Brahmacharya, Grihastha, Vanaprastha, Sannyasa

G

Gandharas	Followers of Lord Mahavira
Ganga Snan	Taking a dip in the River Ganges
Gathabandhan	Tying the wedding knot, a Hindu ceremony in which the mantles of the bride and bridegroom are fastened together
Gathas	Hymns of Zarathushtra – the inspired composition of the poet-prophet
Ghettos	Poor, harsh non-livable environment in which the Jews were forced to live
Gnana	Wisdom
Gnana Marga	Way of wisdom
Good Friday	The day Jesus was crucified

Goshalas	Shelter for cows
Granthi	One who reads the Guru Granth Sahib; the sacred scripture of the Sikhs
Griha Pravesh	A ceremony done on the occasion of one's first entry into a new house
Grihastha Ashrama	The second of the four ashramas, the stage of the householder or married man/woman
Gurbani	The writings/words of the Gurus
Gurdwara	A Sikh temple. It means 'Gateway to the Guru'
Gurpurab	Celebration of the anniversary of the birth or death of a Sikh Guru
Guru	Teacher, Preceptor, Dispeller of darkness
Guru Purnima	The full moon day of the month of *Ashad* (July/August) is sacred to the memory of the great sage, Ved Vyasa who has compiled the four Vedas, the eighteen Puranas, The epics of Mahabharata and the Bhagavata
Gurudev	Great Guru
Gurumukhi	Punjabi script propogated by Guru Nanak Dev

Guru-shishya Parampara	A spiritual relationship between a spiritual mentor and his disciple

H

Hadith	Prophet's actions and words later recorded for future generations to emulate
Hajj	Pilgrimage to Mecca
Halal	Permitted
Hamaspath-maidyem Gahambar	Feast of 'all souls', literally 'coming of the whole group'
Hannyashingyo	Heart Sutra
Haqiqa or Haqiqat	Supreme Truth/Absolute Reality
Haram	Prohibited
Hari	One name of God
Hatha yoga	A stage of physical purification which prepares the body for the higher levels of meditation
Hathleva	A wedding ceremony in which the bride and groom's hands are tied together
Hauravatat	Wholeness and health
Havarshta	Good deeds
Hellenismos	Ancient Greek religion

Hijrah	Migration; in historical terms, the date of Muhammad's flight to Medina, and also the time at which Islam becomes an established religion
Himsa	Violence
Holi	The spring festival of the year observed in the month of *Phalgun* (February/March)
Hudayafa al Yaman	God's tests of the servant by suffering. If he is patient, he will not avoid suffering, but will greet it with a smile, knowing that all that comes from God is good
Hukam	His Will/Order
Hukhta	Good word
Humata	Good thought
Hunafa	Those who turn away
Huppah or Chuppah	A four-poster canopy

I

I Ching	Classic of changes
Ihsan	Righteous living
Ijab	Formal proposal of marriage
Ikebana	An art as flower-arranging

Imam	Islami judge/Trusted community elder who is familiar with Islamic law
Iman	Faith
Imperial Shinto	Associated with the family of the Japanese Emperor in their own imperial shrines
Isa	Transliterated as Jesus
Ishopanishad	One of the Upanishads describing the nature of the supreme being
Itihasas	The great epics of Hinduism

J

Jain	The follower of the Jinas
Janmashtami	The birth of Lord Sri Krishna – the *Avatara* of Lord Vishnu
Jap	Recital of the Name Divine
Japji Sahib	The prayer of invocation of the Guru
Jashan	Celebration
Jataka	Birth stories recounting former lives of the Buddha
Jayanti	Birth anniversary
Jignasu	Aspirant

Jihad	Religious wars
Jihad al-lisan	War of the tongue
Jihad al-nafs	War against one's self
Jihad al-yad	War of the hand
Jihad as-sayf	War of the sword
Jinas	Conquerors, highly evolved and spiritually elevated beings, who had mastered the self
Jiva	Souls and living things
Juche	Communist government of N.Korea and a state religion
Juniz	Nobleman/Gentleman

K

Kabbalah	A school of thought concerned with the mystical aspect of Judaism. It is the mystical branch of Judaism
Kaccha	Shorts to exercise self-control
Kalamallah	The word of God (name of Qur'an)
Kama/ Kamachandra	Physical desires, lust, sensual desires
Kami	Spirit
Kamidana	Public shrine/Home shrine in Japan

Kami-no-michi	Spiritual practices derived from many local and regional traditions of Japan and the Japanese people of the Yamato and Izumo cultures
Kanga	Comb to be used to keep the hair in clean and healthy condition
Kanyaadaan	Ritual in which the bride's father entrusts his daughter to the groom
Kara	Steel bangle
Karah Parshad	Sweet pudding
Karma	Cause and effect
Karma marga	Way of selfless action
Kartik	The month of October/November
Karva Chauth	Hindu festival
Kashi	Varanasi
Kashrut	Jewish dietary laws
Katha	1. Stories of gods/goddesses 2. Religious discourse 3. Oral tradition of narratives
Kathina	Ceremony in which the laity make formal offerings of robe cloth and other requisites to the *Sangha*
Katho Upanishad	A widely known Upanishad that represents a dialogue between an aspiring disciple and the Lord of Death, Yamaraj
Kemetism	Ancient Egyptian religion
Kesh	Hair
Keshava	One of the name for Krishna or God
Ketubah	The marriage contract of Jews
Kevalajnana	Perfect knowledge
Khalsa Panth	Pure sect
Khalsa sikh	Baptized soldier of the Guru's army
Khashathra Vairya	Power and just rule/The supreme Power of God, in the aspect of comes to Him who engages himself in good actions
Khordad Sal	The birth anniversary of Zoroaster on March 26
Khristós	'Anointed' or 'covered in oil'
Kiddushin	The Jewish word for marriage
Kirat Karni	Living an honest life
Kirpan	Dagger-sized sword
Kirtan	Chanting of devotional songs

Kirtan Darbars	Singing of the Sacred Hymns from the Guru Granth Sahib accompanied by music
Kitáb-i-Aqda	Most Holy Book
Kitab-i-Iqan	Book of Certitude
Ko Shinto	Tradition that values the systematic methods of exercise and training. It is also one of the oldest Shinto sects
Koans	Paradoxical puzzles or questions that help the practitioner to overcome the normal boundaries of logic
Ko-ji-ki	Records of ancient matters
Kosher	Food prepared in accordance with the Jewish dietary laws
Kotodama	Words with a magical effect on the world
Kriyavada	The doctrine of action
Krodha	Anger
Kshatriya	One of the four varnas (social orders) in Hinduism. It constitutes the military and ruling order of the traditional Vedic-Hindu social system
Kurukshetra	The Land of the Kurus, the battleground on which the war, was fought between two clans of the Kuru dynasty in the Mahabharata
Kutha meat	Eating meat killed in a ritualistic manner
Kutubullah	Belief in God's books (like the Qur'an and the Psalms of David)

L

La ilaha il Allah	There is no deity worthy of worship except the One True Almighty God
Laja Homa	Sacred Fire
Lalyat Al-Qadr	Night of Power
Langar	Fellowship meals
Laozi	Old Master
Leela	Divine play or game
Lent	A 40 day period of Fasting and repentance in preparation for Easter
Li	Ritual norms
Li Ching	Classic of Rites
Lobha	Greed

Losar Festival or Monpa Festival	A major festival which marks the Tibetan New Year
Lun Yu	Analects of Confucius, a sacred text

M

Madinat al Nabi	The City of the Prophet
Magard	Unmarried man
Magha	The month of March
Mahabharata or Satasahasni	One of the major Sanskrit epics of ancient India, the great tale of the Bharata dynasty
Mahavir Jayanti	The birth anniversary of Lord Mahavira, the founder of Jainism
Mahayana	The School of Great Vehicle
Maidyozarem Gahambar	'Mid-spring' feast
Maidyoshahem Gahambat	Midsummer feast
Maidyaram Gahambar	Midyear
Makara Rasi	Capricorn star sign
Makar Sankranti	The day on which the sun begins to move in *makara rasi*
Mala'ikah	Belief in angels
Manahparyaya jnana	Mental knowledge
Manana	Reflection
Margas	Way/Path. Derived from *mriga*, tracking, searching, following a way
Marifa	Mystical intuitive knowledge
Masnavi	Spiritual book in Persian by Jalal ud-Din Muhammad Rumi
Matijnana	Sensitive knowledge
Matsuri	The worship and honour given to the *Kami* and ancestral spirits
Maya	An illusion
Mehr	The bride has a right to receive a gift from the groom which remains her own property as security in the marriage
Meng Tzu (Mencius)	A sacred text
Micchamidu kadam	Forgiveness
Midrash	A large body of rabbinical material derived primarily from sermons, considered as third group of Jewish Literature
Milinda Pañha	Popular condensation of the *Dharma* dialogue between the Buddhist Sage Naga Sena and the Indo Greek King Menander

Milni	Ceremony in which elders from both sides meet and exchange greetings
Minyan	Communal prayer requires a quorum of ten adult Jews
Mitzvoth	The word used in Judaism to refer to the 613 commandments given in the Torah and the seven rabbinic commandments instituted later making a total of 620
Modaka	Sweet balls of rice flour
Moha	Attachment
Moksha	Freedom from the bond of birth and death
Mori	A few shrines are also natural places
Mujahid	A person engaged in religious war
Mujahideen	Plural of Mujahid
Mukti	Freedom from the cycle of rebirth
Murshid	Master
Murthi	Idol
Muslim Pir	Muslim saint

N

Naam	The name of God
Naam Simran	Meditation on God's name
Nafs	The ego
Najat	Freedom
Naoroze	New Year's day
Naw-Ruz	The Baha'i New Year
Nebi'im and Ketuvim	Law and Writing of the Jewish sacred text
Neijia	Soft/Internal
Nidhyasana	Assimilation
Nihon-gi	Chronicles of Japan
Nikkah	The marriage contract
Nimrata	Humility
Nirankaar or akal or alakh	Formless/Shapeless/Timeless/Beyond sight
Nirjara	The gradual shedding of the weight of *karma*
Nirvana	Liberation from the cycle of birth and death
Nishan Sahibs	The Sikh flag
Nyaya	Justice

P

Paanigrahan	Part of the wedding ceremony in which the groom takes the bride's hand in his hand. It signifies that they will now be together in both good and bad times
Pahlavi Dinkard	Sacred texts
Paitishahem Gahambar	Feast of 'bringing in the harvest'
Pali	A Middle Indo-Aryan language (or prakrit) of India
Palm Sunday	The sixth Sunday of Lent and the last Sunday before Easter. It commemorates the entry of Jesus into Jerusalem, just before his trial and crucifixion
Panj Pyare	Five beloveds
Papa	Demerit
Paramatma	The Supreme Being (The Over Soul)
Parampara	Literally, a great tradition, handed down from one generation to another
Parikrama	Going along a path ultimately to reach back at the starting point
Parinirvana	Enlightenment leading to cessation of cycle of birth and death
Paroksha	Indirect knowledge
Parsis	People from Persia
Parvas	Chapters
Paryushana	A festival which is observed in August/September every year, coinciding with the onset of the South-West monsoon
Pateti	A day of introspection and penitence
Patwari	Keeper of land records
PBUH	The prayer *Peace be upon him*
Phalguna	The month of February/March
Pharisees	A renewed focus on preserving tradition in a new situation
Pir	Sufi master/Saint/Spiritual teacher
Prabhat Pheris	Religious rallies at dawn singing *shabads*, before each important festival
Prajña	Wisdom
Prakash Utsav	Guru Nanak Jayanti

Prakriti	Nature, the matter or material substance from which the Universe is created
Prashneya	Disciples questioning their gurus to clarify their doubts
Pratipada	The commencement of the Jain year
Pratyaksha	Direct knowledge, knowledge obtained by the self without the assistance of an external instrument
Pravachans	Religious discourse
Prayers and Meditations	Important text written by Bahá'u'lláh, in the Bahá'í Faith
Puja	Worship, homage
Punya	Merit
Puranas	Ancient legends and myths which crystallise the teachings of the Vedas. A collection of myths and parables which embody the great Vedic truth
Purnima	The full moon day of the month
Purusha	Spirit
Purusharthas	The four goals of life – *artha, dharma, kama, moksha*
Purvas	Fourteen Jain scriptures that were preached by all Tirthankaras

Q

Qabul	Acceptance of the proposal of marriage
Qadiri, Chisti, Oveyssi, Shadhili, Jerrahi, Ashrafi, Bektashi, Nimatullahi, and *Mevlevi*	The Sufi orders
Qadis	Sharia law judges
Qawwali	Sufi devotional music
Qalb	The heart
Qiblah	The place toward which the Muslims turn their face in prayer

R

Radhasoami	One diverse order of Sikhism
Raga	Attachment
Raja Yoga	Literally the royal union, is concerned principally with the cultivation of the mind using meditation to further one's acquaintance with reality and to finally achieve liberation
Rakhi	Thread of protection
Raksha Bandhan	A bond of protection. On this auspicious day, brothers make a

	promise to their sisters to protect them from all harms and troubles and the sisters pray to God to protect their brothers from all evil
Ramadan	Major religious observances each year
Ramayana	Ramayana is one of the two great epics of India, the other being Mahabharata. It depicts the duties of relationships, portraying ideal characters like the ideal servant, the ideal brother, the ideal wife and the ideal king
Ramnavami	The sacred day that commemorates the birth of Lord Rama, an *Avtara* of Lord Vishnu. It falls on the ninth day of the month *Chaitra* (March/April)
Rasi	Star sign
Religio Romana	Ancient Roman religion
Ren	Humaneness/Benevolence
Ridván	A Festival
Rigveda	The most ancient collection of sacred Hindu verses, consisting principally of hymns to various deities. It is one of the foremost Vedas
Rinzai	Zen sect
Risallah	Acceptance of the Prophethood of Muhammad, a Messenger of God
Rishis	Seer, Sage
Ristakhiz	Rising of the dead
Ruh	The soul

S

Saat pheras	Going around the holy fire place by the bride and groom together. With every round they make one promise to their partner. This way they make seven promises
Sabbath	A festive day, a day of rest, reminding people that in six days God created the world and on the seventh day, He rested. The sabbath day begins at sunset on Friday and ends at nightfall on Saturday
Sadar	Sunset
Sadduccees	New sense of identification and integration with Greek society
Sadeh	A mid-winter festival, traditionally celebrated with a bonfire
Sadhaka	Spiritual aspirant, one who practices *Sadhana*

Sadhana	Spiritual disciplines
Safa	Pure
Sahabah	Companions of Muhammad
Sakahara	Vegetarianism
Sakshi	Witness
Salaam Sin-lam-mim	Safety and peace. Other root meanings of the word also connote "submission" or "surrender" Modern scholars translate the term to mean "losing oneself for the sake of God and surrendering one's own pleasure for the pleasure of God"
Salat	Prayers
Sallekhana	The spiritual decision to choose death
Samadhi	Higher levels of concentrated meditation
Samskaras	Sacraments
Samvada	A philosophical dialogue
Samvara	The breaking of the bonds of karma
Sanatana Dharma	The Eternal Religion (Hinduism)
Sangat and pangat	Congregations of the faithful
Sangha	Community of Buddhist monks and nuns, practising the path of the Buddha
Sankramana	To begin to move
Sanyasa	Renunciation
Sanskrit	A historical Indo-Aryan language, one of the liturgical languages of Hinduism
Santokh	Contentment
Sanyasi	Hindu anchorite
Saoshyant	Saviour
Saptapadi	Seven steps
Satsangs	(1) the company of the "highest truth," (2) the company of a guru, (3) congregation of assimilating the truth
Satya	Truth
Satyagraha	Non-violent resistance
Sawm	Fasting
Sefer ha-Zohar	Book of Splendour
Seva	Selfless service
Shabads	Divine Word, Hymns
Shahadah	Statement of faith
Shahidi diwas	Martyrdom Day
Shakti	Energy

Sharia	Traditional Islamic law
Shastras	Scriptures
Shema	An affirmation of Judaism and a declaration of faith in one God
Shia	A sect of Islam
Shih Ching	Classic of Odes
Shikshasamucaya	Texts, no longer extant in any other form
Shila	Morality
Shin tao	The Way of the gods
Shishya	Disciple
Shiva	A Hindu deity representing the aspect of the Supreme Being who is the destroyer or transformer of the universe
Shiva linga	A symbol for the worship of the Hindu deity Shiva
Shivratri	The great night of Shiva, which falls on the 13th or 14th day of the dark half of the month *Phalguna* (February/March)
Shraddha	Faith, Trust
Shramanas	Members who rejected the authority of the Vedas and the Brahmins
Shramanic tradition	The tradition of continence and austerity
Shravana	Listening with attention
Shrine Shinto	Most popular among the Japanese people, and includes ritual worship offered in over 80,000 shrines all over Japan
Shruti	Sacred Hindu Scriptures which reveal knowledge on the Vedas
Shu	Reciprocity
Shu Ching	Classic of History
Shuddha Advaita	Unalloyed and pure goodness
Shwetambaras	White robed ascetics, who were the followers of Parsvanath
Siddha	Perfect Master
Sikh	Disciple or a learner. (Sanskrit derivation *sishya*)
Simran	Meditation, Remembrance
Siva Purana	One of the major eighteen Puranas (Hindu religious text). It explains the purusharthas (the four goals of life) and the significance of Sivalinga worship
Sloka	Verse
Smrutis	The ancient law codes of the Hindus, also known as the

	Dharma Shastras or the Dharma Sutras. Were composed by Manu, Yajnavalkya, Parasara and Gautama
Sohila	Night
Sol Invictus	The undefeated
Sophia	Wisdom
Soto Buddhism	Zen sect
Spenta Ameraiti	Holy devotion, serenity and loving kindness
Sraosha	Good actions/Sraosha is the Avestan language name of the Zoroastrian divinity of "Obedience" or "Observance", which is also the literal meaning of his name
Srimad Bhagavad	A Hindu scripture which contains conversation between Rishi Sukha – son of Ved Vyas – and King Parikshit, the son of Abhimanyu and the only surviving heir to the Pandavas
Srutajnana	Scriptural knowledge
Srut-kevalis	The persons having the knowledge of Purvas
Stotras	Hymns of praise
Suf	Wool
Sufi	Seeker of wisdom
Sukkah	Like a Shed but instead of a roof it is covered with branches and leaves and inside it is decorated with harvest Festival Fruits
Sukkot	Tents
Sundaram	Beauty
Sunnah	Customs of the Prophet
Sunni	A sect of Islam
Sura	Chapter; The Qur'an consists of 114 chapters of varying lengths
Sutras	Aphorisms
Sutta Nipata	The earliest written canons
Swayambhu	Self-created

T

Ta Hsueh	A sacred text
Tafsir	Interpretation/Denotes commentary of the Qur'an
Taichi	A popular form of exercise
Taichi chuan	A popular form of martial arts
Taiji	Supreme ultimate
Taijitu	A symbol which represents the fusion of Ying and Yang into a single ultimate

Talmud	It is one of the important Jewish texts, a collection of rabbinical writings that interpret, explain and apply the Torah scriptures
Tanakh	Name of the Jewish sacred text
Tan-dorosti	Benediction prayer
Tanha	Desire
Tantric masters	Teachers of life force energy expressed through the human body
Tao	Path/Way
Tao Te Ching or Dao De Jing	A Chinese classic text
Tapobana	Forest of meditation
Tariqah	Conceptually related to *haqiqah* "truth", the ineffable ideal that is the pursuit of the Sufi tradition
Tariqas	Orders
Tarka	Debates and discussions
Tat	That
Tattvas	Concepts
Tauba	Repentance
Tawakkul	Self-surrender
Tawheed	The unity of God
Tawrat	The Judaism, Christianity and Islam regard the first five books of the Bible (Old Testament) as their sacred scriptures. Muslims consider it the word of Allah given to Moses
Terma	Tibetan Buddhist texts regarded as a unique text
Thanksgiving	It is uniquely American. It celebrates a shared meal between Christian Pilgrims and Native Americans. It is not just a religious holiday, but has an interesting semi-religious history
The Seven Valleys and the Four Valleys	Important texts written by Bahá'u'lláh
The Siroza	An enumeration and invocation of the 30 divinities presiding over the each day of the month, according to the Zoroastrian calendar
The Yashts	Worship by praise. It is a collection of 21 hymns, each dedicated to a particular divinity or divine concept
Theos	God
Theragâthâ and Therîgâthâ	Collections of biographical verse related to the disciples of the Buddha (male and female respectively)

Theravada	The School of the Elders
Thina-middha	Sloth and unconsciousness
Til-Gul	Multi-coloured sweets
Tirthankars	Enlightened souls who showed their followers the way to salvation
Torah	Is refered to the entire Tanakh or even the whole body of Jewish writings, it technically means the first five books of the Tanakh
Treifah	Food that violates the Jewish dietary laws
Tripitaka	Three Baskets
Trisna	Desire
Tasawwuf	A branch of Islamic knowledge which focuses on the spiritual development of the seeker under Sufism or studying the life of the prophet
Twelfth Night	Marks the end of the Christmas season

U

Udana	Inspired sayings in verse with a prose introduction
Udasis, the Nirankaris	*Diverse* orders of Sikhism

Uddhacca kukkucca	Restlessness
Ulema	Clergy
Umayyad	Groups in the early days of Islam
Ummah	Community of believers
Upa Purana	A genre of Hindu religious texts consisting of a large number of compilations differentiated from the Mahapuranas by styling them as secondary *Puranas*
Upanayana	A youth's formal initiation into Vedic study under a guru, traditionally as a resident of his ashrama, and the investiture of the sacred thread (yajnopavita or upavita), signifying entrance into one of the three upper castes
Upanishads	The Hindu scriptures that constitute the core teachings of Vedanta
Uttaradhyayan Sutra	Records of final *pravachans* of Lord Mahavira

V

Vaiseshika Philosophy	Is one of the six Hindu schools of philosophy. It has been closely associated with the Hindu school of logic, Nyaya

Vajrayana	The period of the fifth or final period of Buddhism in India
Vanaprastha Ashrama	Life of retirement and contemplation, forest dweller. The third of the four stages in the life of a devout Hindu where he retires to the forest to meditate and contemplate
Vasant Ritu	Spring season
Vassa	Rainy season
Vedanta	Concept of Oneness
Vedas	A large body of texts originating in Ancient India and the oldest sacred texts of Hinduism. There are 4 Vedas
Vendidad	The devout pray in the Fire temples, before the Sacred Fire, and they have immense spiritual power
Vicikiccha	Doubt
Vidaai	Post wedding ceremony in which the bride bids adieu to her family, friends and close relatives
Vidya	Knowledge, Wisdom
Vijay Dashmi	Day of Sri Rama's Triumph over Ravana
Vinaya	Monastic code

Visesha	Attributes
Vishnu	Hindu deity representing the aspect of the Supreme Reality that preserves and sustains the universe
Visishtadvaita Philosophy	Philosophy that combines non-dualism with attributes
Visparad	Collection of invocations or litanies, recited before other prayers
Visuddhimarga	Path of Purification
Vohu Manah	Good mind and good purpose
Vyapada	Aversion

W

Wahdat	Unity with God
Wahdat-ul-Shuhud	Unity of Witness
Wahdat-ul-Wujood	Unity of Being
Waheguru	One God
Wajad	Divine ecstasy
Walima	Public wedding party
Wand chako	Sharing what one has with the community
Wiccans	Trace their roots back to the pre-Celtic era in Europe
Wu wei	Non-action or not acting

X

Xiao	Filial piety

Y

Yagna	Sacrifice
Yajurveda	Second of the four Vedas. It describes in detail various *vedic* sacrifices.
Yasna	A liturgical collection containing prayers addressed to the Supreme Lord and other deities who form the spiritual hierarchy
Yawmuddin	Belief in a Day of Judgement
Yehudah	A Hebrew word from which the word Judaism is derived
Yoga	Union
Yogi	One who practises yoga
Yom Kippur	The tenth day of Tishri is the holiest day of the Jewish year- *Yom Kippur* or The Day of Atonement

Z

Zakat	Tax paid to the government
Zartosht No–Diso	The death anniversary of Zarathustra
Zazen	Posture in which Buddha sat under Bodhi tree
Zealots	Armed revolt
Zen	Meditation – Sanskrit origin *dhyan*
Zhong	Loyalty to one's true nature
Zend–I–Avesta	Interpretation of the Avesta

ABOUT THE AUTHOR

Dada J. P. Vaswani is one of India's greatly beloved and revered spiritual leaders. He is the life-force at the helm of the renowned Sadhu Vaswani Mission, an international, non-profit, social welfare and service organisation with its headquarters in Pune, and active centres all over the world.

Born on August 2, 1918, at Hyderabad-Sind, Dada was a brilliant scholar, who turned his back on a promising academic career to devote himself to his uncle and Guru, Sadhu Vaswani, a highly revered modern day saint, acknowledged in his own time as the spiritual leader of the worldwide Sindhi Community. Today, the Master's mantle has fallen on Dada, whom devotees and admirers look upon as the representative of God on earth, a mentor and guardian of their deepest values and spiritual aspirations.

Dada J. P. Vaswani is a firm believer in the universal religion of Love, Unity, Brotherhood and Service to humanity. Deeply imbued with the liberal and tolerant spirit of the Hindu faith that he was born into, Dada firmly believes that there are as many paths to the Divine, as there are human aspirations. Each one of us can take our own untried, untested, unchartered paths to reach God, and God will meet us half way. This all-encompassing, humane and broad outlook makes him acceptable to aspirants all over the world, who perceive

Dada J. P. Vaswani

him as a non-sectarian, non-judgemental teacher and guide in whom they can repose their faith.

Not only does Dada express the most profound truths in the simplest terms; but he lives and acts these truths in deeds of everyday life; truly, we may say that his life is his message. He *lives* his religion and spirituality, bearing witness to his ideals in thought, word and deed, thus offering a tremendous source of inspiration to everyone who meets him, even once in a lifetime.

A staunch advocate of vegetarianism, Dada has made it his life's mission to spread the message of Reverence for all Life, as advocated by Gurudev Sadhu Vaswani. Under his inspired leadership, the Sadhu Vaswani Mission has made dedicated and sustained efforts to offer various service programmes encompassing the fields of spiritual progress, education, medical care, women's empowerment, village upliftment, relief and rehabilitation, animal welfare, rural development and service of the underprivileged and disadvantaged sections of society. Dada firmly believes in the words of his Master: *Service of the poor is worship of God.*

A fluent, powerful and witty speaker and an inspired writer, Dada is the youngest 91-year old that you can ever meet. His rapport with the youth is truly amazing. He is at home on the world's most eminent fora, as well as in gatherings of students and young professionals, who find his personal magnetism, humility and aura irresistible. Spiritual leader, educationist, philosopher and mystic, Dada J. P. Vaswani represents the very quintessence of India's wisdom and universal spirit.

Everyone who seeks to contact God will find his own way of doing so.

Some Bestsellers by the Author

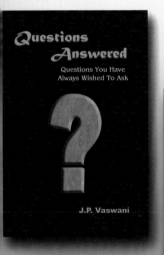

Questions Answered

Questions You Have Always Wished To Ask

?

J.P. Vaswani

Management Moment by Moment

Thoughts that help you to be responsible for yourself, manage yourself and take control of your life

J. P. Vaswani

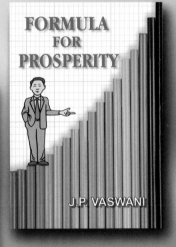

FORMULA FOR PROSPERITY

J.P. VASWANI

An inspiring story for every day of the year

Snacks for the Soul

Stories that will enrich your mind, purify your heart and rekindle your soul.

J.P. Vaswani

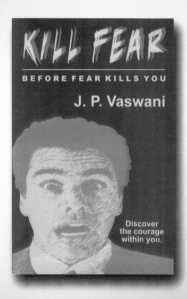

KILL FEAR

BEFORE FEAR KILLS YOU

J. P. Vaswani

Discover the courage within you.

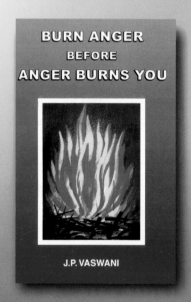

BURN ANGER
BEFORE
ANGER BURNS YOU

J.P. VASWANI

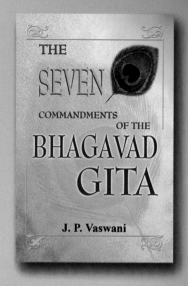

THE
SEVEN
COMMANDMENTS
OF THE
BHAGAVAD
GITA

J. P. Vaswani

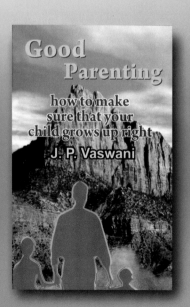

Good Parenting

how to make sure that your child grows up right

J. P. Vaswani

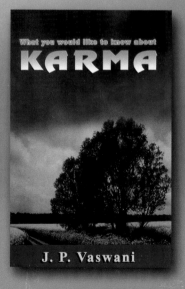

What you would like to know about
KARMA

J. P. Vaswani